THE WIRELESS WEB

How to Develop and Execute
a Winning Wireless Strategy

Bryan Bergeron

McGraw-Hill

New York   Chicago   San Francisco   Lisbon   London
Madrid   Mexico City   Milan   New Delhi   San Juan   Seoul
Singapore   Sydney   Toronto

Library of Congress Cataloging-in-Publication Data

Bergeron, Bryan P.
  The wireless web : how to develop and execute a winning wireless strategy / by
Bryan Bergeron.
    p. cm.
  ISBN 0-07-137359-4
  1. Electronic commerce.   2. Wireless communication systems.   I. Title.

HF5548.32 .B467   2001
658.8'4—dc21   2001030225

McGraw-Hill
A Division of The McGraw·Hill Companies

1 2 3 4 5 6 7 8 9 0   AGM/AGM   0 9 8 7 6 5 4 3 2 1

ISBN 0-07-137359-4

This book was set in Berling by Patricia Wallenburg.

Printed and bound by Quebecor World/Martinsburg.

To Fred

Contents

Introduction

Success, whether in wireless eCommerce or any other endeavor, requires a sophisticated combination of the appropriate technology, a cogent business strategy, a modicum of creativity, and, above all, an ample supply of good luck. In this context, good luck is the direct result of preparing to take advantage of opportunities before they arise. As the Web has taught countless business executives, the conservative wait-and-see approach doesn't necessarily translate into profits when the next "new thing" is on the verge of exploding into the marketplace. The run on domain names, patents granted for what seemed to be obvious Web-based business practices, and the benefits of being first to market have left indelible marks on both the winners and losers in the eCommerce game.

In retrospect, it's easy to see that the infrastructure suppliers of eCommerce were optimally positioned for the wired Web boom. However, few CEOs have the luxury of running a core technology company such as CISCO, Lucent Technologies, or ORACLE. The challenge for the thousands of other eCommerce executives is to somehow introduce a creative, must-have product, position it correctly in the marketplace, and make enough profit to sustain growth and development and provide a reasonable return for investors. In surveying the potential areas for rapid growth and profitability in eCommerce, the wireless Web seems uniquely positioned as the area of future growth. In fact, it's difficult to see how a click-and-mortar company without a wireless touch point will be able to survive.

Wireless computing is being embraced in all areas of business and personal life and takes a variety of forms. Salespeople exchange information via Palm Pilots through infrared links. Accountants use wireless mice and keyboards on their desktop PCs. Students create wireless networks in their dormitories. Executives use cordless and cellular phones and alarm systems at home and in the office. Early adopters use wireless PDAs and smart phones to send and receive short text messages to and from the Internet, including stock quotes, weather forecasts, and flight information. While wireless computing and communications offers a variety of opportunities to small and large businesses, the most explosive growth and intense interest are currently centered on mobile wireless voice and data communications, that is, the convergence of wireless voice and data communications, using the Internet as a low-cost conduit.

By now, everyone has heard of the popularity and apparent success of smart cellular phones in Europe and Japan. For example, in Finland, a country of only 5 million, over 60 percent of the population own a mobile phone, and most use it as their only phone. A Finn's identity is closely attached to her phone, in part because she uses it like a virtual smart card. If a woman wants to purchase a soft drink from a vending machine, she simply dials the number listed on the machine and a soft drink appears. The charge is automatically added to her phone bill. The same is true for banking, trading stock, or simply surfing the Web. All she needs is her cell phone.

But such uses only hint of the possibilities in store for the wireless Web. Given the current trajectory of wireless technology, wireless will eventually redefine the Web itself and the very nature of eCommerce. Today, Ether-Commerce is beginning to infiltrate the essence of the Web. Soon, it will outstrip the wired Web as a touch point. Just as cutting the umbilical cord is a natural and necessary part of the birth process, freeing the Web from the tether of the wired Internet opens up new possibilities that the original Web designers probably never anticipated.

Imagine, for example, that a man walks into a food store with his PDA and has the various vendors bid for his business. Based on his purchasing profile, the five or six companies that supply frozen peas compete for his attention, each offering instant, virtual coupons for their products through the store's wireless intranet. At the checkout, his PDA, which also serves as a cellular phone, transmits the discount data to the checkout computer, along with his billing information. As he walks the aisles, his wireless headphones soothe him with his favorite songs, transmitted to his PDA from the store's local area network. His music preferences, like his food preferences, are communicated to the store's intranet. Once home, he prepares the peas using a recipe that he discovered on the wired Web. This scenario illustrates that whereas the wired Web is information-based, the wireless Web is more transaction-oriented. The man's miniature smart phone, the new charge card of the masses, takes the place of his wallet full of charge cards.

It may be difficult to comprehend, but the wired Web, as new and fluid as it seems, is really a legacy system that has been superannuated by the introduction of wireless technology. Even though it provides needed functionality, the current Web actually hinders moving on to more efficient and useful platforms for information delivery and exchange. Moving to the next stage will require not only overcoming the typical legacy system challenge of having to support the old system while introducing a new system, but overcoming the mental inertia of current Web users as well. This inertia has technical and economic consequences.

Whereas legacy-wired Web users have been accustomed to having free information at their fingertips, the transaction-oriented wireless Web will likely follow the same transaction-based fee-for-service model used by cellular phone service providers. The premise is that customers are willing to pay for information if they can have it immediately. Forums, chat rooms, videos, animations, and extensive databases on the wired Web will take a backseat to just-in-time, just-in-place transactions, navigation, and pure transaction operations that the wireless Web makes possible. Instead of sponsored content, banner adds, and click-through revenue, wireless Web sites will work with value-added transaction fees, akin to the charge and debit card models.

From a technologic perspective, success in wireless eCommerce, while not trivial, seems imminently achievable. Applications of a ubiquitous, wireless communications network backed by millions of pages of information have obvious potential including navigation and communications aids in personal and corporate vehicles; instructions and automatic calls for help in emergencies; replacement for wired networks; interactive, just-in-time and place edutainment for students of all ages; and a variety of mobile and wireless business amenities.

There is considerable technology-related work ahead. Some of the many technical hurdles for wireless computing include a lack of standards; confidentiality concerns; the lack of robust, high-bandwidth network infrastructures; the potential for interference; the question of scalability; fierce competition for the wireless spectrum; and the usual losses associated with small, expensive electronics devices. There is also the technical challenge of managing the convergence of voice and data with traditional hardware that caters to both worlds until the number of smart digital phones and appliances reaches critical mass. Similarly, full utilization of the wireless Web will, in the short term, require businesses to rework their content to contend with diminutive, monochrome, text-only screens. In the long term, user interface tools, such as voice recognition and even heads-up displays, may be the technologic solution to universal use of the wireless Web.

From a business perspective, it's easy to see how a businesswoman would pay a premium for the added convenience of working with a portable, wireless office, using remote voice, email, fax, remote login, and Web surfing any time and from anywhere. There are obvious win-win solutions, such as providing wireless networks for businesses and customers in old, unwired buildings, and providing remote contact for a company's sales, taxi, trucking, or repair personnel. Of course, the real draw of the Internet is grounded in solid economics—it's cheaper than the alternatives. For most operations where the knowledge base of the Web isn't important, any Internet could be used for the majority of wireless computing. However, sending and receiving information through *the* Internet is virtually free to most customers.

The eCommerce CEO should be aware that there are a variety of socioe-conomic implications concerning the increased connectivity that a wireless Web portends.. With emphasis on user interface designs that work with small screens, there will likely be an increased demand for voice recognition and translation software systems. The latter will become increasingly important as business becomes more globalized. In addition, what of the fate of universi-ties, libraries, and other conventional sources of information where every stu-dent has access to the world's store of information at his or her fingertips? How can these potential threats to traditional culture (and to any wireless eCommerce start-up hopefuls) be converted into opportunities?

The successful players in the wireless eCommerce game will be those eCommerce executives who have contemplated these and related issues and are preparing now, carefully carving out niches for their businesses, forming collaborative and strategic alliances, and gaining direct experience with wire-less Web technologies. This isn't to say that every dotCom CEO should immediately jump into the wireless market for fear of missing out on the next gold rush. Rather, it means gathering information now, formulating a strategy, and following that strategy in deciding how and where to act. Readers of this book have taken that first step.

The Wireless Web is a primer on the business and technology of the wire-less Web, from a uniquely eCommerce perspective. It's just as relevant to executives who control companies that either have or are in the process of contemplating a Web presence. To increase the applicability of this book to a variety of audiences, it is divided into three parts. Part 1, Chapters 1 through 3, provides an overview of the current wireless eCommerce environment. This section is intended to bring IT managers up to speed on wireless eCommerce issues, and to provide a review for the wireless eCommerce executive. Part 2, Chapters 4 through 6, describes the technologies involved in networking and wireless computing. This section is intended as a review for IT managers familiar with these technologies, and introduces the concepts necessary for eCommerce executives to communicate intelligently with their IT peers and wireless vendors. Readers well versed in wireless eCommerce principles can save time by reviewing the condensed information at the end of each chapter in Part 1. Similarly, readers fluent in the latest telecommunications principles may elect to read the Executive Summary at the end of each chapter in Part 2.

Part 3 presents the synergy of wireless Web technology and eCommerce. Chapters 7 through 9 provide busy eCommerce executives or IT directors with a road map of how to navigate their business forward in the wireless computing world, from business, technical, and consumer perspectives. This section details what executives can do now within their business to prepare the information infrastructure needed to support a wireless initiative.

With the increasing pressure on eCommerce businesses to produce and demonstrate profitability, the winners will be the executives with strategic advantages, such as a wireless touch point for their customers. They'll decide how to deal with and take advantage of eBooks, cell phone technology, Palm 7 and similar Web-enabled PDAs, and other hardware and software. It's up to the visionaries to formulate and enact a winning plan that will take advantage of wireless Web technology and make their eCommerce initiatives a success. At a minimum, this will require that executives understand and appreciate the possibilities of networks: the telephone network, the Web, and related, enabling technologies. For example, how should a company deal with eBooks? Should it invest in making a component of their Web content compatible with wireless Palm devices? Should the executive look at including Bluetooth technology in her company's next generation of home appliance or audio gear? What about planning for wireless point-of-sale systems for restaurants, theaters, and other retail outlets? Obviously, to make an informed decision, the eCommerce executive must have a working knowledge of both wireless and telephone networks, and an appreciation of the business and technologic possibilities of the wireless Web. To this end, the goal of this book is to provide the reader with exposure to these concepts and more.

Acknowledgments

To my literary assistant and long-time editor, Terry Littlefield, for her technical expertise, encouragement, and mastery as a wordsmith. I would also like to thank my research assistant, Ana Maria de Aljuri, for hard work in providing assistance on this project. To the staff at McGraw-Hill, especially Michelle Williams, my developmental editor. To Rosalind Bergeron, whose experiences with the wireless Web in Europe and Asia, together with her work as a high-technology attorney in Silicon Valley, form the basis for this book.

To my readers and reviewers: Steven Peck, Alliance Manager, Hewlett-Packard; Jim Basillie, CEO of Research In Motion; Richard Bravman, Senior Vice President and General Manager, Wireless Systems Division, Symbol Technologies; Rosalind Bergeron, Vice President of Archetype Technologies; Lucas Cudrigh; Ron Rouse, Director of Educational Computing at Harvard Medical School; and, of course, Gilles, for their time, inspiration, insight, and constructive criticism.

Special thanks to Tony Salomone of Research In Motion Limited; Grant Frederiksen of Everypath; Michael Nobels and Dana Gonzalez of Netmorf, Inc.; Jack Gold of META Group, Inc.; Denise Lahey and Brad Hogan of OracleMobile; Michael Levy of NewMotion Software; Rick Wilhite of FusionOne; Brandon Barber of RadiantLogic, Inc.; Gary Gumbert of AvantGo; Gordon Clyne of Palm, Inc.; Ron Kupkee, Mark Ferrone, and Timothy Brinegar of Symbol Technologies, Inc.; and Ron Sperano of IBM.

Thanks are also due to those who contributed directly and indirectly to the substance of this book. To the pioneers in telecommunications and electronics with whom I have worked over the years, especially Fred Marshall and the staff at Data Comm, Inc.

Part One
ETHER-BUSINESS

1

The Ether World

The great pleasure in life is doing what other people say you cannot do.

Walter Bagehot, founding editor
The Economist

INTRODUCTION

Given sufficient economic incentive, a favorable political climate, and ambitious leaders with the proper entrepreneurial spirit, technologic, business, and political changes usually follow familiar, if not predictable patterns... Initially, there is the original technical innovation, which may be of questionable practical value. The technology is usually advanced by a creative entrepreneur—a change agent—with the vision and genius to combine knowledge gained by others in a new way. This entrepreneur, usually with the help of associates, must also have the time, energy, and money to protect the intellectual property involved, through legal, political, and business channels. Then, there is the actual business venture, championed by an entrepreneur who finds new uses for the innovations, and, in so doing, creates a new infrastructure for distribution.

Early on, amidst enormous speculation and hype, investment monies along with heightened interest and inflated expectations from investors and the public may boost the company's valuation to many times what would otherwise be considered sensible. After key critics and the buying public have experienced and commented on the product or service, there's a consolidation period during which professional managers make the technology work consistently and profitably. At this point, the product or service either takes off or fails in the business arena. Eventually, the cycle repeats itself, as the pro-

3

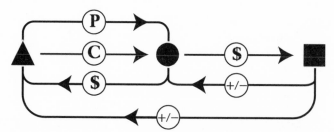

Figure 1-1. Business developments follow a predictable pattern. A new technology is commercialized (C) into a business venture. Profits ($) are reinvested, resulting in new products (P) that can be marketed. A portion of the profits ($) are invested in political areas, preferably resulting in positive feedback (+/−) in the form of environments conducive to both business and research into the core technologies involved in the company. Not shown are the inevitable delays in each pathway.

fessional managers lose ground to a start-up headed by another creative entrepreneur. In some situations, the same entrepreneur has the ambition, vision, genius, and fortitude to move a technology from an idea to a successful company; but this combination of talents is rare in a single person.

Variables ranging from the nature of the technology, the competition, the selling price, the business plan, the expertise of the management team, the creativity and penetration of the marketing and advertising team, the quality and drive of the sales force, and the demographics of the target market all come into play in defining what will survive in the market. Furthermore, the time between the original technologic innovation and a successful business that exploits that technology may be a few months to a decade or more. The interval depends on the nature of the product or service, the lead time involved in production and testing, the time needed for certification or government testing, cross licensing, securing patents, trademarks, and other intellectual property rights, and the ability to find willing buyers. Time to market also depends on the personal energy, motivation, and ambition of the management team. This team may involve a single entrepreneur or, more commonly, a succession of managers with different skill sets and aptitudes.

This process of moving from technologic innovation to a successful business venture is illustrated in simplified form in Figure 1-1. A new technology is commercialized (C) into a business venture. Profits ($) are reinvested, resulting in new products (P) that can be marketed. A portion of the profits ($) is invested in political areas, preferably resulting in positive feedback (+/−) in the form of environments conducive to both business and research in the core technologies involved in the company. Not shown are the inevitable, variable delays in each pathway, or the other variables that affect business success. For example, it's possible for the feedback on business and technology research to be negative because of changes in the political environment.

The rate of technologic innovation is accelerating, in part because developments are rapidly disseminated through traditional print magazines and newspapers, as well as through TV, radio, the Web, and other electronic media. Communications tend to speed the *evolutionary* changes in the improvement of a technology or process, because they provide competitors in the same market with information on how much they need to change to compete. Evolutionary changes are rewarded immediately—positively or negatively—by the marketplace.

Revolutionary changes, such as the Web, have the potential to change everything, including the market infrastructure. The rewards may not be immediate, but the effects on an entire industry can be cataclysmic. Even before events were measured in Internet time, major revolutionary changes occurred when a new technology was introduced. This may happen intentionally, by accident, or as the result of an entrepreneur working on a problem in a peripheral area. The hybrid vigor that results from combining relatively disparate technologies—akin to a biological mutation—often creates a product or technology that overshadows each of the original technologies involved. In other words, the whole is greater than the sum of the parts. The real issue is whether or not the product or service can withstand the ultimate test—in biological terms, survival of the fittest—in the marketplace. If it does, the challenge, at some point, becomes surviving success. For example, the same political and legal structure that protects a nascent business idea in the marketplace through patents, trademarks, and copyright protection, also limits overly successful businesses from monopolizing a market at the expense of competition. Success also tends to decrease the reward for creativity and to attract a risk-averse management team.

Consider the revolutionary developments that occurred in the United States and abroad in the past century and a half, and how the patterns seem to be repeated with each innovation. It's often the case that a technologic advance that results from a focused effort to solve a particular problem becomes the seed for an unforeseen leap in technology that focuses on another challenge. The Web, originally designed as a method of storing, sorting, and accessing documents in a collaborative but closed research environment, has evolved into much more. It now represents a huge store of knowledge and an affordable, globally accessible communications conduit capable of connecting household appliances, automobiles, and people through wired and wireless connections. Not only have thousands of programmers, entrepreneurs, and media consultants made their fortunes on

Web-related businesses, but the social and political landscape of the developed nations has changed to reflect the status of the technologically savvy.

Despite frequent technologic advances championed by visionary entrepreneurs, it takes decades for society to change enough to turn research into commercially viable products, as measured by increased customer demand. Consider some of the more significant events involved in changing the electronic infrastructure of this country, from telegraph to telephone to cable to satellite to the Internet, that led to the wireless Web.

Just 60 years after the United States declared its independence from England, Samuel Morse demonstrated the first telegraph system in New York. The system of wires, batteries, solenoids, and keyers quickly evolved over the next 100 years to include new technologies that allowed increasingly greater coverage of both the United States and connections to Europe. Although voice was never carried over the telegraph, other multimedia—including the text-based Telex and the image-based Wirephoto service—evolved out of the simple clickity-clack of the original electromechanical Morse sounder. Wirephoto was especially popular with the newspaper industry in the 1930s, because it allowed images to be transferred instantly around the country to newspaper owners eager for a photo to include with national and regional headline stories.

In 1876 (the year Lars Magnus Ericsson opened a repair shop for telegraph equipment) another entrepreneur, Alexander Graham Bell, received a patent for the telephone. At the time, it was a technologic oddity with no apparent practical use for the general public. Like the initial customers for Digital Subscriber Line (DSL), cable modem, satellite, and other high-speed Internet connections today, Bell's clients were wealthy business people. Systems were composed of two phones and a private cable, run from one business to another or from a home to a business office. The result was streets choked with private cables strung directly between pairs of phones, because the concept of the telephone network had not yet been invented. However, only three years later, a major milestone occurred with the development of the switchboard—a manual switching system that eliminated the eyesore and expense of point-to-point wiring. This primitive network facilitated B2B communications, since any business phone could be connected to any other phone through the switchboard. The telephone received another boost in popularity among business people when, in 1891, automatic switching for the telephone was patented. This innovation eliminated the expense and slow response of the manual switchboard, and provided ostensibly more private B2B communications.

The quality of life began to improve for consumers when Bell's telephone patents ran out in 1894. While the patents were in place, the average U.S. citizen was only indirectly affected by the new era of communications. The public initially viewed the telephone as a tool for business people and a toy for aristocrats. However, new, competing phone services included the working middle class in their ranks, making the telephone a household appliance in just a few years.

While consumers in the United States were experiencing the advantages of the new telephone technology, Guglielmo Marconi was demonstrating wireless communications using Morse code in 1895. After securing a patent for his system in England, Marconi established the Marconi Wireless Telegraph Company, Ltd., in London two years later. By 1901, a year after American Telephone and Telegraph (AT&T) acquired Bell Telephone, Marconi was transmitting telegraphy successfully across the Atlantic. There was brisk competition between the old wired and new wireless telegraphy services, domestically and internationally, for nonvoice communications. Many young radio entrepreneurs became rich and famous overnight, much like the founders of dotCom start-ups in the 1990s.

The wired telephone was unchallenged as a voice communications device until Lee de Forest invented the first electronic amplifier in the form of a modified version of the newly invented vacuum tube in 1906. In 1907, with the amplifier, de Forest demonstrated that voice signals could be transmitted via wireless. Eight years later, vacuum tube amplifier technology had reached the point that the first successful transatlantic wireless voice communication was held between the U.S. Naval Radio Station in Arlington, Virginia, and a listening post at the Eiffel Tower in Paris. In 1919, the Radio Corporation of America (RCA), founded only a few years before, acquired the Marconi Wireless Telegraph Company. Telegraphy remained popular for decades, even after voice communications became the accepted standard for communications for technical reasons. Telegraphy doesn't require much radio frequency real estate and is audible through static and noise that would make voice communications unintelligible.

Unlike wired and wireless telegraphy, wired and wireless voice technology spun off a one-way or broadcast model. However, the role Bell had envisioned for the telephone—a one-way conveyer of music and other entertainment from concert halls to homes and businesses—was short lived. Theatrophones, which not only carried live opera and other entertainment in stereo, as well as stock reports, live sporting events, up-to-the-minute news reports, and even programming for children, were crushed by cheaper wireless radio. Although several phone-based systems were in place in the United States and Europe by the 1890s, and successful businesses were in place by around 1910 that marketed stereo music on demand, wired services were history within a decade. By the time stereo radio was available to the general public, theatrophones were long forgotten.

By 1923, there was fierce competition for radio listeners, akin to the current competition among Web sites for repeat visitors. There were over 500 radio stations broadcasting a variety of programs in the United States on a crowded range of frequencies encompassing a fraction of the modern AM broadcast band. Because most of these AM broadcast stations were located near the same heavily populated areas, interference from competing stations operating on the same frequency was problematic. The station with the best antenna, most powerful transmitter, or nearest proximity to a potential audience could literally drown out the competition.

Disregarding, for the moment, the potential health risks associated with bathing a population in high-power radio frequency energy from hundreds of sources, static and noise were problematic for a listening public that expected interference-free music, news, and entertainment from their expensive radio receivers. Because many listeners simply turned off their receivers, interference was disastrous for broadcast stations attempting to secure advertising revenues. In response to the ensuing political pressure to do something about the free-for-all occurring in broadcast radio, the U.S. Congress passed the 1927 Radio Act, which created the Federal Radio Commission (FRC) to police the radio spectrum. This regulatory body became the more powerful Federal Communications Commission (FCC) a decade later. These agencies assigned to broadcast stations operating frequencies, antenna specifications, and power limits in order to minimize interference. For example, the FCC was empowered to assign "clear" channels on a regional basis, which barred any other radio stations from broadcasting on the same frequency. This, in turn, eliminated the threat of interference from competing stations. In addition, the broadcast station assigned to the clear channel was licensed by the FCC to broadcast at many times the power of standard stations.

Attention from radio hobbyists and economic stimulus from the military fueled nearly continuous technologic advances in the field of wireless voice and coded communications, especially after World War I. As a commercial venture, broadcast radio became a household item only after AT&T became involved in the radio industry. AT&T used a scheme for networking radio stations in distant cities via telephone lines to create a high-profile network of simultaneous radio broadcasts. This combination of a telephone network with broadcast radio finally made broadcast radio a profitable commercial endeavor. Instead of every radio station investing in resources to create quality content, the big studios in New York and Chicago secured the best talent and made a handsome profit by distributing programming to affiliated radio stations around the United States. Profit was realized by either spreading the production cost to affiliate stations or, more significantly, by giving the advertising-sponsored programming away. Advertisers were eager to use the new business opportunity, which provided a simplified means of disseminating their message to widespread markets. The single point of contact also allowed them to monitor the quality and timing of their advertisements in a way that was otherwise impractical at the time. Advertisers could be assured that a specific advertisement, read by an announcer they preferred, was associated with a particular program aired at a particular time of day.

The AT&T network was eventually so successful that nonnetworked broadcast stations simply couldn't compete for listeners or national advertisers. With a demonstrable method of making money on the broadcast side of the radio industry, RCA invested the profits it had made selling radios to consumers in its own broadcast network, the National Broadcasting Company (NBC), in 1926. The AT&T and NBC networks, and the networks that followed—including the American Broadcasting Company (ABC), a spin-off of NBC—were only possible because of technologies developed by Bell Telephone Laboratories. A competing network, the Columbia Broadcasting System (CBS) was founded in 1927. During this time of explosive growth and competition in network radio, the wired telephone remained the standard technology for public and business communications.

With the network model in place, image broadcasts soon followed voice and music broadcasts—just as voice had followed telegraphy. Regularly scheduled TV broadcasts began in the United States in 1939, nearly a decade before the ENIAC I (the first practical all-digital computer) was developed. The ENIAC, like the radio broadcast equipment of that era, required an entire room just to hold the power supplies, vacuum tubes, and cables.

As a means of mollifying foreign competition, companies in the United States and Europe developed different TV broadcast standards. Although each claimed technical superiority in its own markets, the European standard was clearly superior. The relative differences of these incompatible standards remain today, virtually unchanged from their original specifications. Most TV viewers in the United States aren't even aware of the higher-quality images available to consumers overseas, but assume that domestic TV is as good as it gets. Even viewers of satellite TV in the United States can't take advantage of the superior image standards used in other countries; the TV signal from other countries is "degraded" to the National Television Standards Committee (NTSC) standard so that the images can be viewed on U.S. receivers.

Relying on proprietary standards in order to keep foreign competition at bay worked for only a few years. Asian manufacturers are very successful at producing and selling TV receivers designed for the United States and European markets, which use the NTSC and PAL (Phase Alternate Line) standards, respectively. For these Asian manufacturers, it's akin to manufacturing cars with the steering wheel on either the left or the right side of the car. The original motivation for deciding which side of the car the steering wheel should be on doesn't matter. For these electronics manufacturers, the politics of the situation doesn't concern them—it's simply a matter of meeting the standards for a given market. Today, U.S. domestic production of TV receivers is virtually nonexistent.

As TV began to attract the public's attention, telephone and radio technology continued to evolve. In 1946, AT&T created the Improved Mobile Telephone Service (IMTS), the first mobile radio system to connect with the regular public phone network. This system was mobile, but by no means portable or even luggable. The equipment weighed over 100 pounds—not including the separate car battery needed to power the system. The fixed component of the IMTS, a single, high-power transmitter and a tall antenna, provided a line-of-sight operating radius of about 50 miles. Meanwhile, engineers at Bell Laboratories created the first transistor in 1949. The *integrated circuit* (IC) was invented in 1958, the same year the first active communications satellite was launched. The IC or "chip," which can contain tens of thousands of transistors, made the microelectronics revolution of the late twentieth century possible. ARPANET, the precursor to the Internet, was developed in the 1960s as part of the national defense grid. This communications network was intended to provide a fault-tolerant communications backbone for the military and the government in the event of a nuclear attack.

As part of the Cold War effort, the AM shortwave radio broadcast services begun in the 1930s took on a new significance. A huge infusion of government monies created international radio broadcast systems capable of being heard around the globe. The most notable systems, the Voice of America, the British Broadcasting Corporation (BBC), and Radio Moscow acquired huge, high-powered transmitter facilities and antenna systems that covered acres of land. Hundreds of other international stations were created as well, and programs were beamed to target countries with the aid of elaborate antenna farms. Shortwave listening became an avocation for hundreds of thousands of Americans and for listeners throughout Europe, especially those behind the "iron curtain." Like computer users who surf the Web today, listeners scanned the shortwave bands until they happened on stations that provided the news and entertainment they needed. These noncommercial stations relied on government funding, not commercial advertising, to provide news and entertainment from a particular political perspective.

With advances in computer-based switching and electronic component miniaturization, as well as major innovations in battery technology, work on the cellular radio model began taking shape. A cellular model evolved that relied on a grid of single, low-powered mobile transceivers (combined transmitter and receiver units) that serviced a fixed, limited geographic area and switched from one cell to the next in order to follow the mobile customer. By 1973, Motorola demonstrated a mobile phone, about the size of a modern desktop PC, that worked with a network developed by AT&T. Five years later, the FCC authorized two experimental cellular licenses, one to AT&T and one to Motorola. In a parallel development, the FCC authorized the Specialized Mobile Radio (SMR) service in 1979—a two-way radio dispatch service for use in public safety, construction, and transportation industries. In 1981, the FCC authorized dual wireless/wired cellular licenses, one for wireless and one for wired services in each of several geographic areas. Because competition for licenses was so fierce, the FCC announced a lottery for cellular licenses in all markets below the top-thirty system in 1983, a year after the breakup of AT&T.

Advances in technology, politics, and business became even more interdependent during the 1980s and 1990s. Technologically, transistors, ICs, and other solid-state components essentially obliterated any trace of vacuum tubes and fueled the move toward miniaturization and handheld devices. As engineers became more experienced with new solid-state devices, especially computational systems, there was a shift from analog devices to more capable digital devices. The computer world discovered the value of real time, online transaction processing in the banking, airline, and process-control industries. The resulting systems provide the framework for current Web-based transactions.

In the business arena, this period was characterized by mergers and acquisitions. AT&T, which had previously only leased its equipment to homeowners and businesses, bowed to pressure to allow independently manufactured telephones on its network in 1986. Nextel, a major competitor to the established cellular services, came online in 1991, three years after the birth of the World Wide Web. The FCC authorized the auction of Personal Communications Services (PCS) licenses in 1993 in order to increase competition in areas served by cellular services. In 1995, AT&T made its move to become a major player in the wireless telecommunications arena by acquiring McCaw Cellular.

With the rapid proliferation of electronic products made possible by the new digital technology, the establishment of electronic standards became a political issue. Domestic manufacturers realized that cost cutting and globalization required the establishment of and adherence to standards for the interoperability of components, devices, and systems. With an ever-increasing number of wireless devices competing for the crowded radio frequency spectrum, the FCC began granting licenses in the relatively vacant higher operating frequencies, spurring technologic advances in the microwave frequencies and above. A major political milestone was the passage of the Telecommunications Act of 1996. One goal of this legislation was to increase competition by reducing previous regulations, making it easier for new businesses to enter the telecommunications market. During that same year, the TV industry adopted a volunteer rating system due to public concern over the exposure of children to sex and violence. This is also one of the concerns currently surrounding unrestricted access to content on the Web.

BACK TO THE FUTURE

Fast-forward to twenty-first-century America. Technology stocks account for roughly a third of U.S. stock-market value. Even though the United States lags behind several European and Asian countries in a number of key digital technologies, virtually everyone in the United States is wired for sound—either via FM radio, portable CD, minidisk, or solid-state MP3 players. Personal communications devices are not only part of every businessperson's wardrobe they hold the same status for teenagers that expensive sneakers once did. Parents keep track of their children in the shopping malls via electronic tethers, either in the form of cellular phones or miniature two-way radios. Televisions are as pervasive as clocks in most homes, and the wireless remote controls for

TVs and stereos are so common and inexpensive that they're considered accessories. Free, but limited, broadcast TV competes with for-fee cable and satellite TV services for viewers.

Cellular and PCS mobile phones are so heavily used by commuters that the federal government has investigated their use as a potential driving hazard. Some restaurants restrict or prohibit mobile phone use around other diners. Cellular phones have more in common with the original communicators and tricorders featured on the *Star Trek* TV series than with the luggable mobile phone systems of two decades ago. Mobile phones not only double as pagers and two-way radios, but allow users to surf the Internet, listen to FM radio or MP3 music, and even take pictures. Cordless phones for the home and office are outselling corded models in many markets. Inexpensive handheld and mobile Global Positioning System (GPS) devices have replaced the compass as the navigation tool of choice for hikers and motorists. Television satellite systems now provide hundreds of channels of programming from around the world.

Pocket pagers, smaller and lighter than the batteries that powered the first portable transistor radios, can send and receive messages. Wireless *personal digital assistants* (PDAs), such as the Palm VII, the RIM 957, and the HP Jornada, extend the knowledge base of the Internet to the palm of the user's hand, at any time and from any place. Other handheld wireless devices, such as the colorful Cybiko, are designed to allow teenagers to secretly send text messages up to 150 feet indoors. Motorola's Talkabout two-way pager is more sophisticated, even though it's available in colors from Totally Teal to Raspberry Ice. The palm-size pager with a keyboard is more like a pocket terminal than a pager for the high school and college crowd. Although most digital cell phones can double as pagers, the lack of national telecommunications standards for cell phones and email has kept the pager industry alive. Because carriers cannot agree on standards that will provide interoperability, there are vast areas of the United States without wireless phone service of any kind. This has made the pocket pager one of the few options for staying in touch.

Looking beyond the United States to the global market, mobile phone users in Finland can access Web sites and select pop songs to play as a signal of incoming calls. Finns and Swedes can purchase gasoline by dialing the toll-free number on a gas pump, or a Coke by calling the number on the Coke machine. The charge is simply added to their phone bill. Merita Nordbanken, the large Finnish/Swedish bank, allows its customers to buy and sell securities over their mobile phones. Teenagers use still-image—capable phones from Nokia to exchange photos. In England, Excite UK Ltd. offers local movie listings, stock prices, news, weather, and sports scores. Belgium's Europeaninvestor.com offers customized stock quotes and business headlines. In France, drivers can access real-time traffic information and navigation services through a mobile-phone service unit of Cegetel SA, one of the country's main long-distance phone carriers.

Business people in Japan can read the morning news and then check their bank balance on their cell phone. Waiters in some European cafes use wireless tablets to take orders and process credit and debit cards at the table. In Japan, teenagers and business people subscribe to a service that downloads a cartoon character onto their cell phones daily. Some cell phones are so advanced that people can send and receive email in either Japanese or English, record conversations, exchange information through infrared links, program ringers to play a choice of tunes, navigate the Internet, play games, and even learn English through a daily subscription service. Third-party add-ons, such as stick-on fingernails that flash to indicate an incoming cell phone call, are popular among phone-toting Japanese youth. This activity in the wireless market suggests that it is poised to become the fastest-growing phenomenon in the United States, Europe, and Asia since the Web. However, consumers in Europe and Asia are working with the wireless Web while Web-enabled products are just being released in the United States.

Global and domestic telecom acquisitions and mergers are as active and as hotly debated as the dotComs once were. For example, in the domestic market, Worldcom acquired MCI. Bell Atlantic and GTE merged to form Verizon. Sprint, barred from acquiring Worldcom by a U.S. Justice Department ruling, became an acquisition target of European telecom giants like Deutsche Telekom, France Telecom, and Madrid-based Telefonica. AT&T, forced to consider dumping its consumer long-distance services to get out of debt, played catch-up in the wireless world with Verizon. It's clear that regardless of what happens on Wall Street, activity in the wireless telecommunications market is a global phenomenon, and much of the leading-edge activity—especially in Web-enabled wireless communications—is occurring in Europe and Asia.

The events outlined above are relevant today because they illustrate that the developmental history of telecommunications, like that of the Web, has been circuitous and fraught with technical, political, and business challenges. For example, the Iridium satellite system, backed by telecommunications giants such as Motorola, was a failure. Although the system was successful in providing mobile phone service from any point on the planet, it had to be decommissioned in 2000, just two years after it was put into service. Iridium handheld units were bulky and expensive, the per-minute costs were astronomical, and the system simply couldn't compete with inexpensive, highly mobile land-based technologies. AT&T Wireless, on the other hand, rents specially programmed Nokia cell phones to international travelers that can be used with the same number and features in over 100 countries—at less than 10 percent of the monthly rate charged to Iridium system users.

The telecommunications environment that has evolved since the first telegraph services suggests that there are similar surprises in store for companies moving to the unwired Web. Unlike the virtually unpoliced wired Web, the telecommunications industry is highly regulated. This clash of cultures represents a potential barrier to dotCom executives who are unaware of—and unprepared to provide—the resources required to get things done in the telecommunications business environment created by national and international lawmakers.

The initial success of mobile phones and GPS has been colored by federal investigations into their safety. Not only have these systems been implicated in driving accidents but the radiation from mobile phones may pose a direct health risk. In addition to a $1 million industry-sponsored study overseen by the FDA, mobile phone makers are now required to disclose the radiation levels produced by their devices under a policy adopted by the *Cellular* Telecommunications Industry Association (CTIA), the wireless industry's top trade group. This policy requires manufacturers to enclose information on handset emissions and an explanation of the testing process inside each cell phone box.

Despite the regulatory, technical, and business hurdles, the wireless Web represents a tremendous opportunity for businesses to leverage their existing or future investment on the Web.

ETHER-COMMERCE

Ether-Commerce, sometimes referred to as *mCommerce* or *Mobile Commerce*, is the use of wireless technologies to access content on the Web or to use the Internet as the network for voice and data communications. According to the hype, the business opportunities are virtually limitless. Nearly 100 million subscribers are projected to be connected to one or more cellular networks by 2003.

The future looks especially bright because much of the potential consumer base is already primed for a wireless Web experience. An increasingly large pool of professionals in the United States regularly rely on cell phones for instant communications along with PDAs to plan their day, keep track of contacts, and access the Web. Not only are many potential customers familiar with the technologies underlying the wireless Web but many have come to entrust their data to hardware devices. In contrast, the Web took several years to be accepted by the general population. In many cases, this was simply because the Web was so different from the norm for consumers. This isn't the case in Ether-Commerce, where, thanks to hype from Wall Street and advertisers, consumers' expectations of what is possible today are far greater than the current technology can support.

In simplest terms, when properly executed, wireless Web connectivity provides location-independent access to a virtually unlimited library of knowledge and applications—including decision support tools. A secondary benefit is mobility, or freedom from wires and cables, which enables activities such as remote data acquisition. Of course, the elimination of wires doesn't negate the need to integrate wireless hardware with other systems, provide secure transactions, or guarantee reasonable response times. Despite these and other challenges, the lure of the wireless Web is impossible to ignore. Consider a few of the specific, potentially life-changing and pervasive potential applications in Ether-Commerce:

- **Time management.** A PDA with wireless, networked peripherals can maintain information about how long a woman is on the phone and with whom, how much time she spends watching TV and the type of content she views, and how much time she spends exercising. Web-based personal calendars and to-do lists can be accessed and updated at any time.
- **Just-in-time, just-in-place information.** Instant access to the anytime, anywhere Web can be used to identify and make reservations at the nearest restaurant or hotel, or an appointment at the nearest dentist's office. The user can request that titles of articles from key newspapers be sent to him, alerting him to check the online or printed version of the full article, akin to an electronic version of the front page of the *Wall Street Journal.*
- **eMenus.** A customer can order food or services from a location-specific menu downloaded onto his smart phone (if it has Web access) or wireless PDA when he walks into a restaurant. With a Web-enabled phone or PDA, he can also reserve a table and place his order while he's driving to the restaurant.
- **eTickets.** With a wireless, Web-enabled PDA or phone, potential customers can search for a particular show in their area and then purchase tickets online. The same model could work with similar businesses, such as airline reservations.
- **eCoupons.** Similar to just-in-time time information, stores can provide a woman with custom coupons that appear on her PDA when she enters a retail store.
- **Personal simulations.** A businessman's smart phone can store and document the calories he expends throughout the day and the nutrients ingested at each meal and snack. The system can communicate the information to his physiologic simulation, allowing his health care professional to track and predict his health status in real time.
- **Preview events.** A moviegoer equipped with video-enabled smart phones can preview movie trailers before she buys an eTicket online.
- **Instant ordering.** A listener who hears a song on his radio while driving can instantly order and download the music through a wireless connection to the Internet.
- **eLearning.** Access to just-in-time learning, on-site references, and review materials for knowledge workers in the medical, legal, and engineering professions can reduce errors and increase efficiency.
- **Online auctioning.** A person participating in online auctions can respond to the time-sensitive data at any time and from any place.

Auctioning, one of the hottest activities on the wireless Web, is ideally suited to Web-enabled cellular phones and wireless personal digital assistants.

- **Personal productivity.** Access to email, phone book, calendar, instant messaging, chat, personal trading, mobile banking, and mobile shopping can save time and increase productivity by transforming time spent sitting in traffic and waiting in line into productive time.
- **Remote services.** Continually available alerts and notification, remote monitoring, remote automobile diagnostics, telemedicine, telemetry, service reporting, on-demand video conferencing, virtual collaboration, as well as audio and video on demand can change how people communicate.
- **Financial customer support.** Portfolio and account information, indication of interest, research and alerts, quotes, trading/allocation and confirmation, and analyst reports can be made available via a wireless device, providing investors with the information they need to manage their investments at any time and in any place. Stock trades can be initiated whenever the market is open.
- **Entertainment.** Wireless connectivity between game players will create a new pastime for millions of gamesters. Daily jokes, horoscopes, and other information can be emailed to a mobile phone by subscription.

These applications have yet to make it to mainstream users in the domestic market, but most are enjoyed by those in other countries, early adopters in the United States, and engineers in several research and development (R&D) shops. However, as the Web has demonstrated, if someone can imagine an application, it can be created. The question is when—not if—Ether-Commerce will take off from niche applications for use by the U.S. public.

Quantifying the potential of Ether-Commerce from an eCommerce perspective entails more than determining how much customers are willing pay for the privilege of checking their email from the road. As more companies move to integrate wireless technology into their information technology infrastructure, their executives realize that there are many questions to be answered when formulating a plan to meet the expected demand for wireless applications. These questions include:

Which wireless technology should be used, and will it be compatible with existing management systems? Should the wireless systems be used for content delivery or strictly to support transactions? Which strategic partners should be considered when moving to a wireless Web presence? From an eCommerce perspective, which of the services and information described above will customers expect and be willing to purchase? Will the disparity between the hype and what companies can actually deliver in the near future quash the rush to the wireless Web? Will activities such as online auctions and eTicketing help push the wireless Web past early adopters and into the mainstream? How will developments in Ether-Commerce in Europe and Asia affect the market in the United States? Will technology be able to keep up with customer expectations? What are the global and domestic market projections for the wireless Web? The next section begins the exploration of these and related issues from global and domestic eCommerce perspectives.

GLOBAL ECOMMERCE ON THE WIRELESS WEB

If the current stock market activity is any barometer of the viability of an industry, all indicators point to wireless eCommerce as the next "new thing." Unlike the PC-based wired Web, which has been a predominantly U.S. endeavor, the wireless Web is a global phenomenon—primarily because Europe and Asia have been the test beds for wireless Web development. In Japan, where about 40 percent of the population owns a mobile phone, the wired Web has been leapfrogged; many wireless Web customers have never logged on to the wired Web.

Although the United States is the dominant figure in the world of the desktop PC, domestic wireless voice and data networks are slower and much less extensive than those in Europe and Asia. Unlike most Americans, Europeans and Asians don't limit most of their developments in digital technology to desktop or laptop PCs. Non-PC-based digital appliances, from cell phones to wristwatches with built-in electronic ski passes, vastly outnumber expensive desktop systems.

In Italy, Europe's largest market for mobile phones, almost 30 million mobile phone subscribers outnumber PC-based Internet users 5 to 1. This is only slightly higher than the European average of about 4 to 1. The mobile phone markets with the greatest market penetration in Europe [Finland (about 60 percent), Norway (about 50 percent), Sweden (about 45 percent), and Italy (about 35 percent)] benefit from a wireless standard called the Global System for Mobile Communications (GSM). Subscribers with GSM-compatible phones can access the cellular network in over 130 countries.

Current market indicators suggest that the wireless industries, principally the global telecommunications companies, are growing faster than the Internet ever did, and for good reason. The traditional wired Web, with graphics, animations, video, and sound, may be nice to surf during phone calls or between meetings. However, if a businesswoman is running late for an appointment because she can't locate an office building, a mobile phone can be invaluable. A smart phone can be even more valuable if she can use it to access a map—even one displayed on a postage-stamp-size mobile phone display—indicating exactly where the meeting is being held.

By 2003, over 500 million mobile phones will be in use globally, and only about half as many people will be surfing the Web from their desktop computers. Clearly, mobile computing and information access has the potential to outpace the wired Internet. Perhaps, stated more correctly, the Internet is one of the enabling technologies making it possible for mobile computing and telecommunications to grow so rapidly.

To appreciate the potential of the wireless voice and data communications industry, consider the events of early 2000 in the global telecommunications arena, particularly in Europe and Asia. Britain's Vodafone AirTouch PLC spent almost $200 billion in a hostile takeover of Germany's Mannesmann. France Telecom acquired Britain's Orange, a mobile-phone operator, for nearly $40 billion. KPN Royal Dutch Telecom, the leading telecommunications company in the Netherlands, with over 3.6 million mobile customers, invested heavily in Germany's E-Plus, the third largest mobile operator in Germany. The new entity, KPN Mobile, has a pan-European customer base of nearly 8 million mobile subscribers.

Mobile phone licenses throughout Europe were scooped up at multiples of their original offerings. Stocks of Deutsche Telekom, France Telecom, Telecom Italia Mobile, Ericsson, Nokia, Vodafone AirTouch PLC, and other mobile phone and infrastructure equipment manufacturers remained strong, despite the high-technology sell-off of late 1999 and early 2000.

In Japan, NTT DoCoMo's I-Mode, an optional mobile Internet connection service established in early 1999, is used by a quarter of DoCoMo's 30 million subscribers. This figure represents nearly 8 million subscribers, or over 6 percent of the Japanese population, who use I-Mode to read and send email, check stock quotes, look up train schedules, obtain maps, buy movie tickets, and download and play new ring tones. The revenues of DoCoMo (which means "anywhere"), the publicly traded wireless spin-off of the powerful Nippon Telegraph & Telephone Corporation, are expected to climb sharply as smart cell phones capable of supporting video, and the underlying high-speed communications infrastructure, become available throughout Japan. As it is, DoCoMo is already the world's largest mobile Internet service. Activity in the wireless sector in both Europe and Japan supports predictions that Web-enabled mobile phones and other mobile devices will become the primary means by which customers interact with the Internet in Europe and parts of Asia.

THE MAJOR PLAYERS

As of 2000, the major players in the global wireless Web game fit into one of six categories. There are those that:

- Create the underlying infrastructure, including fiber backbones, satellites, routers, and cellular stations
- Design, develop, market, and support end-user hardware, including wireless PDAs, wireless modems, two-way pagers, and digital mobile phones

- Produce end-user hardware
- Develop operating system software for connecting smart phones and PDAs to the wireless Web
- Develop micro-browsers, the Web interfaces for smart phones and wireless PDAs
- Operate mobile phone and pager networks

In addition to the major players, there are hundreds of ancillary contributors to the wireless Web movement. One class of ancillary contributors that may assume prominence is that of Wireless Enablers. These companies, such as Solutions, Aether Systems, and Datalink.net, sell software and services that take care of the information conversion to and from a variety of wireless devices and networks. There are also thousands of Web developers, quality control groups, Web translation services, data warehouse developers, chip manufacturers, package designers, testing services, and marketing and advertising groups that have a stake in the success of the wireless Web. For example, Texas Instruments, the global producer of *digital signal processing* (DSP) chips for mobile phones, shipped over 200 million chip sets worldwide in 1999. The one thing all these players have in common is volatility.

The companies that design, develop, market, and support end-user hardware aren't necessarily the ones that actually produce the hardware. For example, Motorola doesn't make cell phones and Cisco Systems doesn't make routers. These companies market and support the products, but the products are outsourced to third-party Electronic Manufacturing Services (EMS), an $88 billion business in 2000. The motivation for EMS outsourcing is clear: They can create products faster and cheaper than the contracting company. Companies like Ericsson outsource so they can concentrate on R&D, product design, sales, marketing, and bringing new products to market faster.

As the wired Web has painfully demonstrated, standards are everything. Physical connectivity is worthless with incompatible browsers or operating systems. The Symbian Alliance is one example of a high-visibility standards organization with the mission of creating an environment promoting the proliferation and use of mobile phones. The role of the Symbian Alliance—composed of Ericsson, Motorola, Nokia, Matsushita Communication Industries, and Psion—is to set standard licensing terms and conditions for what they call the Symbian Platform.

Another point to consider is that many domestic companies have foreign investors, and vice versa. Finland's Sonera Ltd. and Hong Kong's Hutchinson Whamopa Ltd. are large shareholders in VoiceStream Wireless Corp., a Bellevue, Washington, company. Japan's NTT DoCoMo is a major investor in the mobile phone unit of Royal KPN NV of the Netherlands.

Five of the largest Electronic Manufacturing Services contractors in the United States are Solectron, Flextronics, Jabil Circuit, Celestica, and SCI

Systems. Solectron, the world's largest EMS contractor, has Cisco, Hewlett Packard (HP), NCR, Nortel, and IBM among its customers. Flextronics is the world's fourth largest EMS manufacturer, and the EMS leader in cell phones, games, pagers, mice, and PDAs. It outsources for Motorola, Palm, Rocket e-Book, Gateway, Philips, Ericsson, Cisco, Compaq, and Siemens. Jabil Circuits focuses on communications equipment and outsources for HP, Cisco, Gateway, Motorola, and Network Appliances. Celestica, which outsources for HP, IBM, and Sun Microsystems, is the dominant EMS contractor for LAN and Internet services. SCI Systems, the oldest EMS contractor, with nearly 40 plants worldwide, outsources for Nokia, HP, and Compaq. EMS contracts can involve significant revenues. For example, Solectron-Nortel and Flextronics-Motorola are $10 billion and $30 billion relationships, respectively.

THE DOMESTIC WIRELESS MARKET

In the world of the wireless Web, the United States has been slow to catch on. Only about a quarter of U.S. citizens own a cellular phone—less than the European Union's 15-member penetration figure that approaches 50 percent. This lack of cellular phone penetration in the domestic market is partly due to the lack of a standardized, nationwide telecommunications carrier. Unlike Europe, where a single phone can be used in Germany, France, or Sweden, a traveler in the United States may have to carry a dual analog-digital phone, deal with roaming charges, or simply do without services in some regions.

Some wireless carriers, such as VoiceStream Wireless, which acquired Aerial Communications, Inc., and Omnipoint Corp., use the GSM standard popular throughout Europe. Most other major U.S. wireless carriers use an incompatible system, usually Code Division Multiple Access (CDMA) and, rarely, Time Division Multiple Access (TDMA). Like U.S. NTSC and European PAL TV, the United States and Europe each have a stake in the success of their incompatible standards. However, except for a few companies like Qualcomm of San Diego, California, that hold patents on the U.S. technologies, there aren't many clear winners for the CDMA standard. Another factor is the shortage of smart phones and other wireless hardware. The Palm VII wireless PDA is one of the most popular wireless devices for accessing the wireless Web in the United States, and even it has limited penetration.

Most mobile phones in the United States can't access the wireless Web, and the new Internet-ready phones are in short supply. In addition to customer resistance created by relatively expensive mobile phone Internet connect charges, there is also a lack of content on the Web capable of being accessed and displayed by wireless mobile devices. Although there are over 15,000 sites available to I-Mode users in Japan, only a small fraction of that number are available for domestic users. Another issue is the volatility of the domestic telecom market. Even though the $155 billion U.S. communications market is significant, the stability of the U.S. market is questionable. For example, AT&T's long-term viability in the long-distance market is questionable as it diversifies into wireless digital communications.

With the feeding frenzy of serial acquisitions and mergers, it's difficult to predict the future in the extremely volatile domestic wireless Web market. However, global players, like Deutsche Telekom, DoCoMo, and France Telecom, may eventually dominate at least a segment of the domestic market by acquiring smaller domestic companies like Sprint or WorldCom, including domestic companies with large overseas shareholders, such as VoiceStream Wireless. There are several potential impediments to such a scenario. A prerequisite for Deutsche Telekom to capture a significant U.S. presence is for the German government–owned company to circumvent U.S. political opposition to a company owned by a foreign government buying a U.S. company. Many foreign telecommunications firms want access to the U.S. market, and buying a domestic wireless company is the fastest way to get it. Unlike wired telecommunications services, which are heavily regulated by state governments, wireless services are a quick and painless way to capture local markets. Collaborative arrangements are another way to gain access to the U.S. domestic market. For example, Sybase Inc.'s mobile computing subsidiary, iAnywhere Solutions, Inc., teamed with Ericsson to develop mobile banking and trading applications that will run on Sybase servers and be accessible via Ericsson mobile phones.

In the domestic market, Verizon is positioned to take the lead in wireless communications. Cisco Systems, Inc. and Intel Corporation continue to grow by supplying the building blocks of the wired and wireless eCommerce infrastructure. Amidst the domestic activity, corporate America is following events very closely in Europe and Japan, as it prepares to compete globally to supply Web-enabled mobile phones, wireless PDAs, and two-way pagers. Even seemingly small political steps, such as the ruling in early 2000 that digital signatures are legally binding, aid the case for wireless eCommerce. Similarly, the lack of browser standards on wireless phones from different manufacturers presents a challenge for software developers, reminiscent of the Microsoft–Netscape browser incompatibility issues. To address this issue, Phone.com, the U.S. company that pioneered the concept of providing a browser on wireless phones, has established a testing center in Belfast, Ireland, to test for browser compatibility. A standard browser environment will simplify and speed the task of developing content for distribution on mobile phones.

Revisiting the theme of repeating patterns in business, technology, and politics, consider some of the domestic players in the wireless Web game and their resemblance to pioneers in radio, network broadcasting, and computing. Microsoft, like the original AT&T, was found guilty of antitrust activity. Palm Computing, like RCA, made its initial mark and its money by selling hardware. In 2000, it reinvented itself as an Internet company. It still sells wireless products, like the original Palm VII wireless PDA, but has poured its energy into developing a wireless infrastructure. Like RCA, Palm Computing diversified into a related and potentially more lucrative market based on a network model it helped develop.

Sometimes technologic innovations fail in the marketplace because they don't meet expectations, even when they perform a useful function. Consider the *artificial intelligence* (AI) market of the past two decades in the United States. In the early 1970s, research in AI techniques at the Massachusetts Institute of Technology (MIT) and other academic research institutions was the next "new thing." All the ingredients seemed to be in place. There was ample funding from the U.S. military and government agencies that were anxious to use AI techniques to guide missile systems, predict nuclear attack scenarios, and translate Russian to English in real time.

However, because of the hype and overblown expectations leveled at AI, it failed in the marketplace. Neural networks, rule-based expert systems, and other technologies that had graced the covers of magazines and propelled unknown researchers to become the heads of companies, disappeared as soon as federal funding dried up. However, work continued with much diminished funding in specific niches, and practical AI applications have been developed for camera systems, copiers, and even in the form of intelligent agents that make shopping through Web-enabled smart phones easier and quicker. This experience with AI suggests that a key challenge with the wireless Web is to avoid the overblown hype (that could quash the movement for decades or longer) through appropriate expectation management. In other words, the challenges of limited screen size, lack of graphics, slow response times, security, lack of content formatted for mobile phone users, browser incompatibilities, and cost must be addressed from a marketing as well as a technical perspective.

The next chapter continues to explore ether-commerce as a natural, evolutionary development of the Internet. It also examines the new wireless Internet in terms of the market drivers and implications of pervasive computing, and reviews the mobile and fixed wireless markets.

EXECUTIVE SUMMARY

Technologic, business, and political changes usually follow familiar patterns. Communication tends to speed evolutionary changes in the improvement of a technology or process, and facilitates revolutionary changes that can redefine and create entire markets. Despite frequent technologic advances championed by visionary entrepreneurs, it may take years or even decades for society to change enough to turn research into commercially viable products.

At the cusp of the twenty-first century, the wireless market is poised to be the fastest growing phenomenon in the United States, Europe, and Asia since the Web. The market is extremely volatile, with companies coming and going, collaborating, and consolidating. Global and domestic telecom acquisitions and mergers are as hotly debated as the dotComs once were at their peak.

Ether-Commerce, the use of wireless technologies to access content on the Web or the use of the Internet as the network for voice and data communications, looks especially bright because much of the potential consumer base is already primed for a wireless Web experience. Applications of wireless eCommerce range from time management, just-in-time/just-in-place information, eMenus, eTickets, eCoupons, and personal simulations, to event previews, instant ordering, eLearning, online auctioning, personal productivity, remote services, financial customer support, and entertainment. Some of these applications are already in use in Europe and Asia, while others are under development.

The wireless Web is a global phenomenon, primarily because Europe and Asia have been the test beds for wireless Web development. The Internet is one of the enabling technologies making it possible for mobile computing and telecommunications to grow so rapidly. The major players in the global wireless Web game are creators of the underlying infrastructure, end-user hardware, operating system software, micro-browsers, and mobile phone network operators.

The United States has been slow to catch on due to the lack of a standardized, nationwide telecommunications carrier, the lack of smart phones and other wireless hardware, and the lack of content on the Web capable of being accessed and displayed by wireless mobile devices. Europeans, in contrast, have a single wireless standard and much more wireless-compatible content to choose from. Despite the apparently sanguine future, the U.S. experience with AI suggests that a major challenge with the wireless Web will be to avoid the overblown hype that could undermine the move to wireless in the United States.

2

Evolution or Revolution?

Life is pretty simple: You do some stuff. Most fails. Some works.
You do more of what works. If it works big, others quickly copy it.
Then you do something else.
The trick is the doing something else.

Tom Peters, business speaker

INTRODUCTION

At a time when Internet start-ups face global cooling, and enthusiastic dot-Com investors are an endangered species, it may seem paradoxical that monies are pouring into telecommunications ventures in the United States and abroad. Even though venture capitalists are raising their standards, start-up firms are withdrawing their initial public offerings (IPOs), and tumbling dot-Com stock prices have crushed the prospects of traditional wired Web start-ups, there is a flurry of excitement around anything remotely related to the wireless Web. This is especially true of the underlying network infrastructure. Although some of the excitement may reflect an overreaction to marketing hype, there are reasonable grounds for a positive outlook on the wireless Web and related technologies. Developments in ether-commerce are a logical extension of the technologic and societal changes related to the Web.

NATURAL EVOLUTION

From one perspective, ether-commerce is a natural—even expected—evolutionary development of the wired Web. Consider the pieces of the wireless Web puzzle that are now in place, or were developed in one form or another during the mid to late 1990s:

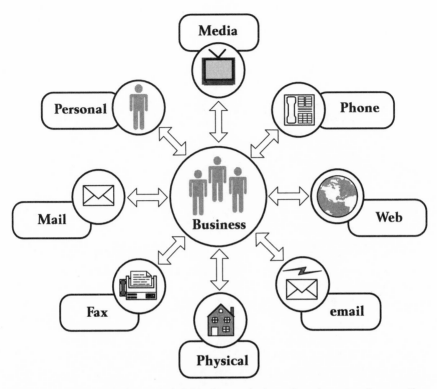

Figure 2-1. Touch points for a typical click-and-mortar business, from the customer's perspective.

Maturation of the Wired Web

The wired Web is a repository of knowledge and information in the form of text, graphics, video, and sound. This information network, originally designed as a document-sharing and archiving system, is the beneficiary of content from physicians and physicists to grade-school students and prison inmates. The Internet, and the Web interface to the Internet in particular, is one of the primary drivers of the wireless Web. Without access to the Web, wireless customers would be limited to private networks controlled by wireless hardware vendors and micro-browser developers. Furthermore, without access to the Web, wireless customers couldn't easily access or modify personal Web content, such as the links listed on their home directory or their Internet-enabled device.

The wired Web is also important because it has served as a test bed for developers and advanced users who experimented with what the Web could offer. Today, most consumers are aware of browsers, hypertext, and the hardware and software tools required to cruise the information superhighway. Just as important, seasoned Web developers recognize the importance of standards, of using the appropriate tools to make the task of programming easier. They have also learned to appreciate and work in Internet time, especially in regard to bringing products to market in a timely manner. A caveat is that Web phones designed to work with proprietary, non-HTML–coded content effectively limit the user's access to the Web. A further restriction, from a global perspective, is that most of the content is in English, and despite the global extent of the Internet, most content is created and used in the United States.

Natural Touch-Point Extension

The movement from traditional click-and-mortar touch points (Figure 2-1) to a business that includes wireless touch points (Figure 2-2) is a natural and obvious one. As illustrated in Figure 2-1, touch points for a typical click-and-mortar business, from the consumer's perspective, include the physical building, personal contact, mail, phone, fax, email, the Web, and traditional media advertising. Depending on the nature of the business, some of these touch points will be more prominent than others, and some may be nonexistent. The natural extension of wired touch points, illustrated in Figure 2-2, includes wireless support for two-way pagers and a variety of phone and handheld devices. In the near future, click-and-mortar companies will consider wireless connectivity as an ordinary, everyday touch point, just as wired telephone and fax services are today.

The Telecom Industry Is Growing, Standardizing, and Coalescing

The next piece of the wireless Web puzzle to fall into place is the proliferation and standardization of domestic and global telecommunications systems. These private networks may resemble the Internet, but typically rely on proprietary hardware and software standards. For Europeans, one positive result of the formation of the European Union (EU) was the standardization of telecommunications in the 15 EU countries. Although there were seven or eight wireless telecommunications standards floating around Europe at the end of the century, today most of Europe has only one wireless standard, GSM.

Even with the deregulation of telecommunications in Europe in 1998, European mobile phone customers don't have to concern themselves with the differences between PCS and cellular services, deal with roaming charges, or determine the extent of coverage areas. In contrast, customers in the United States are confronted with a potentially confusing array of products and wireless telecommunications standards. Despite these and other limitations, business professionals and an increasingly larger percentage of the general population rely on the telecom system for their everyday communications needs.

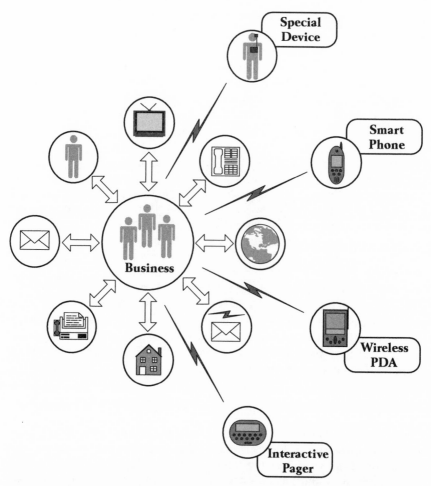

Figure 2-2. Touch points for a click-and-mortar business that includes wireless connectivity is a natural, evolutionary extension of traditional touch points. The wireless touch points illustrated here are special devices, such as wearable computers, smart phones, wireless PDAs, and interactive pagers.

Proliferation of All-Digital Cellular Systems

The replacement of the legacy analog cellular systems popular in the mid-1990s with digital technology makes possible added functionality in the handsets, with options such as caller ID. An all-digital system usually results in power savings as well, allowing for a smaller form factor, or more room for batteries without increasing the size of the unit. Wireless Internet service is only available on digital networks.

Proliferation of Wireless and Cordless Phones

Although the sight may have been cause for alarm a few years ago, it's difficult to walk down a busy city street or across a university campus today without passing someone who appears to be talking to him- or herself. The proliferation of wireless phones suggests that people from all walks of life have come to rely on them for everyday communications—not just emergencies or urgent calls.

Cell phones have not only become a habit; they're a status symbol as well. Everyone from high school and college students to investment bankers sport pagers and wireless phones to keep in touch with friends or business associates. By wearing a cell phone, users imply that they are important enough to be paged and that they have a circle of friends to call. Just as many immigrants in the United States during the early 1900s carried an ink pen in their front pocket to suggest that they possessed the ability to write—although many could not—a cell phone suggests literacy in the modern technology culture. For many in the business world, wireless pagers and phones are simply tools of the trade, and a natural and expected part of everyone's wardrobe.

Widespread Acceptance of PDAs

The success of the affordable RIM, Palm, and CE-based PDAs suggests that people recognize the value of having relatively recent—at least since the last sync operation—calendar, phone, and to-do-list information on hand at all times, even when they're away from their desktop computer. What's more, the popularity of PDAs—whether inexpensive, translucent hot-pink models designed for teenagers to keep track of schoolmates' names and phone numbers, or a business executive's RIM 957—indicates a level of trust in the technology. Most users don't fear that their PDA will suddenly crash, leaving them without their meticulously compiled records. Reliability breeds trust, and trust results in users relying on the technology even more. The success of PDAs has primed users to experience the wireless Web.

Unlike desktop computers, PDAs provide data at any time and at any place, and most importantly, without delay. PDA users have been primed to expect that they can activate their unit, search and retrieve the data they need, deactivate the unit, and return the PDA to its carrying case or a desk drawer, long before a desktop PC has finished booting. PDA users are also accustomed to a much more compact, non-PC interface. For example, although the Palm Pilot's screen real estate is limited, support for handwriting recognition and the simplified user interface make it easy to use. PDA users are prepared to trade limited screen size for a small form factor.

Wireless Is a Déjà Vu Experience

Corporate America and hundreds of thousands of programmers, designers, HTML coders, and database professionals are familiar with the costs, technologies, and nuances of archiving, updating content, and determining the resources needed to maintain a Web presence. The merits and constraints of push services, where personalized content is forwarded to users based on their preferences, provides a starting point for delivering content via smart phones and other mobile Internet-enabled devices. Experience with developing and updating content for the wired Web, and of addressing intellectual property and privacy concerns, will help developers circumvent many of the potential roadblocks on the path to developing wireless Web applications.

Often, the techniques and technologies developed for the wired Web translate directly to wireless Web applications. For example, after years of playing a distant third to Netscape and Explorer, established browser companies such as Spyglass, ICE, and Opera have a new lease on life in the form of microbrowsers. For mobile phone suppliers, a company with years of real-world experience developing and testing browsers counts for more than a hot IPO.

Advances in Electronic Design

Thanks to progress in electronic component design, especially in the area of application specific integrated circuits (ASICs), miniaturization of cellular handsets is now limited by the minimum size of the keypad that users need to enter phone numbers. Whereas early cellular phones were built with hundreds of discrete components and a few integrated circuits, modern units are built around one or two integrated circuits. The simplified design results in cost savings during assembly, as well as a more compact design.

With the latest electronic power management circuitry, power can be supplied to a smart phone or other wireless device for extended periods of time. Thanks to smart power packs, which contain their own microprocessor chips, a cell phone can be powered by a battery pack for 48 hours or more in standby or receive-only mode, and for several hours of talk or Web access.

Proliferation of Miscellaneous Wireless Devices

Another component of the technologic and social foundation for the wireless Web is the proliferation and public acceptance of miscellaneous wireless devices, from garage door openers to TV remote controls. Wireless is no longer mysterious. Increasingly, the tangle of wires stuffed behind every home and office PC is being replaced by a wireless network. Fixed wireless network products like CyberGenie, Airport, and AirConnect are increasingly popular alternatives to wired printer and computer resource sharing. Similarly, Palm Pilot owners commonly beam information from one PDA to another by using the Palm's built-in wireless Infrared (IR) port. Many laptops also sync with Palm Pilot and Windows CE PDAs through IR connections. Kensington and other manufacturers offer wireless, IR-linked keyboards and mice.

Ready Money for Telecom Mergers and Acquisitions

Thanks in part to a healthy European economy, Europe's Internet power-houses—former telephone company monopolies like Deutsche Telekom and France Telecom—are in buying mode. As they are expanding their content and geographic domain by acquiring smaller companies, they are standardizing the telecommunications system. Domestic mergers and acquisitions are frequently fueled in part by foreign investment, since wireless is usually the fastest and least complicated means for a European company to establish a foothold in the U.S. market. Of course, there are also domestic mergers and acquisitions.

Increased Customer Expectations

Consider the fundamental components of a successful wireless Web strategy and how they relate to each other. The prerequisite technical and business achievements, together with customers' experience with wireless technologies and the price points set by similar technologies, not only prepare the foundation for what is technically feasible but also help mold customer expectations.

Taken as a whole, most of these individual contributions portend a positive future for the wireless Web. Consider how mobile computing has been primed by the use of PDAs. With wireless Web connectivity, the process of syncing a PDA with a host PC to exchange data could be a thing of the past, and up-to-date information could be downloaded or accessed in seconds. Wireless devices, from PDA/interactive pagers, TV remote controls, and model airplane controllers, to the handheld product tracking devices used in grocery stores and large warehouses, have been around for years. What's different today is the networking standards that allow the linking of tens of millions of users to each other and the Web. It's one thing to have a wireless remote control that communicates with a TV and another to have a remote control that can access anything on the World Wide Web!

REVOLUTIONARY DEVELOPMENTS

An old cliché for the wired Web is that the Web changes everything. That may be true, but what's also true is that the wireless Web changes everything we know about the Web. The revolutionary aspects of the wireless Web are a result of:

Location Specificity. The design of a cellular system allows the customer's location to be determined within a few hundred meters. This location specificity can be used to assist the customer in locating the nearest theater, hospital, restaurant, or ATM.

Ease of Personalization. With a known phone number or cell location, it's easy for the service provider and, by extension, the wireless Web-site operator, to determine the customer's demographics. If detailed demographic information isn't available, then general information, such as the customer's town of residence, can be used to personalize his wireless experience. Often, this level of customer detail isn't possible on the wired Web without significant user interaction with the site.

New Monetary Models. In some wireless smart phone systems, the hardware vendor is the portal provider. This puts the provider in a position to extract fees from Web sites wishing to be listed on the PDA or cell phone's home page. Some smart phone systems allow the customer to modify her home page by logging onto a Web site. In this system, banner ads and other forms of advertisement are placed on the higher-bandwidth wired Web, leaving the handset free of advertising. The wireless Web challenges the concept of the worth of a Web portal and the value of click-throughs.

New Interface Models. In an almost shocking change, graphics and color have limited importance in wireless Web applications. Free-form hypertext linking also takes on less importance with postage-stamp-size screens. Typical Web-enabled phones can display only three to five lines of 15 to 17 characters of text, plus two or three lines for status and menu information.

Given the nature of the mobile work environment, immediacy of response is of utmost importance. Some delivery vehicles perform better than others. For example, smart phones have a delay or latency on the order of two seconds. Two-way pagers have a 30- to 90-second latency. The current Palm VII has a delay of between 5 and 15 seconds.

Transaction Focus. Because of the nature of the mobile work environment, most wireless encounters are transaction-based (as opposed to information-based). That is, most customers expect specific, concise information with a minimum of delay.

LIMITATIONS AND OPPORTUNITIES

The new wireless Web has its share of both limitations and opportunities. The most significant are listed below.

Bandwidth Limitations

The bandwidth of most smart phones and wireless PDAs used in the United States is limited to less than 14.4 KBps, or about a quarter of the speed of the standard 56-KBps connection to the wired Web. This bandwidth restriction places a practical limit on the amount of information (especially nontext information) that can be sent to and from a wireless Web device in a reasonable amount of time. There are faster services available in parts of Europe and Japan, and all wireless markets have plans for increased bandwidth capacity in the near future. Just as DSL and cable modem companies are finding markets for users desiring greater bandwidth connections to the wired Web, there are opportunities for companies that offer premium wireless bandwidth services as well.

Incomplete Service Coverage. Despite the global nature of the Web and of the telecommunications industries, coverage for the wireless Web is far from global. With the exception of Japan, most countries, including the United States, have spotty wireless Web coverage. This is especially true when the mode of communications is considered. There is no single, nationwide wireless operator that blankets the United States with coverage. Because of the nature of terrestrial radio, even a covered area is usually dependent, to some degree, on the effects of structures, foliage, and weather-absorbing radio-frequency (RF) energy.

For example, coverage for Palm devices through Palm.Net, also known as BellSouth Mobile, is limited to about 230 U.S. cities. In addition, some areas require the user to be outside to transmit, while some areas have enough coverage to allow indoor transmit and receive wireless connectivity. BellSouth Mobile's major competitor, Motient (www.Motient.com), uses a different network, but provides similar coverage patterns. In some instances, laws and regulations obstruct coverage. For example, cell phone use is barred in certain hospital wards and on most airplanes because they have the potential of interfering with medical or aircraft navigation equipment.

Scarcity of Content. Content may be "king" on the wired Web, but on the wireless Web, content is the undisputed supreme ruler. Content written specifically for the smaller Palm Pilot or cell phone display is sparse. Even content designed for NTT DoCoMo's wildly popular I-Mode is limited to thousands, not millions of sites. While there are software tools that automatically convert wired Web content into content suitable for smaller, low-bandwidth displays, the results are often aesthetically deficient, and the content isn't easy for the user to access. Content designed specifically for a particular device—that is, content formatted not only for the bandwidth and screen size but the application as well—is of far greater value to users than generic content originally designed for the wireless Web.

Lack of an Installed User Base. In Japan, where mobile phones and wireless Internet access are the rage, only a little more than a third of mobile phone users made the move to Internet-mode (I-Mode) phones by the end of 2000. The number of Internet-capable mobile phones in the United States is even lower. As in Japan, U.S. customers upgrading to wireless Web access will need to discard or trade up their current mobile phones, which may be in perfect working condition, and sign up for a more expensive monthly service plan. In Europe, the relative expense and scarcity of the latest generation of Wireless Application Protocol (WAP)-enabled phones have increased interest in and use of alternative net-access protocols, especially Short Message Services (SMS), a means by which short messages can be sent wirelessly to handheld wireless devices. This turn of events has not only been a boon to

SMS providers but also to the customers who can access the Web without making a new investment in hardware.

High Customer Cost. The increased cost of Web-enabled hardware and Internet access service is an impediment to global wireless Web use. In the United States, the tiered-access service-charge model, where subscribers receive a given number of minutes for a flat monthly rate, is common. Cellular providers frequently offer business customers "free" nights and weekends, as a means of attracting customers while shifting the cost burden to business.

More progressive Internet access companies offer volume-based services. Palm.Net offers several access options, ranging from a minimal monthly charge that includes a small amount of data transfer, to a significant monthly charge for unlimited access. In the United States, monthly charges for unlimited wireless Web access are about double the cost of comparable wired Web access.

Changing Communications Standards. Communications standards are changing worldwide. These changes are driven by technologic as well as business and political pressures. For example, wireless telecommunications in Europe and China use one standard or protocol, Japan has another, and the United States has several. As global mergers and acquisitions continue, either the European or Japanese standard will likely emerge as the global standard.

It's difficult to predict which communications standard will eventually win in the global market. As the VHS versus Beta, Mac versus PC, or the ac versus dc power wars illustrated, simple technologic superiority isn't necessarily a good predictor of a technology's success. However, even if global telecom standardization were to occur immediately, there are plans for increased bandwidth and media capacities in virtually all wireless markets. For subscribers to take advantage of this increased capacity, they'll eventually have to upgrade their handsets, and the infrastructure will need to be upgraded as well. In other words, periodic change in wireless access is inevitable.

Although there will likely be some cost resistance among consumers, if the added functionality offered by a successive generation of devices is enticing enough, customers will opt for the new services. Consider the incremental sale of wired modems. Virtually everyone with Internet access in the United States upgraded from 14.4- to 28.8- to 56.6-K modems as soon as they became affordable. This opportunity for continuing sales assumes that the wireless telecommunications industry can mirror the tactics used by the personal computer industry, where customers are enticed to upgrade to faster, slimmer, and more powerful laptop computers, even when their existing laptops are perfectly serviceable. Many customers are willing to pay handsomely for an incremental increase in functionality, especially if time saving or increased ease of use is involved.

Security. Wireless communications are inherently less secure than wired communications. Not only are wireless devices susceptible to viruses and the other data-threatening plagues of wired devices but the communications can be intercepted and, with the appropriate software tools, decoded.

As it is, the FBI has taps on all Internet Service Providers (ISPs) and can intercept any communication, whether it originates from a wireless device or a wired desktop system. Third-party workarounds, such as sites that encrypt and reroute email and other data, are popular on the wired Web. Encryption and other security measures are likely to be even more popular on the wireless Web than they are on the wired Web.

The next section dissects the new wireless Internet, and the remaining part of this chapter examines how wireless connectivity redefines the Internet for developers and users. It identifies the wireless market drivers, explores the phenomenon of pervasive computing, and assesses the mobile and fixed wireless market.

THE NEW INTERNET

Wireless and mobile Internet connectivity is an enabling technology for transforming the current workforce—especially the segment that deals with sales and knowledge management—into a mobile information society. The focus on personal, any time and any place communications made possible by wireless technology is driving the redefinition of the Internet. The new focus is more on personalized services and transaction support, and less on surfing the Web for multimedia games and references.

The individual and personal nature of the cell phone is a key to the transformation of the Internet into the back end of a personal information appliance. A cell phone, unlike the PC in a home or office, tends to be carried by its owner. As a rule, people don't share cell phones, but carry them on their person for their own communications. This personal relationship with a device that provides a telecommunications link is in part responsible for transforming the Internet—simply because the user's demographic information, including telephone number, is available to the service provider. This knowledge, properly leveraged, can be used to provide the subscriber with personalized, location-specific information, such as directions to the nearest service station.

The proliferation of smart phones—mobile or cell phones with the ability to browse the Internet, receive and send faxes and email—is also redefining the Internet. Users expect personalized, relevant, concise information, whether for personal navigation, eCommerce, or personal time management, and they expect it instantly. From the service provider's perspective, these expectations represent a demand for services that can be delivered when and where subscribers want them.

Enabling Technologies

The enabling technologies of the new Internet include new, high-speed wireless networks, new protocols for sending data to and from wireless devices, new operating systems, and technologies for providing short-range wireless connectivity between peripherals and wireless devices. Although these and other technologies are discussed at length in Part II, Wireless Wonders, they are introduced below:

Wireless Networks. The wireless networks developed and supported by the telecommunications industry define the potential of the wireless devices connected to specific networks. Just as analog cellular was eventually superannuated by all digital systems, the basic, slow-speed wireless networks are slowly evolving into next-generation high-speed communications channels capable of supporting multimedia services, like video. The alphabet soup of evolving network standards that will be described in Part II, such as GSM (Global System for Mobile Communications), GPRS (General Packet Radio Service), HSCSD (High Speed Circuit Switched Data), EDGE (Enhanced Data for GSM Evolution), and WCDMA (Wideband Code Division Multiple Access), represent the telecommunication industry's attempt to provide service in the most efficient, interference-resistant, bandwidth-sparing means possible.

Wireless Protocols. The Wireless Application Protocol (WAP) makes information and services on the Internet accessible to new, WAP-enabled wireless devices. That is, WAP provides connectivity to the Internet. In the United States, Amazon.com and Yahoo are two of the first large companies to provide wireless connectivity to their Web sites through WAP.

In Europe, wireless phone users without new WAP-enabled phones are using the older, but readily available and inexpensive, Short Messaging Service (SMS) to access the Internet. Potential WAP competitors, such as Sun Microsystem's Java 2 Micro Edition (J2ME), will appear on wireless phones from NTT DoCoMo and Lucky Goldstar. Until a clear winner appears, it's likely that these and other protocols will coexist on wireless devices. If protocols such as J2ME become accepted standards, they have the potential to redefine the post-PC era of computing.

Symbian Alliance. Readers will remember from Chapter 1 that this alliance of major wireless equipment manufacturers—Ericsson, Motorola, Nokia, Matsushita Communication Industries, and Psion—develops and promotes an operating system for wireless information devices. The core of the Symbian Platform is a nonproprietary, scalable operating system called EPOC, which defines issues such as Internet connectivity and the nature of the customizable user interface. The EPOC operating system links software applications and provides a consistent development environment for wireless developers.

Bluetooth. A standard and a protocol, named after a fierce Viking king of the tenth century renowned for uniting the kingdoms of Denmark and Norway, defines and enables short-range wireless communications among electronic devices. That is, Bluetooth links devices. For example, Bluetooth is designed to support wireless connectivity among laptops, smart phones, printers, PDAs, and peripherals. A Bluetooth-compatible smart phone could access a phone number from a Bluetooth-enabled PDA without the user having to manually access and transfer the information to the cell phone from the PDA. Similarly, a woman with a wireless headset containing a microphone and ear mike could operate the smart phone in her car, either from the driver's seat or from the comfort of her Jacuzzi with the car parked in her garage. At the end of 2000, there were over 1,200 companies who had joined the Bluetooth consortium, including most of the major telecommunications and hardware vendors.

Increased Infrastructure Demands

In seeming defiance of Wall Street's opinion of dotCom start-ups, Internet traffic continues to grow at exponential rates, even without a significant contribution from wireless Web traffic. In this environment, customers are demanding higher-quality, higher-bandwidth connections to the Internet. This current reality, together with the projected demands associated with exponentially increasing wireless Web traffic, is fueling infrastructure growth and boosting the valuation of infrastructure technologies, such as fiber-optic communications, to levels unheard of at the height of the dotCom era. Optical fiber infrastructure companies, such as Nortel Network Corporation, are enjoying multipliers of 40 and higher. This represents an opportunity for companies like Microsoft that will offer software solutions to linking databases and servers with wireless applications. Infrastructure capacity will become critical as wireless connections make demands of applied service providers (ASPs) connections, serving transaction-oriented applications to millions of wireless devices.

New Services

The New Internet is partially defined by the broad range of new services made possible by personalized, just-in-time data access. As described broadly in Chapter 1, these services focus on immediate, location-specific, personalized communications. Content ranges from personal navigation, personal health and security, personal time and knowledge management, entertainment, edutainment, and eLearning, to eCommerce and social networks. Not everyone will be interested in purchasing a Coke from a cellular-enabled vending machine, but this is only one example of the potential of the wireless Internet. For example, the concept of a wireless wallet—something that customers keep with them at all times so that important information and money are at their fingertips—seems intuitively attractive.

The introduction of new services is limited more by developer imagination and customer expectations than technology. For example, the all-woman Finnish band Nylon Beat released the first hit single for mobile phones, "Not Guilty," as a cell phone ring. This unlikely use of a cell phone generated significant money for the band, and signaled the onrush of new mobile entertainment options ranging from video games to games for video communities.

New Players

To avoid losing the lead they established on the wired Web, Amazon.com, Yahoo, and the other wired Web powerhouses are making their presence known on the wireless Web. One of the earliest eCommerce transactions supported on the wireless Web was the ability to order books from Amazon.com. In addition to the established dotCom players, the wired Web is becoming home to telecommunications giants like AT&T and Deutsche Telecom, and to wireless equipment manufacturers like Motorola. These new players bring a different transaction and time-oriented focus to the Web.

One player obviously missing from the major players on the wired Web is Microsoft. While Microsoft has had a great deal of leverage working with PC manufacturers because of its operating system software, it hasn't fared as well in the mobile wireless market. Microsoft is a minor player in the micro-browser business, having been snubbed by the major cell phone provider companies like Nokia. In contrast, once prominent wired Web-browser companies, including Spyglass, ICE, and Opera are developing micro-browsers for Web-enabled appliances. Opera, for example, developed the micro-browser for Ericsson's Screen Phone.

Microsoft is working with Ericsson with the aim of bundling its micro-browser on Ericsson's phones. The company is also working with smaller cell phone players, such as Samsung, toward developing a micro-browser based in part on its CE operating system. Unfortunately for Microsoft, CE has yet to be embraced by the cell phone manufacturers. However, Microsoft does have a chance to become a major player in the wireless market, primarily as a back-end system for companies such as British Telecom and NTT DoCoMo, Inc.

New Interface Paradigms

The postage-stamp-size display panels on smart phones require a rethinking of Web access interface design. The tiny form factor of current smart phone displays is a challenge that may eventually be addressed by some combination of pen computing (as is used by the Palm PDA) and voice recognition.

Affordable voice recognition systems, which allow a businessperson to open a word processing document and dictate a letter with reasonable accuracy, are now available from several vendors, including IBM, Lernout & Hauspie, and Philips. These PC-based systems can interface directly with Web browsers, allowing anyone to perform searches and other routine tasks with speech control. Recent advances in speech recognition technology have moved the price/performance ratio of speech recognition systems to the point where powerful, affordable systems are becoming attractive alternatives to the conventional mouse and keyboard. The greatest challenge to overcome is that wired Web browsers are optimized for point-and-click operations, not speech recognition. Using speech recognition with a wired Web browser is akin to directing someone who's blindfolded to "go right three steps, stop, go forward six steps, stop, go back one step, stop."

The issue with large vocabulary, continuous speech, PC-based voice recognition systems is that they're extremely resource intensive and require far too much computing power to run on a device like the current Palm Pilot. A typical system requires a hundred megabytes or more of disk space, at least that much RAM, and a fast processor to operate properly. The only portable option these vendors offer is a handheld, digital voice recorder about the size of a digital cellular phone. Voice recognition vendors are reportedly working on an ASP-type voice recognition system that would offload most of the processing to a remote server. The advantage of using a non-PC device, such as a smart phone, is that the interface limitations of the current wired Web browsers don't have to be addressed. Smart phones represent a blank slate as far as interface design goes. User expectations haven't been solidified yet, leaving the options open for alternative, innovative interface designs that needn't resemble anything on the wired Web.

A major concern with smart phone interface designs surrounds the graphical user interface (GUI), or what the user sees and interacts with during the normal operation of the wireless device. Good graphical interface design for a browser such as Internet Explorer on the wired Web, or any PC-based application for that matter, is considered an art. It is an art that is difficult to master, which is one reason great Web designers are in demand. Even subtle differences, such as the color, size, and style of the font used on a Web site, can have a profound impact on how visitors perceive the site and the company it represents.

In developing a graphical interface for a site intended to be viewed on a large color monitor, accomplished Web designers take into account dozens of subjective and objective factors. They need to know what sort of image the business wants to project to its customers: carefree, serious, or responsible? Similar information is necessary for a Web designer to determine the modes of interaction (mouse versus pointing device) that a Web site should support. Considerations include the role of mental models (the metaphors that give the GUI meaning) in the interface, the appropriate level of graphic complexity (a balance among the need to focus customers' attention on some aspect of the site, hardware limitations, and the resources necessary to create the interface), the optimal mix of power versus the ease of learning that should be provided, and how to provide situational awareness (informing users where they are, where they can go, and where they've been). Then there's the issue of localization—making a Web site equally appealing to customers in other countries who may speak other languages. Not only is accurate textual translation an issue, but subtleties such as the colors used in graphics and buttons can have a profound effect on the perception of the site.

As important as all of these factors are in the design of a wired Web site, current hardware and bandwidth limitations require that these issues be put aside for now. Until higher bandwidth connections are generally available, animated, colorful graphics on smart phones, wireless PDAs, and similar wireless devices aren't practical. For the immediate future, wireless devices have to support a "retro" look, primarily using text lists. Perhaps the best way to handle the limited bandwidth dilemma is to use wired devices in conjunction with desktop-access Web content. For example, suppose there is late-breaking news in an area of interest to a subscriber. This might appear on her smart phone display in the form of a text alert. (It might say something like "Stock Alert.") The subscriber acknowledges and stores the alert with a simple keystroke. When she returns to her office or home computer, a Bluetooth connection between the subscriber's PC and cell phone is automatically established, and the URL associated with the full text and graphics stock alert appears on the computer screen.

New Business Models

Business on the wireless Web is centered on speed, location, and personalization. For the foreseeable future, the wireless Web is being optimized for transactions. In terms of these transactions, consider the value of pushing personalized, preferred information, as well as a variety of applications, to customers.

The transaction paradigm doesn't necessarily decrease the significance of the PC as a component of the wireless Web. Subscribers can be enticed to use wired Web connections through personalized portals, which can contain banner ads and other forms of advertisement. Whether or not advertisements can be successful on the wireless Web proper is debatable, especially if users pay for per-minute connections. The wireless Web challenges the concept of pay for connect time, versus a charge for the amount of data downloaded. Some wireless suppliers, such as Palm.Net, do offer connection plans based on volume, not connect time. The per-KB connect charge will drop as more competitors enter the wireless market.

WIRELESS MARKET DRIVERS

According to the Gartner Group, over 1.2 billion Internet-enabled cellular phones were in use worldwide by the end of 2000. In contrast, the growth in domestic PC sales declined. Even Microsoft is looking to the wireless Web and other Web-enabled applications for its future growth. As the number of mobile Internet users outnumbers PC users worldwide, there will be a concomitant shift in eCommerce from wired PCs to Internet-enabled mobile devices.

As the wireless promise satisfies the demand for just-in-time information, new opportunities in the consumer market will materialize. When a person with a wireless tablet or smart phone can buy books, download music, monitor news, buy and sell stocks, read and send email, check sports scores, book a flight, check her bank account balance, or call her financial analyst, why would she spend money or time reading a newspaper in the morning with her coffee? Following the "if we build it, they will come" mentality, consumer expectations will redirect the flow of capital away from more traditional businesses such as the newspaper industry to wired devices, such as eBooks, and wireless software and service providers.

For the modern commuter, a significant amount of time is spent in transit to and from work, shopping, and in business travel, so everything takes on a time-critical aspect. To capture the demand for instant gratification for products and services, cell phone retail outlets are almost as plentiful as Starbucks in many areas of the United States. Just as fast food has taken off in the United States, consumers will gladly pay to be connected to their friends, coworkers, or suppliers at any time and from anywhere. The perceived value of instant access to information is a function of the type of information and the role of the customer in managing that information. For example, up-to-the-moment stock quotes are invaluable to a day trader. For a businessman lost in traffic in downtown New York City, the relative location of a meeting site is critical. The value of just-in-time data is application and situation specific.

The worldwide adoption of wireless technology and demonstrated worth of the Internet is a significant market driver. It's obvious to subscribers and investors alike that the Web is a virtual information megastore that provides a tangible value to anything that can tap into the knowledge base. In addition, the wireless Web is increasingly perceived as a necessary touch point by most click-and-mortar businesses.

PERVASIVE COMPUTING

As the United States evolves into an "information everywhere society," the wireless Web will look very different from the prewireless one. More importantly, the effect that pervasive computing will have on society is likely to be profound. From the U.S. perspective, careful monitoring of how wireless technology is affecting the lives of workers overseas will provide information on what might be in store for the United States, including the way pervasive wireless technology will alter customer attitudes and expectations.

At the outset, pervasive computing seems like nirvana. A businesswoman can maintain constant contact with her home office, through voice, email, or fax, to and from anywhere and at any time. Her ability to change flight reservations without standing in line at the airport terminal and receive a last-minute quote from an office associate before a critical meeting can increase efficiency and accuracy. With the proper data acquisition equipment at home, she can use her smart phone to control the lights in her house, adjust the aquarium's water temperature, and measure the temperature, relative humidity, and wind speed at her summer home.

However, paradise can have its demons. As anyone who has worn a pager knows, the advertised weight of only six or eight ounces for these devices is a gross understatement. Even the lightest, thinnest electronic pager can feel like a 50-pound weight when it's perceived of or used as an electronic leash. Pervasive computing and communications are desirable and sometimes life-saving, as long as the user has the option of turning the equipment on and off, or at least of being able to call or not call, when necessary. From an employer's perspective, having an employee who works at home or who travels a lot available at a moment's notice can be critical. Providing that last-minute information for a proposal or bid can make the difference between celebrating the signing of a business contract over a good meal or spending a quiet evening in a cheap hotel.

Another minefield on the wireless Web is the issue of privacy. Many privacy advocates object to the FBI's ability to track a subscriber's location by tapping into the cellular phone system. However, the same capabilities used by the FBI allow companies to determine a cellular caller's location, and provide him with location-specific information that may be of great interest. The issue, from a societal and marketing perspective, is how much wireless subscribers are willing to put up with in order to enjoy the benefits of wireless connectivity at home and work. One risk is that wireless customers may eventually reject the personal privacy costs of living and working in the wireless world without some sort of financial reward. This doesn't seem to be the case in Japan, where the I-Mode has captured the younger generation by providing games and communications on demand. As will be discussed in Part III, Convergence, a prerequisite to achieving a state of pervasive computing is creating a homogeneous, standardized wireless infrastructure in the United States.

MOBILE AND/OR FIXED WIRELESS

The concept of wireless communications, including access to the wireless Web, isn't limited to accessing the Web through a smart phone, wireless PDA, or two-way pager. Wireless communications extend into small geographical areas, such as a home or office, much the same way cordless phones extend the reach of the telecommunications network. The concept of local roaming—moving freely with a laptop, for example, from one office to another without having to reconfigure local network settings—is catching on in many businesses and at home. Wireless docking stations and keyboards remove the clutter from a work desk, and ultimately increase workspace efficiency. Even cordless phones, which aren't necessarily connected to the Web, are becoming necessities in the workplace. In some parts of Europe, the concept of fixed and mobile phones doesn't apply, because most people own one phone—a wireless model—that they use for all calls. Along a similar line, a few hotels in Silicon Valley offer wireless network connections. Guests don't deal with modem connections and incomprehensible switchboard glitches. They simply check out a PCMCIA wireless modem card, stick it in their PC, and start checking their email.

Several vendors offer fixed wireless networks that allow multiple PCs to access a single DSL or cable modem port from wireless connections. In addition to saving money on connect charges, users in an office or home setting can access their laptop from one location to the next. In addition, new hires can usually be added quickly and inexpensively to the fixed wireless network, without the time and resources needed to run additional cables.

Although the wired Web is evolving rapidly, and the most profound hardware and software solutions are still under development, there are dozens of hardware solutions available today, each focused on a particular niche of the wireless market. There are wireless modems that allow any laptop or handheld computer to access the wired Web. These PCMCIA cards are equipped with antennas and can be used like a wired PC when connecting to the Web. No special software is required—just an access account with an Internet service provider—and the patience to surf the Web using wired Web browsers at very slow speeds. There is the pace-setting Palm VII, which provides the functionality of the popular Palm organizer in a somewhat hefty form factor. In addition, there are also third-party modem manufacturers, such as Novatel Wireless, that market the Minstrel Wireless IP Modem for pre-Palm VII devices. A variety of vendors market snap-on modem adapters that connect personal data assistants (PDAs) to the user's cell phone to provide wireless Web connectivity.

Smart phones with a variety of features, from built-in PDAs to MP3 players, address the teen market. Two-way paging devices, like the RIM Interactive Pager, allow businesspeople to send and receive email when a phone call would be inappropriate. Smart phones with built-in pager functionality obviate the need for someone to carry both a pager and a cell phone. As a dedicated text input/output device, however, two-way pagers provide a keypad that is much easier to use for composing email messages.

In the long term, many wireless add-ons, such as wireless modem cards and snap-on modems for the current generation of PDAs, will be unnecessary thanks to technologic advances and the consolidation of individual wireless devices. Consider the proliferation of IR remote controls in the typical U.S. household, each specific to a particular piece of equipment. Most homeowners replace three or four remotes with a single, easy to use universal remote. Similarly, there will be a demand for a single device that can replace wireless phones, interactive pagers, wireless PDAs, and other specialized wireless devices—each with its own battery, password, mobile Internet provider, and billing account.

Some forward-looking manufacturers are providing the infrastructure for wireless options within their current products, obviating the need for customers to purchase third-party products later on. For example, Apple Computer includes a built-in wireless antenna system in its laptop series, in the event that the computer owner decides to upgrade to a wireless network.

If the concept of smart phones displayed by Nokia and other smart phone marketing companies has any bearing on reality, the future wireless communications device will be a thin, portable unit that provides functionality through a user-definable pen-based interface. This device, or something like it, may eventually sound the death knell for interactive pagers and PDAs. It will provide virtually infinite functionality because of its user-fconfigurable user interface and its ability to run programs running on Web-based servers, through an ASP interface.

The next chapter examines the economic aspects of the wireless Web, including a look at the current and future stakeholders in the wireless economy, the frenzied feeding pattern of mergers and acquisitions, the Eurasian advantage, and the business opportunities for companies supplying hardware and content.

EXECUTIVE SUMMARY

Even though Internet traffic continues to grow at an exponential rate, the explosive growth in domestic PC sales and Web-related start-ups has cooled to the point that investors are increasingly hesitant to assume the risk of a dot-Com failure. However, in ventures related to the wireless Web, dotCom fever is as hot as ever—monies and other resources are pouring into any application that has a wireless Web component. This is especially true of infrastructure providers, such as companies involved in fiber-optics communications components. The Web infrastructure is critical, since all traffic, whether wireless or wired, eventually travels through the wired infrastructure.

The wireless Web represents a natural and expected development in that the technologic, political, and business foundation for success in the wireless Web is in place. This foundation includes maturation of the wired Web; the standardization and coalescing of the telecom industry; the proliferation of all-digital cellular systems; the increased acceptance and use of PDAs and other portable, personal data devices; experience with the wired Web; advances in electronic design; the proliferation of miscellaneous wireless devices; and the ready availability of money for mergers and acquisitions. There are also revolutionary developments, including the ability to specify user location, the ease of personalizing services, new monetary models, new interface models, and a focus on transactions.

Some of the more significant limitations and opportunities associated with the wireless Web include limited communications bandwidth, scarcity of content crafted for the wireless Web, lack of a significant installed user base compared to the user base afforded by the wired Web, high customer costs, and the challenge of moving standards.

The "new" wireless Internet is defined by enabling technologies, including wireless networks, the wireless application protocol (WAP), self-governing bodies like the Symbian alliance, and the Bluetooth standard. The new Internet is also defined in part by new services, such as personal navigation and new players from the global telecom community. The wireless Web also brings with it increased infrastructure demands, as well as demands for new services, new players, new interface paradigms, and new business models.

Wireless market drivers include the number of cell phones in use, the projected cell phone use in the near future, the just-in-time delivery of content, and the time-critical nature of information. The work-anywhere attraction of pervasive computing carries with it a threat to personal privacy. Despite the current technologic limitations, mobile and fixed wireless services provide real benefit to users today, and promise even more in the future.

3

Money Matters

*The most successful businessman
is the man who holds onto the old just as long as it is good
and grabs the new just as soon as it is better.*

Robert P. Vanderpoel

INTRODUCTION

Assuming that the wireless Web is, in fact, the next "new thing," just who is going to make a profit, and by doing what? As the dotCom experience has taught many start-up executives, timing and execution are almost everything. The rush on catchy URLs made some early prospectors millions of dollars overnight, simply because they had the foresight to claim potentially valuable URL real estate before someone else. In the wireless Web world, the real estate involved is the RF spectrum that extends across national boundaries. The money involved in securing licenses for the next generation of cellular phone service makes the cost of even the most expensive dotCom URL pale by comparison.

From a business perspective, things look promising for companies even peripherally involved with the wireless telecommunications industry. Consider that cell phone use by U.S. business travelers has been growing at about 30 percent per year for the last two years. Following this trend, the global market for mobile devices will be well over 1 billion by 2003, with a majority of those devices connected to the Web. Not only will this level of Web access overshadow wired Web access significantly but it also promises a substantial revenue stream for companies involved in the wireless Web. For example, in Japan, I-Mode customers pay a 25 percent premium to be connected to the Web, as compared to regular cellular phone users. Not surprisingly, at the start of the new millennium, Nokia and NTT DoCoMo were the most valuable companies in Europe and Japan, respectively. And look at what happened with the two largest cell phone operators in Europe: Vodafone AirTouch's $163 billion takeover of Mannesmann was the largest ever! Vodafone's commitment to Britain's network infrastructure alone was $8 billion.

Even though the business prospects for the wireless Web seem almost as limitless as the Web itself, picking the wrong technology, or using the best technology for the job with the wrong business strategy, or simply bringing a product or service to market too soon can spell disaster, even for the big players.

The Iridium fiasco is one such example. Iridium LLC, the world's first global satellite and paging company designed for handheld mobile phone users, filed for bankruptcy in early 2000 and was at one point prepared to destroy its network of 66 low earth-orbiting satellites. When the system went live in November 1998, it seemed less of a technical marvel than when it was conceived. A subscriber with a portable, but by no means slim, handset could make a call from anywhere on the globe. As with most businesses, there was competition from the start. GlobalStar and ICO offered similar services using different and less expensive systems. To make matters worse, the voice service available through Iridium didn't seem so leading edge compared to the Internet and email services available through more popular GSM-compatible mobile phone systems.

A postmortem analysis suggests that Iridium failed on several points. First, despite its early mover advantage, the Iridium service was too expensive. Second, Iridium was initially marketed only to wealthy business travelers—ignoring the more lucrative and receptive professionals in the maritime, oil, and gas industries. Even though deep-pocketed Motorola, a company fluent in the workings of the telecom industry, was one of the major backers of Iridium, it failed. Despite this temporary setback, Motorola continues to invest heavily in satellite communications, underlining the confidence the major players have in wireless as the future of telecommunications.

Motorola may yet see some profit from the Iridium project, in the form of the new company, Iridium Satellite, which purchased the $5 billion assets of Iridium LLC for $25 million. Motorola will make or license the production of handsets and satellites for the new company, which has a $72 million contract for two years of satellite service.

This chapter focuses on the economic aspects of the wireless Web from the perspective of the stakeholder businesses that stand to profit from the inrush of capital, energy, and ideas. It also examines the pattern of mergers, acquisitions, and alliances that forms in the volatile wireless market as companies jockey for position, leverage, and radio spectrum licensing.

STAKEHOLDERS

The types of companies that stand to benefit most from the wireless Web gold rush are the companies that create the underlying infrastructure, manufacture or supply end-user hardware, develop operating system and application software, and operate the communications networks. The roles of these first-tier stakeholders, and the more significant second-tier stakeholders in the wireless Web arena—including government, content providers, and service providers—are described in more detail below.

Telecom Giants

The cash-rich giants of the telecommunications industry, including Vodafone AirTouch (the largest cellular operator in the world), Telecom Italia Mobile (the largest domestic operator in Europe, with over 20 million subscribers in Italy), Tercel (Portugal's second largest ISP), Libertel (the second largest operator in the Dutch market), and Finland's Sonera (the world leader in wireless encryption), are investing feverishly. These and other companies are paying whatever it takes to upgrade their systems so they can not only participate in but also control the next generation of wireless telecommunications. There is a similar, but less frenzied, feeding taking place in North America. Players include AT&T Wireless, BellSouth Corp., Motient, Nextel, Sierra Wireless, SBC Communications, Sprint PCS, Verizon, and several start-ups.

For telecommunications carriers that own and operate the cellular networks that transport voice and data to and from wireless devices, upgrading for the future wireless Web entails the acquisition of next-generation cellular licenses throughout the United States, Asia, and Europe. The lofty expenditures for licenses are rationalized by even loftier goals—to become the Cisco of the wireless world. The eventual winners in Europe and Asia will certainly influence the industry in the United States, whether through acquisitions, mergers, and partnerships with U.S. companies, or by setting the global wireless standards for the wireless Web. The economic risk that the telecom giants face, aside from competing with each other, is dealing with the debt accrued from acquiring subscribers at a cost of between $350 to $1000 each, including next-generation spectrum licenses.

Government

In order for the telecom giants to secure their positions in the next generation, they continue to spend billions at government auctions for high-capacity cellular licenses. Consider the positive effect of huge cash flows on regional and national governments as Vodafone and others competed for the 64 third-generation licenses throughout Europe. Every telecommunications carrier, regardless of its past profitability, depends on next-generation licenses for its future viability.

To the delight of local governments, the telecom powerhouses are uniquely positioned—and have deep enough pockets—to continue a bidding war for a pan-European presence. Not only has building a pan-European network entailed paying governments handsomely for the coveted licenses but the government's windfall is compounded by secondary gains of increased tax revenues and the creation of local jobs. When the United Kingdom auctioned off five third-generation (3G) wireless licenses in 1999, it raised over $33 billion, about ten times what was expected. Similarly, the German auction for 3G licenses in 2000 raised $46.25 billion. Furthermore, the windfalls haven't been limited to Europe. The domestic PCS spectrum, auctioned off in 1994 and1995, raised $7.7 billion for the U.S. government. Most analysts expect the FCC's 2000 auction for 422 licenses to be even more lucrative.

While the situation isn't as dire in the United States, for most European mobile operators, obtaining a license isn't an option—it's a matter of life or death. Failure to obtain a next-generation technology license effectively locks such mobile operators into a relatively low-speed wireless network. A mobile operator limited by current technology faces extinction. In addition to securing the appropriate licenses, the winners in the wireless Web struggle will be those companies with the largest subscriber base, the right mix of customers, quality management, and an ability to react to changes in the marketplace in Internet time.

Although the government auctions for wireless licenses have left some bidders in debt, governments have been winners, at least in the short term. The risk is that, although the various European, Asian, and U.S. governments may be cash rich in the short term, the long-term effects on local economies are less certain. Unless the debt-ridden companies are managed expertly, they may not be able to grow themselves fast enough to survive in the long run— even with licenses for next-generation wireless connectivity.

Infrastructure Builders

The companies ultimately responsible for the wireless Web's infrastructure, such as Cisco, Powerwave, WorldCom, Ericsson, and Nortel, are well positioned to benefit economically from the wireless Web explosion. Given their expertise and continued involvement with the wired Web, the telecommunications infrastructure builders are the key to the success of the wireless Web. These companies are essential because the infrastructure is the primary rate-limiting factor in determining how rapidly the global markets can evolve. This evolution involves moving from the relatively slow-speed first- and second-generation telecommunications network connections to the third- and fourth-generation network systems and beyond. The next generation of networks will be capable of supporting voice recognition, video, and other bandwidth-intensive interfaces that will eventually supplement or obviate the miniature, text-oriented displays found on first-generation devices.

Barring the collapse of the Web and the dotCom industry, the future success of infrastructure builders is relatively secure given the constantly increasing traffic load of the dotCom and wireless voice industries. In addition, the wireless Web is a new driving force injecting money and energy into this industry. The main economic risk to information builders is primarily from domestic and foreign competitors vying for market share.

Application Developers

The wireless Web represents an open frontier, ready for the taking by capable, creative application developers, especially for those with expertise in developing programs for wireless devices that follow the ASP model. These applications reside on remote servers and execute locally within a generic browser environment connected to the wired or wireless Web. There are ample valued markets for wireless Web—enabled applications, such as messaging systems that communicate physicians' orders to pharmacists, so prescriptions can be filled and waiting for patients when they arrive at the pharmacy. In addition, there are markets for many of the same applications that run on standalone and Internet-enabled PCs. Among the most popular applications are antivirus utilities, personal databases, calendars, to-do lists, and other time management applications. As the wired Web has demonstrated, the ASP model can be successful for products ranging from Web-based games to office utilities. The ASP model is not only cost-effective, but the rapid time to market this model means that developing and deploying software across the Web on a variety of hardware platforms can truly happen in Internet time.

The greatest initial opportunity for application developers appears to be in porting wired Web applications to wireless devices, including applications that target specific wireless devices. The financial risk for application developers is related to the fast-changing market, and, correspondingly, short product life cycles. The wireless device standards, including display sizes and capacities, will be in flux for years. As a result, developers will have to write for a rapidly moving target, anticipating future hardware and firmware characteristics.

Working under the constraints of a moving-target platform is a normal and expected part of software development, given the periodic upgrades in operating system software and browsers every year or so. The challenge with developing applications for the wireless Web is the volatile product cycle and the rapid pace at which the changes in standards are likely to occur during the early phases of evolution.

Content Authors

On the Web—wired or not—content is king. However, with the introduction of any new computer-based system, applications and content typically lag behind hardware innovations by months, or even years. As IBM and Apple Computer learned from their first personal computer offerings, hardware doesn't sell well without software, and software developers and content authors don't write for specific hardware platforms that don't have a large user base. Because of this chicken-and-egg phenomenon, hardware vendors are doing all they can to encourage development on their platforms. They are providing content authors with everything from heavily discounted hardware, developer seminars, documentation, and joint marketing opportunities, to t-shirts and coffee mugs. One company, Nokia, established R&D centers in Belgrade, Helsinki, and Sydney to help develop entertainment content for its cell phones.

The enticements for content authors to publish their work on the Web are more obvious. Consumers either pay for content directly or, more commonly, indirectly through advertisers who pay for banner ads at a rate that is a function of the amount of traffic a site handles. In this regard, the wireless Web resembles the wired Web at an early stage of development. While the wired Web has more content than one person could possibly read through or experience in a lifetime, the wireless Web has very sparse content. The first companies to develop and publish interesting content for the wireless Web will have an opportunity to capture customers before the amount of available content explodes, as it did on the wired Web.

There are two direct routes open to content authors. The first is to create content de novo, using tools designed specifically for wireless access, such as those that follow the WAP standard. However, in part because WAP doesn't live up to expectations, and because authoring in these environments is too challenging for those who simply want to provide content, the other option is to reformat or translate wired Web content. Although the wireless Web, at its full potential, is much more than a repackaging of the wired Web, the fastest time to market involves reformatting HyperText Markup Language (HTML) documents from the wired Web to fit, for example, the layout of a RIM wireless PDA.

Many wired portals are paying to have their sites reworked to make the content they host more suitable for displaying and searching on handheld devices. Software tools for converting existing Web content are available from vendors such as Everypath (www.everypath.com) and NetMorph (www.netmorph.com). As described in detail in Chapter 5, these transcoders translate content originally developed for the wired Web for different screen phones, PDAs, and interactive pagers.

With the wireless Web industry trying desperately to attract customers, there is a wide-open market for content authors and translators. The risk for these developers, who may spend many months mastering a particular authoring language or environment, is that tools will eventually be available that make content development as easy as using a word processor. This scenario is typical of tool development in the PC industry. For example, many authors learned HTML early on in the Web's history. However, a few years later, tools such as Microsoft FrontPage and Adobe's GoLive put the power of Web publishing into everyone's hands. Until that happens with the wireless

Web, content authors and translators will be able to charge a premium for their services.

Content Providers

As the wired Web has demonstrated, excellent content is necessary, but not sufficient, to attract traffic to a site. Spending millions on a Super Bowl commercial is one approach, but an option open to more companies is to collaborate with a service provider to reach target audiences. For example, Barnes&Noble.com negotiated contracts with the service providers Verizon and AT&T so a link to Barnes&Noble.com would be listed prominently under shopping headlines on the cell phones that Verizon and AT&T support.

Because of the display and keypad limitations of the current generation of smart phones, the wired Web approach of making a URL known around the globe isn't enough. Users not only have to know the URL, but they have to take the time to type it in. Even if a businesswoman's favorite online bookseller is Barnes&Noble, she's probably not going to spend a minute or more keying in a name when a link to Amazon.com is only a keystroke away. The challenge for content providers is to secure links on as many wireless devices as possible—within economic reality—and this means working with a service provider. On the wireless Web, the service providers make the rules.

Service Providers and Portals

On the wired Web, user dependence on the top portals or information gateways, such as America Online (AOL) and Yahoo, has been very lucrative. Many wireless portals, sometimes called *content aggregators* or *formatters*, follow an obvious strategy, instituted by Sprint and other wireless service providers, of creating an ISP and portal wrapped into one. Service providers set up browser environments that include links to other sites, email, information personalization, and a list of online retailers. Service providers act as gateways to Web content, since they work with device browsers to present preselected content menus. In other words, they both define and control the links to Web content. Examples of wireless service providers that run portals include AT&T Digital PocketNet Service by AT&T, Mobile Web from Verizon, Yahoo Mobile from Yahoo, MSN Mobile from Microsoft, and Wireless Web from Sprint.

Consider what happens when a businessman signs on to Sprint's Wireless Web service. He is first greeted by Sprint's home page, where there are links to Web portals, such as Yahoo and AOL. In exchange for their prominent position on the wireless screen, these Web portals share revenue with Sprint when it sends customers their way. For companies like Amazon.com, Sprint acts as a value-added reseller. For subscribers, these services are either free or available for a minimal monthly cost. The content providers pay fees for being listed. Amazon.com, BarPoint.com, JDJ Direct, ESPN, E-Trade, Fidelity Investments, and TicketMaster are examples of companies that have contracted with Verizon to display links to their Web sites. This approach has been attempted before on the wired Web, but the first generation of wired ISPs moved too slowly to compete with the more nimble, yet entrenched companies like the then youthful Yahoo.

Portal owners, by virtue of their control over the information gateways to the Web, can effectively censor Web content. Wireless portal companies charge more for space on the front screen, just as wired portals do. Start-up screens for PDAs and Web phones may be owned by huge players, such as AOL and Microsoft, effectively blocking competition from services with less political or financial clout. Subscribers may find it easy to look for books under Barnes&Noble.com, but almost impossible to navigate to Amazon.com, depending on how the portal owner has the browser home page configured. Service providers that follow this model will eventually face the same type of antitrust claims made against Microsoft for bundling its Internet explorer browser with every PC sold. Perhaps in realization of this, some portal owners do not ascribe to the combined ISP-portal service model. For example, U.S. West's Web portal, BrowseNow, allows subscribers to configure their wireless start-up screen from their PC.

Search Engine Developers

One of the earliest success stories on the wired Web was that of search engines that somehow managed to make the millions of pages of Web content accessible in a standardized way. As a result of the work of companies like Yahoo, users could quickly search for and access Web content without having to know a specific URL beforehand. Although the Web content available using a smart phone isn't anywhere near the amount of information available on the wired Web, there is an increasing demand for fast, efficient search capabilities.

In the new wireless market, the established wired Web search engine developers, including Yahoo, are being challenged by start-ups like Oracle's OracleMobile and Phone.com Inc.'s Myphone.com, which are completely focused on the wireless Web. These heavyweight contenders for the wireless Web search engine arena provide added value by basing search results on user preferences. As a result, the number of keystrokes needed to access a site is minimized. Saving keystrokes on a smart phone saves time, and that's worth money to most users.

The smaller search engine start-ups, such as MobilID, which provide services that list local restaurants and events based on user preferences, face stiff competition from the heavyweights. In addition to facing competition from other companies specializing in search engines, the carriers are also creating their own wireless Web portals. The competitive landscape is further clouded by the way search engine companies make money. In addition to collecting a fee from phone carriers, the search engine companies extract a fee from companies they list in search results. The challenge for independent search engine developers is to sign up enough carriers who either don't have the resources to create their own wireless portals, or who will pay a fee in order to be able to compete with the carriers intent on creating and controlling their own portals.

The DotComs

Virtually every dotCom in existence has a financial stake in providing a wireless touch point for its customers, regardless of whether the dotCom supports a B2C, B2B, or some other business model. This includes traditional and customer relations businesses that have only recently become click-and-mortar establishments by adding a Web touch point. Even a nontransaction-oriented Web site that's little more than a comprehensive information listing, such as an online magazine, can profit from the wireless Web by adding wireless transaction capabilities. Without a means of specifying the exact information required, a reference Web site, for example, is essentially off-limits to a wireless device. It's unreasonable to expect that someone commuting to work on a bus would scroll through hundreds of postage-stamp-size screens of text.

Consider the value of adding a wireless touch point to a dotCom's wired medical portal that specializes in providing references for its clinician members, including drug and disease management information. The static textual information on the Web site could be reformatted for transaction-based Web phones and wireless PDA access. Because scrolling through hundreds of miniature pages of drug-to-drug interactions would be too time-consuming for clinicians, a transaction-based application optimized for wireless access could be developed. The application could allow clinicians to enter the names of the drugs and would return a list of potential reactions and precautions, formatted for their wireless PDA or cell phone. For more in-depth information, clinicians would be directed to the references on the comprehensive wired Web site. In this scenario, investment money for development and operations could come from managed care organizations interested in minimizing costs and from pharmaceutical firms. Both would benefit indirectly by helping clinicians promote the safe use of drugs, including detecting drug-to-drug interactions among their subscribers.

The overall financial incentive for dotComs (including click-and-mortar companies) to include a wireless Web touch point is to increase traffic to the wired Web site, thereby increasing potential advertising revenue. A second incentive is to build on the services provided by the wired Web site with value-added functionality: a billable service. Consider the wired touch point of a firm offering a wired push service that provides subscription-based alerts and short bulletins that are customized for the subscriber's needs. For example, a short text message like "NOK up 1 $1/4$," accompanied by a special ring, could alert the subscriber to an increase in the stock price of Nokia. She could then either opt to buy or sell stock or read more information from her cell phone. Alternatively, she could go to the dotCom's main Web site on her PC for the details behind the stock price change.

Transaction Businesses

All businesses, by definition, are transaction-based, and transaction-based dotComs, as well as countless click-and-mortar businesses, have the potential to profit from just-in-time, location-specific business from wireless customers. Transactional online sites, unlike show-and-tell marketing and advertising-oriented wired Web sites, survive not by simply attracting visitors to their sites, but by achieving a high conversion rate—the number of business transactions, such as book purchases, relative to the number of visits. Amazon.com and Barnes&Noble.com don't benefit from customers checking the price of a book and then going to their neighborhood Borders bookstore to purchase it.

Virtually all transaction-based businesses, on- or offline, have the potential to profit from a properly implemented wireless Web presence. For example, QXL.com, Europe's largest online auction company and eBay, the U.S. equivalent, offer wireless access to online auctions. The challenge is to provide customers with fast, efficient service while maintaining a reasonable return on investment (ROI). Establishing a reasonable projected ROI for developing and maintaining a wireless touch point is especially relevant, given the high cost associated with being an early adopter of technology. Examples of transaction-oriented businesses positioned to benefit from a touch point with a likelihood of a positive ROI include the following.

Restaurants. The better (higher margin) eating establishments stand to gain the most, initially, from location-specific advertising to potential patrons. Connectivity can be used to provide menu selections and, with the advent of 3G bandwidth and larger graphic displays, images of the dishes available. Wireless devices can be applied to everything from locating a restaurant to selecting items from a menu. The customer's selection can be communicated directly to the kitchen and suppliers, following the choice board model. A *choice board* is a Web-based, multiuser ordering system in which a customer's order is sent to suppliers along the entire supply chain. For example, not only would the chef be notified of an order, but the companies that supply ingredients to the kitchen as well.

Wireless choice board style systems have been in place for years in some resorts, such as Disney World in Orlando. At some of Disney's outdoor restaurants, waiters take orders with the aid of wireless tablets, moving from one table to the next, but never wasting time walking back and forth between customers and the kitchen. The order, communicated via wireless to the kitchen and the serving staff, is delivered by a second waiter to the appropriate table when it is ready. The order is also communicated to a procurement program that subtracts the ingredients necessary to prepare the order, then initiates a reorder of ingredients and supplies when the level drops below a predetermined value. In the restaurant business, there are opportunities for system integrators, especially those with experience in the restaurant industry. The economic risk is that low-volume, low-margin restaurants won't be able to compete.

The choice board system at restaurants at some Disney resorts, as well as similar systems used in Europe, illustrate several points that most transaction businesses have in common. Consider the old-fashioned speaker and microphone system of ordering food popular in the 1950s. With the wired version, a woman who wants a burger simply buzzes the order taker and orders her meal by speaking into the tableside microphone. A few minutes later, a waiter delivers the order and collects the cash or credit card. If the woman uses a credit card or doesn't have the correct change, then the waiter makes yet another trip to the table.

Even if the original order taker keyed the order into a computerized restaurant management system, there are several important advantages to a wireless scenario. First, if the wireless restaurant system is properly configured, there's no error-prone, dual entry of data. That is, once the waiter checks off the customer's selection on the wireless tablet with his stylus, the order is entered into the restaurant system computer and displayed on the chef's screen. Second, the wireless restaurant management system acts like a choice board on the wired Web. When the waiter orders a meal, messages are sent to the kitchen staff and the suppliers, which may be across the street from the restaurant or in another state. In other words, when a customer orders a burger, then the beef patty supplier is notified of a sale, as is the bakery. Everyone in the supply chain is aware of the raw materials need to construct a burger, and the suppliers know to replenish the restaurant's supplies when certain raw materials drop below a preset quantity. Third, record-keeping overhead is reduced, since the wireless system tracks every transaction. In addition, because only one or two wireless pads are used, there is a potential cost savings over having to build and install dozens of wired tableside stations.

Most importantly, and perhaps most paradoxically, the use of wireless technology allows for more personal service with the same number of employees. The one order taker is no longer hiding behind a speaker microphone, but is out in front of the customers, smiling, and creating an air of trust and, hopefully, loyalty. One final point is that, compared to the alternatives, using a wireless pad to take orders looks cool—and customers will pay for cool. At Disney, cool is almost expected. Similarly, witness the popularity of the Apple iMac and G4 cube computers. People didn't buy these systems because they run Microsoft Word any better than a PC clone that sells for $500 less; they bought the Apple products because of cool product design. The same goes for the IBM NetVista. IBM's ads for the NetVista, like Apple's, don't tout computer speed or hard drive capacity, but focus on the "look."

Another example of the value of "cool" is NEC's 20-inch flat screen LCD monitor. When the panel was first introduced, it was available in putty or black, the only difference being color—and price. The black model listed for about 15 percent more than the putty model—the price of cool.

Hotels. Mobile travelers with access can poll a specific area or hotel chain for room rates and locations. Customers select a hotel, based on personal criteria, and the hotel then provides a detailed map or driving instructions. The transaction is recorded and automatically forwarded to the customer's company, along with billing information. The customer then receives an electronic verification of his stay, including room number, before he enters the hotel parking lot. Hotels not listed on the wireless Web will be increasingly passed by, as more mobile travelers begin to rely on the wireless Web for locating rooms. The opportunities for software developers, hardware developers, and vertical integrators to provide these and other services is balanced by the economic risk that the overhead and complexity of the initial wireless system may be too great for all but the largest hotel chains.

Emergency Services. The wireless Web isn't only for business and leisure. It can provide necessary and, at times, lifesaving assistance. A "911" equivalent can be established for cellular phones that not only pinpoints, within a radius of about 500 feet, where the call originates but also the identity of the caller. Directions and prenotification to the nearest emergency room can also be provided. The subscriber's demographic information, including electronic medical records, can be forwarded to the emergency room for review before she arrives. In the area of emergency services, there are opportunities for using wireless to create networks that connect hospital units, ambulance services, and cellular phones, much like the mobile emergency services. The economic risk is that the emergency service staff will be turned off by having to rely on and carry yet another piece of equipment.

Media and Entertainment. The media and entertainment industries represent a large, untapped market for location and user-specific connectivity. A variety of user-specified goods and services can be sold, including interactive games, news and information services, music, gambling, electronic ticketing services, and adult entertainment.

Strong sales of Nintendo's Gameboy and Sony's PSone mobile game machines demonstrate that the wireless game market is significant. MP3 music downloads, video games, and other entertainment will be among the largest revenue generators of wireless providers. Nokia ships games with some of its wireless phone models. Some Ericsson phones sport a scaled-down version of the Tetris game. In Finland, even extensive text-only interactions with adventure games are the rage, as are jokes and dating services.

Fortunately for game developers, most can leverage their expertise on the PC and the wired Web into creating games for the wireless platforms. The market for portable, pocketable entertainment devices includes school-age children. There is the risk that unknown, unwired competitors will cannibalize sales of game consoles. Some analysts postulate that the telephone giants could overtake the Segas and Nintendos of the world.

Retail. The huge brick-and-mortar retail industry, once thought to be at risk from the dotComs, is uniquely positioned to benefit from technology. There are virtually unlimited possibilities for integrating wireless commerce with every retail operation. Because of the location and user specificity possible with wireless technology, companies like GeePS are offering to deliver targeted sales messages to shoppers within the vicinity of a particular store. This service can even be provided on a store-by-store or market-by-market basis. Location-based marketing can be used to deliver messages to customers who access them by wireless phonepagers and PDAs. In other words, they can become part of an orchestrated promotion to reinforce advertising and promote customer loyalty.

Another wireless application is to employ the smart phones as digital wallets. In other words, use the wireless phone's memory to store and forward information about purchases and demographics. An issue regarding the use of cell phones in retail operations is that everyone's user profile is still considered private. This is a negative for businesses and a positive for consumers.

Travel and Transport. The mobile professional will become virtually inseparable from the wireless Web. For the mobile traveler, the ability to check flight availability, make last-minute travel arrangements, and obtain the local forecast, all translates to secondary gain for the airline industry. Happier travelers travel more on a particular carrier. In the war for customers, airlines that provide the best, easiest access to travel information win customer loyalty. Similarly, ancillary travel services that provide online guides for locating restaurants, entertainment, and fuel represent additional financial opportunities. These specialized travel portals, paid for by the vendors they represent on a per-transaction basis, vie with larger, horizontal portals for business.

Just as the wired Web has changed the airline reservation industry, with discount tickets and last-minute ticketing available online, the Web is poised to transform the online ticketing industry again. Consider that Southwest airlines alone sold over $725 million worth of tickets online in 1999, and in the same period, United Airlines sold $268 million. These online Web sales figures represent more than a potential market for travelers with access to the wireless Web.

In addition to supporting the business traveler, wireless communications holds great potential for the commercial transportation industry as well. For example, the Omnitracs system, developed by Qualcomm in the 1980s, was the first satellite-based mobile communications and tracking system for the transportation industry. It's still used today to track and communicate with over 300,000 commercial vehicles worldwide. With the system, trucking companies can track each truck's progress from pickup to drop-off, as well as maintain real-time contact with drivers. The result is not only time and cost savings. The degree of control and certainty that it enabled has opened up new markets for the trucking industry, including accounts with manufacturers that demand just-in-time delivery.

Banking and Finance. Online banking, one of the first transaction-supporting services of the wired Web, is also one of the first services offered to wireless Web users. Initiated by Japanese and European wireless service providers, mobile banking promises to be a lucrative business for both financial institutions and the service providers that charge transaction pass-through fees. Consider that Paine Webber had $140 billion or 33 percent of total customer assets in online accounts in 1999. Similarly, Bank of America had 14 percent of its customers, or 2.1 million clients, enrolled in online banking in 2000.

Security Solutions Providers

One of the greatest challenges for the wireless industry to overcome is that of security. Not only must the transactions be secure from eavesdropping, but someone with a stolen wireless device must be prevented, through the use of some type of personal identification verification system, from directing the financial transactions of others.

Wireless devices provide particular security challenges due to their portability. They present an opportunity for someone with the appropriate equipment to intercept or at least monitor communications between the mobile unit and the base station. Companies that provide encryption technologies, such as Finland's Sonera, stand to gain enormously, since every secure mobile device requires security. Encryption makes even sensitive transactions like stock trading and bank account management relatively safe on wireless devices. Companies that develop other security measures, such as personal identification verification through biometrics—the use of a thumbprint to validate a credit transfer, for example—have opportunities as well, as long as they can work within the confines of a cellular phone or PDA form factor. The challenge for these companies is to provide secure transactions on enough devices. Not only would successful attacks result in sensational news coverage but they would also undermine the integrity of cellular phones in any financial transaction.

End-User Hardware Suppliers and Developers

As the number of features provided by a generation of cell phones is superceded by the next, available at the same price or less, the EU will probably enjoy a high device turnover rate. This pattern follows the PC model, where faster, more powerful machines are always six months away, and devices are obsolete the moment they're turned on. Whether this is a form of planned obsolescence on the manufacturers' part, or a reflection of user expectations, the result is a brisk market for hardware suppliers and developers.

It is clear that the lure of continually increasing functionality will sell more phones, following the PC model of producing faster and more powerful machines. For example, early adopters of phones were quick to pick up analog systems for safety reasons, especially for use while traveling. After customers became familiar with cellular technology and began to rely on it for some day-to-day communications, subtle differences in cell phone models began to matter. Portability became a major factor, creating a demand for thin, light-weight phones, such as the Motorola StarTac series. Clarity of communications became an issue, as well as convenience features such as caller ID and other services normally found on wired phones. With clarity, caller ID, and other services available on digital phones, old analog units were soon replaced by digital models.

Now the push is to provide Web access on the wireless Web. This move requires that customers upgrade their existing cell phones again. For many customers, the history of cell phone use in the United States represents a new phone purchase every 12 to 18 months. This is a greater turnover than is experienced in the PC industry, where CPU upgrades average every 18 to 36 months.

Bigger, brighter screens are on the horizon. In addition, U.S. companies like Texas Instruments and Intel are gearing up to produce chip sets for mobile phones. Nokia and others are loosely following the PC model of creating continuous demand by introducing models that provide enough incremental value that users will upgrade their existing equipment on a regular basis. The risk that chip suppliers face is not being able to meet demand, much the same way that periodic RAM shortages strangled PC sales.

Interface Developers

The various and varied displays on smart phones, PDAs, and two-way pagers present a very different and difficult problem for interface designers. Interface developers for the new wireless formats who can work around these difficulties will be in demand in any company that wants to move onto the wireless Web.

In addition to graphic interface developers, there are classes of companies that stand to benefit directly from the wireless Web. For example, as voice recognition and synthesis become major components of the next-generation cellular interface, the voice recognition software companies such as Lernout & Hauspie, IBM, and Philips stand to gain considerably. In the United States, Sprint PCS supports a service called *voice commands*, where a cellular phone responds to a customer's voice. Not only does the system handle commands for up to almost 3000 numbers, but subscribers can edit their entries by voice as well. This capability bypasses the limitations of the typical cell phone graphical interface. The opportunities for these and other companies that offer user interface components will increase as they move to a system that uses a thin client architecture in which most of the processing is done on a server.

Despite a long maturation curve, voice recognition is starting to take hold in general computing and for users with specialized problems. One indication of the new status this potential tool holds for the wireless Web is the quick growth of Lernout & Hauspie, a major force in voice recognition software. Despite subsequent managerial and financial turmoil, this Belgian firm went from a tiny company headquartered in a trailer in the middle of a cow pasture to a multibillion-dollar company with offices located worldwide in only a few short years due to the increasing popularity of voice recognition technology.

Vertical Integrators

Vertical integrators in areas such as medicine, law, education, and transportation have opportunities to leverage the standards established on the wired Web and extend the legacy systems used in these areas. In medicine, wireless technologies have been tried for years, with a very poor return on investment. Fragile, expensive, nonstandard hardware was one limitation. Another was the high cost, in part because each system was based on a proprietary networking infrastructure and operating system. With the advent of standardized hardware and Web connectivity, vertical integrators provide most of the tools needed to implement a wireless component for most businesses. Unfortunately, vertical integrators could become entangled in standards wars, resulting in extended implementation time and potential failure.

Consider the economic benefit associated with integrating wireless Web capabilities in law enforcement. When the next generation of cell phones becomes commonplace, the FBI and other government agencies will be able to monitor the location of the cell phone (and therefore the owner) at all times. G3 phones are intended to be left on continuously, not just when the subscriber wants to place a call, so a cell phone can be polled for its position at any time. Such devices will provide cost savings to law enforcement agencies in manpower and time when trying to locate a suspect. The economic risk to law enforcement is minimal.

In the area of education, wireless devices can provide a means for students and faculty to collaborate in real time, inside or outside the classroom. Students can provide real-time feedback to a lecturer regarding level of interest, relevance of content, and other suggestions that would allow the teacher to modify her presentation accordingly. Similarly, real-time testing, requiring frequent participation from students or listeners can gauge whether or not the listeners are grasping the concepts. The result is a more attentive student body and more data for analysis.

The advantage of wireless over a wired Web connection, given the current pace of hardware development, is lower cost. Initial wireless educational systems are being targeted at schools, such as the project initiated by MindSurf, a company started by Sylvan Learning Systems, Inc., and Aether

Systems, Inc., to enable eLearning services over wireless devices. In addition to charging for the programs themselves, these companies can charge clients to train their personnel, initially through the cost-savings of providing on-site training.

Wireless Enablers

Companies involved, directly or indirectly, with the two-way conversion of information to and from wireless devices and networks will be in tremendous demand as long as there is content on the wired Web that must be available on the wireless Web. Wireless enablers allow a content provider such as a click-and-mortar business or dotCom to maintain a single version of their information and make it available on a variety of wireless platforms. Similarly, this makes the process of transaction translation seamless for the restaurateur, widget developer, or online bookseller. Given that millions of dotComs could be potential customers for this service, this market seems like a low risk. The more technical aspects of this technology are described in Chapter 5.

The downside for wireless enablers is that, as a stop-gap measure, they have a limited life span. There are two developments that will eventually negate the need for enablers. The first is the eventual appearance of automated software tools that provide enabling translation, especially Web sites that provide real-time or ASP-style programming. The second, and most devastating, is that once wireless networks and devices conform to one or two standards, enablers will be competing directly against every ISP and ASP on equal ground.

The major advantage of using a wireless enabler is that content providers only have to maintain a single version of a document. For example, a medical site that lists current drugs and prices for consumers doesn't have to concern itself with updating the price on multiple databases or Web pages each time there is a change. A single entry takes care of every touch point, whether wireless or wired.

Pager Companies

For pager companies, the wireless Web breathes new life into a technology that faces obliteration by the cellular phone industry. Thanks to interactive email, two-way pagers have experienced a resurgence of interest in the United States. Pagers have an edge over cellular phones in nonvoice applications, such as email, and they typically have a superior keypad for entering short messages. Pagers, unlike cell phones, also enjoy virtually total coverage in the United States The downside for pager companies is that, as more digital phones have the ability to double as pagers, the overhead and inconvenience of carrying and maintaining an additional electronic device will discourage pager use.

Advertising Industry

Advertising and eCommerce certainly have a place on the wired Web. As dot-Coms quickly demonstrated on the wired Web, the shotgun banner ad approach simply didn't warrant the cost per thousand (CPM) requested by the online advertising agencies. Personalized ads, made possible by Web sites that either track user preferences with cookies or ask consumers outright for their preferences, are more effective.

Consider the value of knowing where a smart phone subscriber spends her weekends. If, based on weekend calling or monitoring patterns, she is known by the wireless portal operator to visit a particular mall a few miles from her house, this information probably has considerable value to the shop owners in the mall. Together with other subscriber demographics, such as email address or cell phone number, marketing firms representing specific stores in the mall could send directed advertising to the woman, in the form of paper flyers, email messages, or a message on her cell phone. However, such practices, while potentially lucrative, face potential opposition. There continues to be a hot debate on the rights of companies to create dossiers on consumers without their knowledge and then sell the information to third parties.

While companies like DoubleClick received a lot of media attention for the intentional use of consumers' data gathered without their knowledge, other companies, such as America Online, have maintained a low profile. America Online, for example, maintains information on over 21 million subscribers, including demographics, credit card numbers, and where they spend their time within its service. Although AOL is not currently in the business of selling consumer data, it sells names and addresses to bulk mailers, and buys information about subscribers for targeted advertising. Some service providers intentionally track subscriber movements, with their knowledge, and sell the information to third parties. In return for the extensive personal profiles that result, subscribers are given free Internet access. The same model will extend to the wireless Web.

The diminutive smart phone screen does leave room for imaginative advertising. Banner ads, where the name of a retail outlet is pasted across a screen isn't likely to be appreciated when the cell phone is clipped to a businessperson's waistband or carried around in a briefcase. A better option is to use proximity-based multimodal advertisements. For example, when a businessman is within two blocks of a McDonalds, an audible advertisement noting a special is announced over his cell phone. This system assumes a user-definable filter that accepts only certain messages; otherwise driving down the highway with a cell phone turned on would be akin to listening to a radio station that featured nothing but advertisements. For advertisers, it's a boon, simply because customers are most receptive when they're looking for something specific—like lunch. That's the time for a restaurant such as

McDonalds to pay for an advertisement. The success of just-in-time, location-specific advertisements will depend on changes in the billing structure for cell phones. In the United States, most cellular users are charged for airtime, whether or not they initiated the call. Like faxes and collect calls from vendors, subscriber-funded advertisements from a cell phone are not appreciated.

Stockholders

As in the wired Web, all of the current and projected activity surrounding the wireless Web is certain to provide investors with an opportunity to profit from the stock market. As the dotCom experience has also illustrated, however, there is ample opportunity to lose money as well. The stocks to watch include the telecom giants and infrastructure builders, which should experience modest growth for the foreseeable future. As is frequently the case with a brick-and-mortar firm adding a wired touch point, the traditional business profitability may be temporarily depressed due to the start-up cost of a dotCom operation. For example, Staples, the office supply chain, initially saw its profitability fall because of the investment required in its Staples.com touch point.

Customers

Customers—everyone from schoolchildren toting candy-colored PDAs to executives sporting the lightest, thinnest cell phones—are the ultimate beneficiaries of the developments in wireless technology. For example, school-age children who have not been exposed to the Internet will have affordable, easy access to the Web. Executives will have affordable, multimedia communications on the Web. In addition, there are hundreds of thousands of field service engineers who need access to mission-critical information on demand from any location. And many stockholders and employees will benefit indirectly from some phase of the wireless boom.

The wireless Web value chain, arranged in order of increasing customer value, includes network, device, and infrastructure developers, as well as customer services and solution integrators. At each point in the value chain, technology, people, and resources come together to provide solutions that ultimately benefit customers—and virtually everyone is a customer.

MERGERS, ACQUISITIONS, AND ALLIANCES

The use of cell phones in the United States is less than half that of Europe and Japan combined. For the cash-rich European and Japanese telecom giants and service providers, the U.S. market represents a huge, untapped opportunity for expansion and globalization. The possibility of adding U.S. companies, such as VoiceStream Wireless Corp., to their future subscriber base is extremely attractive; but that base will only be available within a finite window of opportunity.

Dates for the anticipated next-generation wireless network launch vary from country to country, with the United States trailing Japan, Australia, Western Europe, and Hong Kong. The issues aren't simply technological, but political as well. For example, the anticipated date of between 2002 and 2003 for next-generation wireless technology to appear in the United States assumes that licenses can be obtained, and that the spectrum can actually be used. However, in the United States, many broadcasters hold licenses for spectrum designated for the next-generation system until 2006.

The standards adopted by the United States and other countries that lag behind Western Europe and Japan will be defined by the technologies used in those countries. As such, European telecom companies, such as Deutsche Telekom, are bidding over $20,000 per subscriber for U.S. territories. While this overvaluation seems ludicrous at first, if the potential subscriber base is considered, the investment drops down to a more reasonable $250 to $650 per subscriber. More importantly, the potential to significantly alter the standards mix in the United States also positions the right investors to secure global dominance. That is, owning major U.S. markets would allow a European company to promote GSM, the European wireless standard used by only 10 percent of U.S. subscribers—primarily VoiceStream subscribers.

Similarly, if NTT DoCoMo were to win major telecom positions in the United States, it could use the leverage of the U.S. market to extend its standard worldwide. NTT DoCoMo is forming alliances with U.S. companies such as AT&T Wireless Group, Microsoft, Sun Microsystems, and investing heavily in telecom companies in Hong Kong and Europe. Its aim is to spread its new standard, a direct competitor to GSM called W-CDMA, worldwide. In this regard, the United States represents the swing vote, with enough potential customers to make the European or Japanese standard the global one.

Although international competition may not bode well for U.S. companies such as Sprint, Verizon, WorldCom, and SBC Communications, for subscribers, the real or perceived threat of competition will have a positive impact. Domestic companies will have to provide services enjoyed by European and Japanese subscribers in order to compete. And, if a European telecom gained control of the U.S. market, then U.S. subscribers would have access to technology that's faster than what's available in the domestic market. For any of this to come to pass, however, European and Japanese telecom companies will have to merge with, acquire, or form alliances with U.S. companies that have access to spectrum licenses.

Mergers and acquisitions are by no means limited to international companies preying on the disorganized U.S. market. For example, chip manufacturer Intel has been diversifying by acquiring wireless companies. Similarly, WorldCom has become a powerhouse primarily through buying other companies and making more of their assets than their previous owners. However, regulators in the United States and Europe have a habit of attenuating the megamerger mentality.

Given the turmoil in the wireless market, a number of companies have decided to minimize their risk by forming alliances, similar to the ones used in the PC arena, where standardized components and bus architectures paved the way for inexpensive cards and peripherals.

THE EURASIAN ADVANTAGE

In evaluating the economics of the wireless Web, it's impossible to ignore the lead Japan and Europe have over the United States. Europe and Asia are the leaders in wireless technology, and both are well positioned in emerging wireless markets. As the European economy pulls ahead of the cooling U.S. economy, the United States is left in the uncomfortable position of playing catch-up in the world of the wireless Web. Although the United States doesn't compete directly with companies like Deutsch Telecom for subscribers in Germany, the wireless Web is a global business, and what affects Deutsch Telecom affects U.S. businesses, too. Foreign investment in the United States can dramatically alter the makeup of the U.S. network infrastructure, from determining which companies will own and run the infrastructure to the communications standards used with cellular handsets.

In the evolution of the wired Internet, the domestic infrastructure was in place before there was a critical mass of content and applications to make the Web a commercially viable entity. However, on the wireless Web, the opposite condition holds true; the domestic wireless infrastructure is in a relative shambles. But even though device-specific content lags behind what customers in Japan and Europe have access to, there is a storehouse of content in digital form residing on the wired Web. Unfortunately, this information is out of reach of most wireless devices in the United States. In addition, the infrastructure lags behind where it needs to be in terms of bandwidth and connectivity to support the interactivity and content that wired Web users are accustomed to.

The access to capital, engineering excellence, and the technological lead of Japan, Germany (and other European countries), and Finland is difficult to ignore, despite the historical lead of the United States in exploiting technologies in the marketplace. On the bright side, telecom companies in the United States can learn a lot from observing the international markets.

Consider Japan, the second largest mobile phone market. NTT DoCoMo of Japan has the advantage of experience with millions of subscribers on its I-Mode phones. One reason I-Mode is so popular is that there are over 20,000 Web sites that have been specially modified so they can be viewed on a small phone screen. From an economic perspective, not only is I-Mode attracting additional revenue, but I-Mode phones, used by about a quarter of DoCoMo's customers, bring in substantially higher revenue per customer compared to phones sold without the I-Mode's interactive features. In addition, DoCoMo makes money by charging a transaction fee of about 10 percent for every eCommerce transaction. This approach, which has been highly successful for DoCoMo, is in sharp contrast to some of the U.S. telecom carriers who are positioning themselves to be gatekeepers to the Internet. DoCoMo's approach, an apparently successful one, is to make it easy for outside Web developers to make their sites I-Mode friendly. The more Web sites that support I-Mode, the more valuable I-Mode phones are to consumers, and the more I-Mode customers sign up for the DoCoMo service.

International activity isn't limited to the EU and Japan. Koreans enjoy cell phones with services that surpass what most Americans have experienced. Cell phone activities in countries such as Korea and Taiwan will become increasingly significant as companies from these and other countries enter the international market. From the consumers' perspective, this should be a welcome change, and wireless device prices should plunge overnight. Unfortunately, many domestic producers will be unable to compete on price or quality. Similarly, for U.S. telecommunications companies hoping to invest in foreign companies or governments, China, Eastern Europe, Australia, and developing countries represent opportunities as well. As a result, the market for some of these players is largely uncertain and fraught with political problems that will likely take many years to resolve. For this reason, the leaders in the wireless world (Europe, Japan, and, in third place, the United States) have the potential to define standards and develop the technology to the point that deploying a wireless system in another country will simply be a purchase decision on the consumers' part.

ETHER-COMMERCE WRAP-UP

This chapter ends Part I on ether-business for the wireless Web. The discussion underlined the relative position of the United States in the global economy of the wireless Web, and looked at how important it is for the United States to follow economic developments of the wireless Web in Europe and Asia. It also emphasized the relative importance of government regulations and licensing to the survival of wireless Web companies—a sharp contrast to the relative free-for-all on the wired Web.

Part II, Wireless Wonders, introduces the myriad technologies related to the wireless Web, with a focus on the practical aspects of these technologies from an executive decision-maker's perspective. Chapters 4 through 6 will provide an overview of the technologies involved, with just enough technical detail to give any CEO or CIO the knowledge they need to speak intelligently and confidently with vendors and executives in the telecommunications industries, and to make informed decisions about which technologies and approaches make sense for their business goals.

EXECUTIVE SUMMARY

The wireless Web may well be the next "new thing," but cashing in on the euphoria is going to take more than securing a highly desirable URL. Unlike the wired Web, the telecommunications networks that will support ether-commerce are highly policed and subject to local, state, regional, and federal legislation. Claiming territory on the wireless Web will be much less like the western gunfight of the dotCom era and more like a dentist appointment. Companies willing to pay the price for RF spectrum licenses, technology licenses, and the hearts of customers stand to win big.

In addition to the obvious winners in a wireless utopia—the telecom giants, infrastructure builders, and wireless handset manufacturers—others also stand to gain. Those that should benefit directly and indirectly include two-way pager companies, which have been given a new lease on life with the advent of Web connectivity; the millions of existing dotComs; portal owners, such as Sprint Wireless; a variety of transaction-based businesses, from travel and banking to ticketing; and the entire advertising industry, from dotComs to newspapers to radio. Of course, the ultimate beneficiaries, subscribers, will determine if the services provided by the new wireless technology fill their needs for instant gratification and time and cost savings.

Significant funds will change hands in the many mergers, acquisitions, and alliances. Enormous sums of money are being spent on next-generation wireless licenses in Europe and, to a lesser extent, in the United States The United States is playing catch-up to both Europe and Asia, where money, engineering excellence, a technologic lead, and a hot European economy are pushing the wireless Web forward. The immature domestic infrastructure in the United States also limits its global influence. Globally, a short-term lack of content and a wireless handset hardware shortage temporarily limits demand for and access to the wireless Web, but it also presents a huge opportunity for content developers and translators and hardware manufacturers.

In addition to those who secure the appropriate licenses, the economic winners in ether-commerce will be the companies with the largest subscriber base, right mix of customers, quality management, and the ability to react to changes in the marketplace in Internet time.

Part Two

WIRELESS WONDERS

4

Network and
Wireless Technologies

*For the things we have to learn before we can do them,
we learn by doing them.*

Aristotle

INTRODUCTION

When the telephone was first introduced to the general public, long distance meant calling the next town. Because electronic amplifiers weren't yet available, the feat of sending a feeble audio signal over a distance of 10 to 20 miles was accomplished by using specially constructed telephones and, most importantly, high-quality, low-loss cables to connect one special phone to the next. Instead of signals running over barbed wire, from farmhouse to farmhouse with local phone traffic, long-distance calls traveled over cables that were carefully constructed of low-resistance copper wire. Furthermore, the cables were insulated from—and supported by—tall poles designed to keep them off of the moist earth, away from branches and anything else that might interfere with or attenuate the audio signals they carried.

Even with this level of attention paid to minimizing the amount of audio signal lost in the phone system, calling someone in another state, much less across the country, was out of the question with unamplified point-to-point cabling. To get a message from one end of a state or region to another, human-operated relays were established. An operator—often the town postman or other official—took a written message from a customer, called the next town, and dictated the message to an operator, who in turn called the operator in the next town down the line, and so on. This process was continued until the operator in the town of the person intended to receive the message was reached. This arduous process changed with the advent of electronic amplifiers used to boost the audio signal every 20 miles, or more. These "repeaters" made it possible for an audio signal to travel from one end of the continent to the other without human intervention.

The development of long-distance wireless communications in the United States has a similar history. Even as late as the 1970s, it was common practice for military personnel stationed overseas to contact their family and friends in the United States via human-operated relays. For example, a private in the U.S. Army stationed in West Germany wishing to contact relatives in San Francisco—but without the funds to pay for a long-distance call—would place a local call to a radio operator in West Germany. The operator would contact an operator in, say, New Jersey, who would in turn contact a radio operator in San Francisco. The radio operator in New Jersey could hear the other two operators, but the operators in San Francisco and West Germany could not hear each other directly. By using specially designed equipment to connect his radio to the public telephone network, the operator in San Francisco would call the private's relatives and connect the two parties. Of course, not only could the three operators hear everything that was said between the private and his relatives, so could anyone else with a shortwave receiver.

Unfortunately, this system of manually relaying or repeating messages from one station to the next, while providing a humanitarian and inexpensive service to military personnel and others stationed overseas, was unreliable. The reliability of long-distance, terrestrial-based wireless communications, like the weather, is difficult to predict. In the high frequency (HF) bands, which are frequencies between 3 and 30 million cycles of a radio wave or megahertz (MHz), and for distances greater than line of sight (about 100 mi or 166 km), communications depends on the state of the ionosphere. The efficiency with which the ionized atmosphere or ionosphere acts as a mirror for HF radio signals is affected by the sun's ultraviolet light, the time of day, the exact frequency of the RF signal, the season of the year, and even the sunspot cycle.

The reliance on point-to-point HF (3 to 30 MHz) wireless technology for global communications diminished rapidly with the advent of automatic satellite relay stations, the proliferation of wired transcontinental communications cables and networks, and the demand for rapid, reliable, personal communications. Today, privates stationed overseas use their calling cards and wireless phones that operate at 800 MHz or above to make long-distance calls home, and generals use secure direct satellite links to the Pentagon.

Except for the security precautions used with the generals' communications link, the technologies in the two communications examples are virtually identical. Wireless communications over any appreciable distance is rarely totally wireless. Even a cell phone call across town to another cell phone typically involves a wired communications link between the two cell stations handling the calls for each subscriber.

The cell is the fixed transmitter and receiver that sends and receives messages from wireless mobile phones, and connects these phones with the public telephone network and, more recently, with the Internet. Few "wired" communications of appreciable distance are fully wire based. For example, a transcontinental phone call from the United States to Europe might entail a hybrid system of a microwave link from one bank of a river to the next or across a mountain range with a satellite link and perhaps a laser link between skyscrapers. (Microwave communications are generally considered to use the frequency band between about 1 and 20 gigahertz (GHz). Whether a call contains voice, data, or both, there's likely to be a mixture of wired and wireless technologies involved.

This chapter begins Part 2, "Wireless Wonders." Chapters 4, 5, and 6 present a synopsis of the major technologies involved in the wireless Web, including topics from networking and RF communications principles to wireless Web communications protocols and software development tools. The focus is on the practical aspects of the technologies involved, and on providing a ready reference for the alphabet soup jargon the reader is likely to encounter in contracts and advertisements. The glossary at the end of this book provides an added resource for deciphering the technological information involved.

Readers who are fluent in wireless communications and networking technologies may wish to simply review the Executive Summary sections at the end of this and the following two chapters. They can then skip ahead to Part 3, "Convergence," which describes the convergence of the technologic, business, and political forces in the development of the wireless Web.

THE PHYSICS OF COMMUNICATIONS

A scene from *Funny Lady* starts with a ruthless businessman interviewing prospective painting companies for the job of refinishing several hundred chairs in his nightclub. As part of the interview process, he has the fastest, most skilled painter from each company come to his nightclub and paint one chair—at their cost. The impeccably dressed owner glares at his stopwatch as each painter carefully brushes on glossy black enamel, taking care not to drip any on the white dropcloth. The businessman has done his homework—at least on the financial end of things—and he knows the going rate for painters. He takes the salesman of the winning company aside and offers him the going rate for painting his chairs, based on the painter's winning time. The salesman begrudgingly accepts, remarking that the owner really knows his business. Confident that he has negotiated a winning contract, the penny-pinching nightclub owner walks away, off to attend to some other detail of his business.

The salesman walks away as well, even more confident. He pats the painter on the back and compliments him on a job well done. The salesman then asks the painter to get some help to take the chairs out back where he can *spray paint* them. The nightclub owner is unaware of the technology available to the paint company. His negotiations are based on the cost of two man-weeks of labor, for a job that requires only a few man-hours of work—with the right technology.

Any technology, whether a paint sprayer or cellular communications system, is simply a consistent way of producing meaningful results. It happens that most technologies, no matter how complex, are built on a foundation of basic principles. For example, the technologies involved in communications, whether between two neighbors talking on a phone to each other or between a NASA astronaut and Mission Control, are based on a handful of physical principles. These principles, outlined below, include signals and information content, operating frequency, modulation, bandwidth, and noise. With wireless communications, there are additional principles to consider, including field strength, antennas, receiver sensitivity and selectivity, signal absorption, signal propagation, and interference. In order to avoid the nightclub owner's mistake, it's important for a corporate decision maker to at least be familiar with these underlying principles so she can intelligently select the approach most appropriate for her company's needs.

Signals and Information Content

At the simplest level, communications is about moving energy from one place to another. This energy—a beam of light, a burst of RF energy, or the sound of a drum beating—when sent in a controlled way, can serve as a signal capable of imparting information to the receiver. Of course, the energy sent from a sender or transmitter to a human or electronic receiver takes on meaning only if the signals follow a mutually agreed-upon language—a standard syntax and character set—and a protocol or set of rules regarding how the language is used. The amount of information that can be conveyed by an RF signal is a function of the operating frequency, the bandwidth of the communications channel, the manner in which the signal is generated, the error correction and compression schemes used (if any), and the amount of noise in the communications system.

Operating Frequency

The operating frequency is the quantitative description of the RF wave used to carry information, often referred to as the carrier frequency. The operating frequency ranges from 10 to 20 Hz used for submarine communications to microwave signals used to communicate with satellites. For example, many first- and second-generation cell phones in the United States operate at a frequency of about 800 MHz. Because frequency allocations by the FCC started at the lower end of the spectrum to contend with the crowding in the AM broadcast bands, increasingly higher frequencies tend to be allocated to new services. As such, many new services operate in the ultra-high frequencies (UHF) of 300 MHz to 3 GHz and super-high frequencies (SHF) of 3 to

30 GHz) bands, where 1 GHz is equal to 1000 MHz. However, even these bands are crowded. For example, the personal wireless system called Bluetooth operates at 2.4 GHz, which is in the same band allocated for industrial, scientific, and medical (ISM) applications.

Since the UHF and SHF frequencies used for wireless phone communications are not normally reflected back to earth by the ionosphere but travel off into space, terrestrial communications is limited to line-of-sight distances under ideal conditions. As such, the potential for a wireless phone service in the United States to interfere with a wireless service of any type in Europe or Japan is minimal. It follows that the international governing bodies who negotiate international agreements on frequency allocation are more concerned with the lower frequencies that can traverse the globe than they are with those used for line-of-sight communications. This stance is reflected in the different frequency assignments for cellular services in Japan, Europe, and the United States. For example, the European GSM system operates in the 1.8-GHz band, whereas U.S. cellular and PCS services occupy the 800-MHz, 1.7-GHz, and 2.3-GHz bands. This lack of a global frequency standard means that for a European communications company to be successful in capturing the U.S. market it would still have to deal with dual-band phones because the frequencies licensed for use by the United States and Europe are different—even for the same type of service.

Modulation

In order to impart information to a receiver, an RF wave must be varied through a process called *modulation*. Modulation commonly involves changing the amplitude (intensity), frequency (cycles per second), or phase (rhythm) of a beam of light or radio signal in accordance with the information intended to be communicated to a receiver. Amplitude modulation (AM) and frequency modulation (FM) are used in broadcast radio throughout most of the world.

One of the key distinctions in defining modulation is whether it's accomplished through analog or digital means. The majority of wireless phones in use in the United States use analog modulation techniques because of the huge analog legacy systems that span the country. To use the new digital services, many cell phones in the United States are dual-mode devices, capable of working with either digital or analog networks. These phones default to analog services if there are no digital services available. Most modern cell phones and all PCS phones are completely digital.

Bandwidth

One of the basic physical principles of communications, and the focus of virtually every wireless company that is looking to the next generation of wireless systems, is bandwidth. In the context of the wireless Web, bandwidth is a measure of the information-carrying capacity of a communications system. Note that bandwidth applies to an entire communications system, since the bandwidth of a system is limited by the software or hardware component in the communications chain with the narrowest bandwidth. The more information that has to be transferred from one location to another, the greater the bandwidth requirement of the communications system.

Bandwidth is commonly expressed in bits per second (bps), where a bit is equal to a binary unit of information—a "0" or a "1." Dividing the number of bits/second by 10 provides an approximation of the equivalent number of characters per second. For example, 10 bps is equivalent to about one character per second. Images require much more bandwidth than text.

Where bandwidth and the wireless Web are concerned, a picture really is worth a thousand words—or more. As in the wired Web, it seems inevitable that everyone wishing to work with graphically rich content on the Web will require more bandwidth than they have access to (or can afford). The pictures, video sequences, and music that appear on a typical Web site require much greater bandwidth than even lengthy text-only email messages. The desire to download and share music and images across the Internet is the driving force behind DSL and Cable Modem use on the wired Internet and next-generation (G3 and above) wireless technologies.

Bandwidth and speed are often used synonymously. A high-speed connection is by necessity a high-bandwidth one. However, a high-bandwidth system, though capable of handling high-speed communications, may not be used to capacity because of some nontechnical constraint, such as licensing. The bandwidth of wireless systems is usually measured in Kilobits per second (KBps) or even Megabits per second (MBps), corresponding to sending or receiving a thousand or a million 0's and 1's per second, respectively.

Primarily because of the work of C. E. Shannon, a scientist working at Bell Laboratories in the 1940s, it's now understood exactly how bandwidth and the maximum amount of information that can be communicated are interrelated. Shannon discovered that a signal—whether a human voice, MP3-encoded music, or streaming video on the Web—requires a medium that provides a bandwidth equal to about double the highest frequency of the information to be communicated. Often, this information is processed or manipulated in a way that minimizes the bandwidth requirement without losing too much of the original information. For example, telephones are designed to carry voice frequencies only up to about 1500 Hz, even though the speech of most adults contains frequencies up to 5000 or 6000 Hz.

Because bandwidth is so precious, engineers and physicists have toiled for countless hours to determine how to squeeze as much data as possible through a connection with a given bandwidth. Fortunately, human speech is full of redundancies, including pauses, ums and ahs, and repetitions, all of which can be removed or compressed to increase information throughput.

There are also redundant variations in the loudness or amplitude of speech that can be used to reduce bandwidth requirements. A variety of data compression algorithms are available to minimize the bandwidth requirements and allow content to be sent and received across the wireless Web that would otherwise be impractical.

Voice frequencies used for public telephone communications are limited to a band of between 300 and 1500 Hz, corresponding to a bandwidth requirement of only 1500 Hz x 2 or 3000 Hz. In contrast, if the full range of human speech were used, the bandwidth requirement would be 6000 Hz x 2 or 12,000 Hz. In other words, limiting the bandwidth of the speech signal to 3000 Hz allows four channels to exist in the space that would have been occupied by the higher-fidelity signal.

This limited bandwidth of the phone system is one reason that "on-hold" music sounds so miserable over the phone; all of the higher frequencies above about 1500 Hz are cut off. In addition, the 3000-Hz limit also accounts for the slow progression of online modem connection speeds, from 300 to 1200 to 9600 to 14,400 to 28,800 and finally 56,000 (56K) bits per second. The current maximum modem speed over regular telephone lines, 56K bps is only possible because of elaborate, high-speed compression and error-correcting communications techniques that were perfected and standardized over several years.

Signal Loss

No matter how carefully constructed the communications system, signals are eventually degraded and attenuated. Every cable and connection is associated with signal loss. Infrared signals are absorbed or reflected by a piece of cloth or paper, and RF signals are attenuated by walls. Eventually, unless an amplifier is used appropriately and in the correct part of the signal path, a signal will be lost; that is, become indiscernible from noise. Recall that the old phone systems were limited to 10 or 20 miles primarily because of signal loss, even with high-quality phone cables.

Digital systems are somewhat better than analog systems at maintaining signal integrity, in part because distortions aren't added to the signal with each stage of amplification, as is the case with analog signals. With an analog amplifier, the background noise is amplified along with the desired signal. In addition, distortion and noise are added to the desired signal because of the limitations of the technology.

Noise

Unwanted, meaningless data, due to random electrical fluctuations or other factors, are an inescapable component of communications. Electrical noise can be due to natural disturbances, such as lightning or manmade sources, such as the operation of a car engine. Even the vibration of molecules at room temperature in everyday objects contributes to electrical noise. Most wireless devices, from cell phone receivers to home audio receivers are designed to work with noise—as long as it's considerably lower in strength than the communications signal. The relationship between the strength of the desired signal and that of the background noise is commonly referred to as the signal-to-noise (s/n) ratio. The higher the s/n ratio, the better. Digital communications systems, such as the second-generation cellular phone system in the United States, are less affected by noise than analog systems. This is due in part to a variety of error correction and regeneration processes that can be applied to digital signals.

WIRELESS COMMUNICATIONS BASICS

Building on the physics of communications, the next step is to understand the characteristics specific to wireless. It's important to note that, from a communications perspective, it doesn't matter if information flows through a cable run from Boston to San Francisco, in a beam of IR light between a TV remote control and a TV receiver, or in an RF signal beamed from a satellite to a satellite TV dish. The principles of information content, modulation, noise, and bandwidth apply equally. However, wireless communications involves a few additional technologies and principles not normally associated with wired communications, including antennas, the concept of field strength, receiver sensitivity and selectivity, absorption and propagation of RF signals, and interference.

Field Strength

The intensity of a radio signal emitted by an antenna or other radiator, commonly called the *field strength*, falls off with the square of distance from the source. That is, assuming there are no obstructions between a transmitter and a receiver, doubling the distance between a transmitter and a wireless PDA results in a drop in the field strength of the signal to $(1/2)^2$ or $1/4$ of the original value. The more powerful the signal fed to the antenna, the greater the field strength created by the antenna and, all else being equal, the greater the operating range of the communications system. For those users concerned with the potential health effects of cellular and PCS phone use, the relationship between field strength and distance means that doubling the distance between the antenna and their head—through the use of a headset or by using a car window or rooftop-mounted antenna—reduces the field strength to $1/4$ of the original value.

Antennas

The wire or other apparatus used to radiate and receive radio waves from space has several important properties: radiation pattern, efficiency, selectivity, and gain. The radiation pattern for the short vertical antenna found on most cell phones is normally omnidirectional in the horizontal plane. The radiation pattern for the fixed, tower, or rooftop-mounted cell antenna is usually omnidirectional in the horizontal plane as well, but may be directional depending on the proximity of adjacent cells. If one cell is likely to cause interference with a neighboring cell, the radiation pattern can be directed away from the neighboring cell with special antenna designs. Similarly, a satellite transmitter antenna may be focused broadly on a particular region of the continent, but the receiving dish antenna is usually tightly focused on the satellite's signal. Terrestrial microwave links typically employ two highly focused dish antennas for security and for the increased signal strength—referred to in relative terms as *gain* or in absolute terms as *effective radiated power* (ERP)—provided by the dish antenna design.

The efficiency of an antenna as a radiator of energy, and as a receiver of RF energy from space, is related to the physical size of the antenna relative to the operating frequency. For optimum transmitting and receiving efficiency, the length of the antenna on a handheld phone should be some multiple of 1/4 of the wavelength of the operating frequency. Actually, the minimum effective wavelength of an antenna is $1/2$ wavelength. In the case of a cell phone or wireless PDA, the metal chassis of a handheld phone and, to some extent, the hand of the user, form the other $1/4$ wavelength of the antenna. That is, together, the $1/4$-wave antenna and the chassis-human holder create a $1/2$-wavelength antenna.

Wavelength and frequency are related by the formula:

$$\text{wavelength}_{\text{meters}} \times \text{frequency}_{\text{MHz}} = 300$$

where wavelength is measured in meters and frequency is expressed in megahertz. The 300 represents the speed of light or any other electromagnetic wave, such as a cellular radio signal, in space. That is, regardless of the frequency, a radio wave will travel approximately 300,000,000 m/s through space. Since the frequency is expressed in MHz in this equation, the speed of radio waves traveling through space is represented by the figure 300.

For example, if the operating frequency of a wireless PDA is 300 MHz, then, by the formula above, the wavelength equals 1 m, since 1 (meter) × 300 (MHz) = 300. That is, in 1 s, the wireless PDA would generate 300 million electromagnetic waves, each 1 m in length. If the PDA's frequency were 600 MHz, then in 1 s it would generate 600 million electromagnetic waves, each $1/2$ m in length.

Based on the above formula, at 300 MHz the theoretical or electrical wavelength is 1 m. At 900 MHz, one wavelength is $1/3$ m, and a $1/4$-wavelength antenna would be $1/4$ of $1/3$ m or 8 cm (3 in). Although the physical length of an antenna is 2 to 3 percent shorter than the theoretical or electrical length, at 800 MHz, the frequency used by most domestic cell phones, the difference between electrical and physical length is negligible. The optimum physical length for a $1/4$-wavelength antenna for 800-MHz cell phones is about 9 cm

($3^{1}/_{2}$ in). Adding multiples of $^{1}/_{4}$ wavelength to the antenna length has the effect of focusing the radiated energy in the horizontal plane, parallel to the ground, where it can do the most good. Radiating energy above or below the horizontal plane, that is, where the cells are located, is simply sending energy into space or into the ground.

The commercial relevance of optimum physical antenna length is that, because of differences in the cellular operating frequencies used in Europe, Japan, and the United States, there is an added cost to manufacturing antennas for specific markets. In other words, not only must wireless phone manufacturers contend with differences in the electronics contained in cell phones destined for different markets, but the physical packaging (antenna length, for example) must change as well. Even in the domestic market, antennas designed for 800-MHz cell phones aren't suitable for 900-MHz PCS use. This difference applies to the fixed wireless base antennas, as well as to those used with handheld phones. For consumers, this means that moving from a cell to a PCS service provider entails changing their car phone antenna to a shorter 900-MHz model, as well as replacing their phone unit.

In addition to the simple vertical antenna found on cell phones, there are a variety of complex configurations, such as dish antennas, which have their own constraints on efficiency and radiation patterns. Many of these larger configurations are associated with directivity, gain, and a greater degree of selectivity, compared to the simple $^{1}/_{4}$-wavelength antennas used on handheld cell phones. Directivity is the ability to create greater field strength in one direction compared to another on transmit, and to receive signals with greater efficiency in one direction compared to another. Using a vertical antenna longer than $^{1}/_{4}$ wave—a $^{5}/_{8}$-wavelength antenna, for example—provides gain over a $^{1}/_{4}$-wave antenna because the signal strength is focused in a narrower beam. Multielement antennas, such as the aesthetically vacant TV antennas that graced many urban rooftops prior to the introduction of cable TV, also provide gain. Dish antennas can have enormous gain and directivity, allowing secure terrestrial communications as well as terrestrial-satellite communications using minimal power and receiver sensitivity. For example, Qualcomm's Omnitracs satellite-based mobile communications and tracking system relies on truck rooftop-mounted dish antennas to maintain real-time contact with drivers.

The selectivity of an antenna is a function of how well it responds to the frequency of the desired signals and how well it rejects others. More selective antenna designs are an obvious advantage in a metropolitan area where there is an abundance of potentially interfering RF signals from other services. Manufacturers typically offer a selection of omnidirectional and directional antennas to provide coverage patterns that meet the specific requirements of a particular installation.

Since wavelength is inversely related to operating frequency, the use of higher operating frequencies allows for shorter, lighter, less obtrusive antennas, without compromising on the efficiency or operating range of a wireless PDA or phone. Not only are small antennas necessary for practical mobile communications but small, unobtrusive, fixed cellular antennas can be placed throughout a city—on rooftops, atop telephone poles, and along highways—without spoiling the view.

At the VHF (30 to 300 MHz) frequencies used for broadcast TV and other services, antennas may need to be several feet in length for optimum efficiency. An efficient antenna system, especially for transmitting, is critical for a handheld cellular phone or wireless PDA in order to provide adequate range with the minimum power (and therefore the minimum battery drain) that's consistent with reliable communications.

Receiver Sensitivity and Selectivity

Two interrelated qualities that describe the receiver component of wireless devices are sensitivity and selectivity. The sensitivity value indicates the ability of a receiver to pick up weak signals. All else being equal, a more sensitive receiver will be able to pick up a signal a longer distance from the source. Both sensitivity and selectivity are desirable characteristics of a receiver. However, a more sensitive receiver may also be more susceptible to noise and interference. Selectivity is the ability of a receiver to distinguish desired signals from adjacent signals, as well as from noise and other interference. Selectivity can be a major factor in the performance of a receiver, especially when the potentially interfering signals are much stronger than the desired signal. For example, the frequency allocated for Bluetooth, the very low-power, personal network communications system, is adjacent to the "dirty" RF band allocated to microwave ovens. Since microwave ovens can create 1000 watts or more, and the Bluetooth system operates on mere milliwatts (1/1000th of a watt), the Bluetooth system receiver must be selective enough to operate effectively even when bombarded with several milliwatts of nominal leakage from a microwave oven.

More sensitive, more selective receivers are generally larger, heavier, require more power, and are more expensive to build and design. Mobile cellular systems (car phones) have more latitude in their design, given that power and size limitations are relatively lax compared to micro-thin handheld cellular or PCS phones.

Signal Absorption

The UHF radio waves used for cellular communications are subject to absorption by objects and structures between the cell and the handheld device. Trees, water vapor, rain, cars, metal beams, metal plumbing, and electrical wiring all absorb radio frequencies to varying degrees. The result is that a cell phone used in an open field has a greater range, and therefore doesn't require as many closely spaced cells (fixed transmitters and receivers), compared to a wireless phone used in, say, downtown Manhattan.

Absorption is a function of the RF used, as well as the nature of the potentially absorbing obstacles in the radio signal's path. For example, many experts consider the radio spectrum near 700 MHz, which is currently licensed to UHF TV broadcasters in the United States, to be optimal for third-generation (3G) wireless services because of the relatively low absorption of 700-MHz signals by buildings. At 800 MHz, the frequency for 2G cellular services in the United States, radio signals are absorbed by vegetation and bounce off the ground and buildings.

Signal Propagation

Radio waves tend to propagate or travel through space in predictable ways. As noted earlier, at the frequencies used for cellular communications, propagation is mainly line of sight, free of the effects of the ionosphere.

At the UHF frequencies allocated to the wireless Web, radio waves often behave with less predictability. For example, the signal from a cellular phone might follow an elevator shaft, only to be directed to another building where it causes interference with a computer monitor. Conversely, the same computer, operating at or near the cellular phone's operating frequency, might generate an RF signal that blocks the cell phone. Similarly, the RF signal from a mobile phone used in an office building might be reflected by partially silvered glass.

Interference

The RF spectrum isn't the open frontier it was a century ago. Today, virtually every frequency band is allocated or licensed to services ranging from commercial broadcast to fire, police, and cellular phone use. With all of this "radio pollution," interference from neighboring services is not uncommon, especially since radio signals from various sources can interact to create new signals that interfere with cellular phone service. Harmonics or multiples of the operating frequency of a device can create unexpected interference. A laptop computer operating at 1 GHz can emit harmonics at 2 GHz (2 × GHz) and 3 G MHz can wreak havoc on wireless communications using the same or nearly the same frequencies. As noted above, receiver selectivity and sensitivity as well as antenna selectivity can be manipulated to lessen the likelihood of interference from neighboring signals.

A COMMUNICATIONS MODEL

To illustrate the communications principles described above—which will be applied directly to wireless Web communications in the following chapters—consider this communications model. The model consists of a long, semiflexible tube, black (corresponding to a binary digit of value 0) and white (corresponding to a binary digit of value 1) marbles, a means of inserting marbles in the upper end of the tube (the sender or transmitter), and a means of observing the marbles as they exit the bottom of the tube (the receiver). Signals can be sent down the tube by one of several approaches. Groups of, say, three marbles can be inserted in rapid succession at the top of the tube, followed by a brief pause, and then three more marbles, and so on. With three marbles, messages or words composed of six different characters can be sent (for example, 000, 001, 011, 111, 110, or 100), corresponding to the possible color combinations of three marbles.

Assume that gravity is constant, so the rate of marbles falling down the tube doesn't vary from one moment to the next, and that initially the diameter of each marble is just slightly smaller than the diameter of the tube, thereby preserving the pattern of marbles inserted at the top. Given these assumptions, the maximum number of marbles that can drop freely from the tube per second, corresponding to the maximum frequency, is primarily a function of marble size. The smaller the marbles, the more that can fall through the tube in a given period of time—in other words, the higher the frequency. That is, the frequency used in this system is the reciprocal of marble size. Big marbles correspond to low frequency, small marbles to high frequency. The rate at which a marble moves through the tube is fixed by gravity, just as signals travel through space and copper wire at a speed of about 300,000,000 m/s.

The maximum communications throughput of the model, corresponding to the maximum number of marbles that can be handled by the system, occurs when there is virtually no space between adjacent marbles. However, as the space between characters (sets of three marbles, for example) is decreased, there is an increased likelihood of error. A marble intended to be associated with one character could be knocked adjacent to the set of three marbles corresponding to another character. Without some sort of memory device to keep track of the total marble count and therefore which marbles belong to a character, utter confusion may result. The operator will have to shut down the model and restart it at the point of the last known good character.

The transmitter in this simple, single-tube system consists of two cylinders, one containing new black marbles and one containing white ones. There's a slider bar with a hole in it below the mouth of the containers. The slider bar is moved in unison with a time-varying analog signal, such as a human voice or other sound, releasing black marbles as it moves left, and white ones as it moves right. That is, the slider apparatus, analogous to an RF modulator, converts an analog signal into a digital one, just as a digital telephone takes analog voice signals and converts them into digital signals. In a cell phone, this process is accomplished with a chip called an analog-to-digital (A-to-D) converter.

In the model, noise is represented by the variability in the rate of release of marbles at the bottom of the tube. This variability can be due to a variety of internal factors, ranging from changes in the length, diameter, or elasticity of the tube due to changes in ambient temperature, humidity, or simply aging—the same factors that affect electronic components. The tube could shrink and become brittle with age, slowing the marbles down as they traverse its length. External factors include earthquakes and other sources of low-frequency vibrations, such as nearby traffic, which may affect the motion of marbles relative to the tube.

In addition to noise, the model illustrates other imperfections typical of communications systems. For example, the model is lossy, in that marbles wear a little and pick up debris from the tube wall as they travel down the tube. Bright white marbles become dull, and dull black marbles take on a dusty gray color. In this model, marble color saturation corresponds to field strength, with bright white and darkest black corresponding to the highest field strength. At some point, the marble color (corresponding to signal field strength) may become an ambiguous gray. The receiver may not be able to accurately distinguish an originally white marble from an originally black marble, introducing errors in the message. Fortunately, digital technology supports the concept of lossless regeneration.

A marble regenerator, which corresponds to a repeater in a communications system, takes dirty marbles in one end and produces clean marbles on the other. Even though digital systems are superior to analog systems in many respects, they aren't perfect. Errors are possible with the regeneration process when the input is ambiguous. The parallel would be a repeater placed too far from the signal source in a wireless communications system. There are ways of resolving this sort of ambiguity, including error correction techniques, as described below. Of course, an analog repeater or amplifier would simply replicate the input pattern in the output, including the gray tone. The very process of analog amplification will introduce a bit of gray into each marble in the output pattern, as well. Eventually, after many stages of analog amplification and lossy travel through the communications system, the original signal will be lost, corresponding to all gray marbles, with varying shades of gray.

With a few modifications, the original communications model can illustrate the concept of interference. The addition of a few adjacent tubes that carry marbles is equivalent to crowding in the RF spectrum. Assuming that the tubes are somewhat elastic, and that adjacent tubes are touching, the motion of marbles down one tube can upset the progression of tubes down the other. Two neighboring tubes, one to either side of the main communications tube can cause even more interference with the movement of marbles down the main tube. The obvious solution to the interference problem is to keep the other tubes away from the main tube—a feat normally accomplished in the real world by FCC licensing and frequency assignments for different services. Using a more selective receiver is another approach to minimizing interference.

To illustrate the concept of the bandwidth limits of a communications system, assume that there are small fenestrations or perforations along the length of the communications tube, appreciably smaller than the diameter of the tube. Recall that in order to increase the throughput of the communications system—that is, increase the KBps figure—one approach is to decrease the size of the marbles. However, the holes limit the minimum marble size that can be used in the model, corresponding to the maximum frequency of an RF signal that can be used in a real-world communications system.

Assuming that the model is limited to a single, fixed-bandwidth tube, one way to increase the information throughput is to use some form of information compression. Recall that signal compression is what allows a 56-KBps modem to operate on a telephone line that can only handle a noncompressed signal at about 1200 Bps. In the model, compression is represented by a process that shrinks and encapsulates each character or group of three marbles into a clear sphere the size of the original marbles. That is, a single transparent marble containing three miniature marbles corresponds to a character. Each marble may contain three white, three black, two black and one white, or two white and one black marbles. In the real word, the parallels to the compression process would be accomplished by high-speed computer-enabled digital signal processing.

Even further increases in information throughput of the model could be achieved by shrinking the marbles so that more could fit in the tube at the same time to the point that the marbles approach the size of the tube perforations. That is, the bandwidth of the tube still limits the maximum frequency of marbles traversing the tube, just as the bandwidth of a communications channel does for RF signals. The length of the original message, relative to the tube length, diminishes significantly, becoming shortest when a higher frequency is combined with encapsulation and shrinking of the marbles. Recall that tube length is equivalent to time, since propagation time through the tube, like the propagation of electrical signals through a cable, is fixed.

Further increases in information throughput can be achieved with additional tubes, which effectively increases the bandwidth of the model. In moving from a serial to a parallel model, the tubes can be used in a variety of ways to increase signal throughput. One use is timing. Instead of spaces between characters (or, if the compressed marbles are used, between groups of characters or words), a marble can be dropped down the timing tube to indicate the start of a new word. Furthermore, the color of the marble signifying the start of a new word can be used for error correction. For example, a black marble can signify that the word being sent is composed of an odd number of individual black marbles. A white marble sent down the timing tube can signify an even number of black marbles is contained in the following word. If the error correction marble doesn't agree with the marble count of a particular word (the checksum), then the sender can be asked to resend the word.

With the increased information-handling capacity of the model provided by using multiple tubes, there may be idle periods during which there are no marbles flowing down the tubes. This excess bandwidth capacity can be used as added communications channels for additional users. The tubes can be multiplexed, or shared by multiple users, with the addition of an address tube. In the multiplexed communications model, a transparent marble with some combination of compressed black and white marbles, corresponding to the identity of each owner, is released at the start of every three-character word. In this way, words belonging to separate messages, each intended for a different recipient, can be sent and received. The cost is the additional overhead of selecting and sending the appropriate marble down the address tube and of interpreting it at the receiving end. In addition, there is the bandwidth occupied by the timing and user ID marbles, which could otherwise be used for data. However, this overhead is acceptable, given the power and flexibility that addressing and error correction provide.

Note that in a real-world communications system, the equivalent of parallel tubes can be created with a variety of encoding schemes that don't actually involve multiple, parallel wires. Of course, providing the virtual equivalent of parallel connectivity, along with features such as error checking and multiplexing does make for a more complex system. Not discussed, for example, is the complexity of the receiver, which has to handle address recognition as well as performing the checksum calculation for error correction.

Continuing with the marble communications system analogy, the wireless equivalent of the communications system. Marbles from the centrally located base transmitter (equivalent to the fixed cell) are launched into the air before traveling down a communications tube to all receivers within range. The range of the cell, a function of the power fed to the antenna from the transmitter, is represented by the velocity and trajectory of the stream of marbles.

Objects in the path of the marbles can drastically reduce the operating range (absorption), and marbles from other communications systems can knock the marbles off course (interference). In this wireless model, funnels correspond to antennas, with the funnel shape determining selectivity. A funnel with a wider mouth corresponds to a system with less selectivity; a narrower mouth corresponds to greater selectivity.

Note that while every receiver receives the same stream of marbles, the receiver only recognizes messages that contain the appropriate user ID. In the model, the filter rings at the base of each funnel (antenna) represent this mechanism. In this and most other respects, the basic operating principles of the airborne (wireless) model is the same as the initial tube (wired) model. For example, there are bandwidth limitations on both the sender's side and the receiver's side, represented by perforations in the transmitter and receiver tubes. The primary exception is that receivers are mobile. As discussed below, this seemingly small variation makes all the difference in the world to consumers.

THE VALUE OF MOBILITY

From a business perspective, the difference between wired and wireless communications is that wireless gives the user freedom of mobility, and therefore value over and above that of wired communications. Sometimes the value of mobility is primarily a matter of convenience and timesavings, such as the ability to make an important call from a cell phone instead of taking the time to go out in the rain to make a call from a phone booth. The same holds for a wireless garage door opener versus one with a wall-mounted switch that must be pressed for access, or a TV or stereo remote control. In addition to the convenience factor, wireless also makes some things possible that are otherwise impossible. For example, the remote control of model airplanes, cars, and even control of interplanetary satellites would not be everyday occurrences without wireless communications technology.

Bandwidth, a measure of the maximum information-carrying capacity of a communications system, is only one of several factors that defines the usability of a wireless system. For example, a trader on the stock exchange trading floor needs a wirelesscommunications system that provides virtually instantaneous response. However, even with more than adequate bandwidth, response time can be lengthened simply by virtue of the distances involved between the sender and the receiver. Communicating via satellite, for example, might take several seconds for each exchange of information. The point is that, while bandwidth limits the maximum throughput of a communications system and makes rapid response possible, the system must be designed to take advantage of the bandwidth available, within the limits of what the customers want and can afford.

The issues of bandwidth, range, power, and cost can be illustrated by examining the typical wireless phone or PDA. First of all, the handheld unit has to be light, the battery must be able to supply the energy requirements for several days, the range has to be sufficient to allow the phone to be used indoors and outside of the city, and the phone needs to be relatively immune from interference from other remote control systems or unrelated devices. Finally, for the system to be successful in the marketplace, not only does it need to be easy to use and provide the proper mix of features, it also has to be affordable.

The features and affordability of any wireless system depend to a great degree on the nature of the underlying infrastructure—the communications network—that provides the support and connectivity to resources on the public telephone network and the Internet. A review of several aspects of networks and networking that are relevant to the wired and, increasingly, the wireless Web follows.

NETWORKS

A network is simply a means of connecting devices in such a way that they can share information. Connecting to the most celebrated network, the Internet, with fast, secure, mobile communications technology is viewed by many as the means to providing added value over strictly voice communications. Without a connection to the public telephone network or the Internet, a cell phone is just an expensive walkie-talkie. As described below, there is a plethora of competing technologies focused on providing subscribers with the most impressive, high-speed connectivity to the Internet and public telephone network possible. Before exploring the bells and whistles, a grounding in network principles is in order.

As introduced in Chapter 1, one of the first networks was born out of the need for point-to-point wiring for the telephone. Not only was point-to-point wiring an eyesore—streets were littered with huge bundles of cables hung from telephone poles—but the cost of this approach was far too prohibitive for all but the most affluent businesspeople. A telephone network with a manual switchboard at its hub or center made it possible for *anyone* with a telephone connected to the switchboard to talk with anyone else on the network.

Since the early networks with manually operated switchboards, networks have evolved to service a variety of other appliances, from the PC to wireless PDAs and cell phones. Networks are most commonly described on the basis of the following: their architecture; the types of signals they handle; the speed that these signals flow through the network; the topology or physical layout of the network; their geographical extent; the protocols or communications standards used; the application, such as supporting the Web or telephone communications; and the details of physical connectivity, such as satellite or wireless PDA communications. These categories are described in more detail below.

Network Architecture

Network architecture describes the framework for interoperating on networks—the rules that allow sharing of information among different types of computers and other devices, regardless of their design or operating system. That is, architectures describe the cables, transmission services, the services provided to the network applications, and how they can be put together. Network architectures are often confused with the protocols that run on them. Protocols are specific implementations of services that follow the rules of the underlying architecture.

Examples of network architectures are Open System Interconnection (OSI), IBM's System Network Architecture (SNA), and Transmission Control Protocol/Internet Protocol (TCP/IP). TCP/IP, originally developed by the U.S. Department of Defense, the dominant architecture today, provides the logical connectivity for the Internet. Like OSI and SNA, TCP/IP uses a layered approach to networking, starting with the top level that deals with applications, and ending with the bottom layer that deals with hardware issues. An example of a network application for TCP/IP is the ability to publish Web pages. The lower layers handle connections between devices and the routing of information.

Signal Type

From the perspective of the wireless Web, the major distinction regarding signal type is analog versus digital signals. Most computer networks are fully digital. However, the domestic public telephone network, one of the largest and oldest networks in the United States, is predominantly analog. Even the majority of wireless telephone networks are analog, albeit with an interface to digital networks to provide caller ID and other functions made possible by digital technology.

Although only about a third of cellular telephone traffic in the United States is digital, there is stiff competition from the all-digital PCS service (the intent of creating the PCS service in the first place was to provide cellular operators with competition to move things along), as well as all-digital carriers such as Sprint. Digital communications services, on average, require less battery power, offer improved sound quality, and offer a level of privacy and security that's difficult to match with analog networks.

Data Transfer Rate

The distinction between high-speed versus normal-speed networks is a relative one, and one that, like PC clock speeds, changes every few months. What was considered high-speed six months ago is considered slow today. Even so, most would agree that a dial-up 56K-modem speed represents a benchmark for normal speed connectivity on the public telephone network, whereas ISDN, Satellite, DSL, and Cable Modem represent the higher end of speeds possible. The speeds possible with these wired network technologies range from a rather modest 128 KBps for ISDN to over 7 MBps for DSL. Network data transfer rate or speed is normally tied to specific network services, either by technologic limitations or, more often, by licensing restrictions. Increased speed requires an increase in bandwidth, potentially resulting in interference with other services that share the spectrum.

In the wireless world, what constitutes normal speed in the United States is painfully slow—anywhere from 9 to 19.2 KBps. Even the third-generation (G3) wireless network services, considered high-speed at 384 KBps to 2 MBps, are slow compared to high-speed wired services. Given the market that G3 services is projected to open up, it's a concern in the industry that even high-speed wired network services have yet to tame streaming video and other services that slower G3 wireless connectivity is supposed to provide.

It's important to recognize the features and limitations of the most common high-speed or broadband network service, in part because they are competing with fixed wireless service for the "last mile" connection in the United States and Europe. High-speed network services have yet to become commonplace in Europe or the United States. Less than 1 percent of Western Europe has high-speed Internet access, and the figures aren't much better in the United States. Reasons range from expense, long delays for installation, and unavailability. In Europe, lack of high-speed wired network access is seen as an opportunity for Wireless Local Loop (WLL) access. This fixed wireless solution may extend the wired Web to the home and small business in a way that was impossible before because of the monopolies that controlled the last mile of cable from the telephone office to the home. Paradoxically, wireless technology may finally bring the wired Web into the homes of Western Europeans at the same time the United States struggles to achieve the level of wireless service enjoyed by many Europeans.

The most significant high-speed network alternatives in the United States are ISDN, Cable Modem, DSL, T1, and Satellite. At 128 KBps, ISDN (Integrated Services Digital Network) services provide about double the bandwidth of a standard 56-KBps modem. Even though the high initial and monthly costs, difficulty associated with setup, lack of general availability, and only modest bandwidth improvements over a 56-KBps analog modem have limited the appeal of ISDN, it does allow both voice and data flow over a standard phone line. A key characteristic of ISDN is that it is symmetrical, in that upload and download speeds are the same.

Cable modems use the same cable and much of the communications electronics used for cable TV. Cost is typically a little less than DSL. Download bandwidth, the connection bandwidth for images and other content coming from the Internet to a desktop PC, is typically between 3 MBps and 10 MBps. When uploading data to the Internet, bandwidth is between 1 and 2 MBps. A smaller upload bandwidth isn't normally a problem if the user is sending text emails and mouse clicks. A cable modem is a natural for the home if the subscriber has cable TV, but it may be inappropriate for a business unless it's already wired for cable TV. The downside of cable is security, in that everyone in an area shares access to the same information.

A Digital Subscriber Line (DSL) lets users send data at about $\frac{1}{2}$ MBps and receive data at over 7 MBps, depending on the type of DSL service available. Like ISDN, DSL can simultaneously handle voice and data over standard phone lines. Since DSL is only available within a four-mile radius of a telephone switching office, it's typically not an option in rural areas.

For years, the standard for reliable, secure, high-speed connectivity has been the T1 line. A T1 line is a dedicated, high-speed cable, typically composed at least in part of fiber optics, that delivers at about 1.5 MBps. The only real problem with a T1 line is cost, which can be several times that of other high-speed network services. For rural connectivity, a satellite network connection may be the only available option. Satellite downlinks provide moderate speeds of only about 400-KBps connectivity. This technology provides point-to-point, narrow-beam (secure) communications between the satellite and the user's dish antenna. Satellite networks are more expensive than alternative systems, in part because of the added cost of the antenna and receiver system, but may be the only option available in some communities.

Topologies

Regardless of whether the media that is used to connect devices on a network is copper wire, fiber-optic cables, or wireless, there are a variety of established physical configurations or designs that have become standards for networks. The archetypal configurations are point-to-point, star, ring, and bus. Other physical configurations are common as well, including ARCnet, Switched, Daisy Chain, and Mesh. It's important to note that the physical topology may be very different from the logical topology. For example, it's possible to establish a logical star network even though the cabling is arranged in a bus configuration. In addition to these "pure" topologies, there are hybrid and irregular topologies as well.

In theory, an enterprise selects one physical topology and extends it throughout the organization. In practice, few networks are original; there's always some legacy system to deal with, which is often composed of several network configurations glued together to solve some long-forgotten problem that a company's IS department faced in the past. A patchwork of network topologies—referred to as a hybrid or irregular topology—can also develop in new networks as well. Perhaps the graphics department wants to install a group of Macintosh computers with their own star network topology, including several wireless devices, in an otherwise all-PC shop. Similarly, the R&D group may need to install its own network of Silicon Graphics workstations. A small cluster of devices connected together, with or without connection to a larger network, is often called an *ad hoc network*. Two laptops connected to a printer through a wired or wireless network would normally be considered an ad hoc network. Each topology is associated with benefits and tradeoffs regarding centralization, cost, maintenance and troubleshooting, scalability, security, speed, and stability. For example, point-to-point networks work best for a handful of devices, whether local or spread out over thousands of miles. As Alexander Graham Bell discovered before the advent of the switchboard, a point-to-point network topology doesn't scale very well.

In the star topology, all data are routed through a central machine or hub. That is, the star topology is structured for centralization; failure in one connection or leg of the star should not affect the others. Networks set up in a star configuration are therefore easier to manage, but tend to be slower than the other topologies, because every message must pass through the hub.

In the ring topology, information is passed from device to device in turn, when permission is given. The ring topology, often referred to as *token ring*, usually involves passing a token around the network to identify which device on the network has a matching address. The bus network simply links devices to a common signal channel. Note that the physical and electrical topologies can be totally different from each other, even on the same system. For example, a logical star network can run on a physical bus topology.

Geographic Extent

In addition to physical topologies, networks tend to be categorized in terms of their particular geographic configurations, which in turn lend themselves to particular types of physical connections. For example, connectivity configurations include wireless, wired, fixed, mobile, terrestrial, and satellite. Examples of actual implementations are handset-to-satellite, mobile-satellite, terrestrial, and maritime.

The most common geographic network descriptors are PANs, LANS, WLANs, WANs, and MANs. Personal Area Networks (PANs) have a very limited range, on the order of a few meters, and tend to be somehow attached to the user. Wearable computers typically rely on PAN technologies to provide communications between the various components of the computer and peripherals. A form of PAN defined by the Bluetooth standard is called a *piconet*, and multiple independent piconets combine to form a scatternet.

As the name suggests, a Local Area Network (LAN) connects computers in a single location, such as an office or a car. Car-based LANs, which may contain a mix of wired and wireless connectivity, are expected to increase dramatically in popularity, assuming legislation against a Web-enabled office on wheels isn't forthcoming. Wireless LANs (WLANs) are commonly used in fixed wireless services, based on either IR or RF signaling. Wired LANs tend to be high-speed networks used to connect, for example, printers, scanners, and other peripherals with computers on a network. RF WLANs have a range of up to a few hundred meters—much less if based on IR technology—and typically handle speeds of up to 10 MBps. LANs are often implemented with symmetric topologies such as the star or ring.

The archetypal Metropolitan Area Network (MAN) is a high-speed intra-city network that links multiple locations with a metropolitan area. MANs operate from 1 MBps to 200 MBps. MANs can be wired and increasingly include a wireless component. At the next level of geographic coverage is the Wide Area Network (WAN). WANs are used to connect disparate networks, often located in different states or across the globe. For example, the major telecommunications carriers have WANs connecting the West and East coasts of the United States. WANs consist of multiple local networks tied together, typically using telephone company services. WANs may connect users in different buildings or countries. They tend to have irregular topologies, often built around point-to-point wiring, satellite, and cellular telephone networks. Although high-speed WANs are commonplace, wireless WANs tend to be limited to about 20 KBps.

Network Protocols

Protocols are specific implementations of services that follow the rules of the underlying architecture, providing the logical connectivity among devices on the network. The role of a protocol is to make certain that messages sent over a network reach their destination. Modern devices are capable of handling a variety of protocols so they can be used in different parts of the United States and with different service providers. For example, the OmniSky Minstrel wireless modem designed for the Palm V supports TCP/IP, UDP, PPP, and SLIP protocols. (See the Glossary for details.)

One of the most important network protocols for wireless Web work is IEE 802.11b, the industry standard for LANs. This protocol provides 10 MBps throughput with a maximum range of about 300 m (1000 ft). This standard forms the basis of many home and office-based wireless networking products that can extend connectivity to the Web through a variety of hand-held devices and laptops.

Application

The two major application areas for network technology relevant to the wireless Web are internetworks, including the Internet, and the public telephone systems. To the dismay of appliance manufacturers and trademark lawyers, sometimes the word for a technology or device comes to stand for the generic device. For example, many people go Rollerblading instead of inline skating, spinning instead of indoor cycling, and at one time owned a Frigidaire instead of a refrigerator.

It's the same with the Internet. A collection of interconnected networks is called an *Internetworks* or *internet*. There are many internets, but only one Internet. An *internet* is simply a collection of LANs connected to WANs. Because of the potential for confusion, the term *internet* (lowercase i) is often avoided.

Wired Web users, except for those connecting to an Internet service provider or ISP via a modem, have largely ignored the telephone network. The network uses computer-controlled exchange switches, which are roughly equivalent to operator switchboards, but operate much more quickly and without human intervention. A central technology in the telephone network is the Private Branch Exchange (PBX). A PBX is the electronic equivalent of a local switchboard operator, interconnecting telephones and other devices in a local area with a telephone switching system. Most larger companies have their own PBX, allowing outside customers to call a single number, and then connect to a particular line in the company by using an extension number. In this way, one telephone line can be leased from the telephone company, replacing potentially thousands of direct lines.

Essential Network Jargon

Every executive working in the area of wireless technology has to have a grasp of the networking jargon that describes much of the enabling infrastructure. A reasonable vocabulary for an executive engaged in negotiations with a network vendor might include terms like 100BaseT, Application Server, ATM, Backbone, Bridge, Client-Server Architecture, DNS, Fast Ethernet, Firewall, Gateway, Linux, NIC, Repeater, Router, Server, Switch, and Thin Client. These and other networking-related terms are defined in the Glossary.

DISCUSSION

Technologic issues aside, most users don't care or even know which standards their wireless phones, PDAs, or two-way pagers use until they have to switch providers or use their wireless devices while traveling outside of their home territory. Their concerns, and the concerns that will continue to drive business in the wireless Web, are full, consistent coverage, data transfer rates that meet their needs, and reasonable prices. Regardless of advances in bandwidth and other technical issues, availability and connection costs will be the main factors affecting wireless usage for the foreseeable future.

The next chapter builds upon the basic communications and networking technologies discussed here and examines the technologic trajectory of wireless communications as it relates to the wireless Web.

EXECUTIVE SUMMARY

The technologies involved in communications are based on signals and information content, operating frequency, modulation, bandwidth, and noise. Other factors in wireless communications are field strength, antennas, receiver sensitivity and selectivity, signal absorption, signal propagation, and interference. Most of the technologic advances that pertain to the wireless Web have to do with supporting multiple users in a challenging, bandwidth-restricted environment adjacent to potentially interfering signals.

Wireless communications relies heavily on both wired networking technologies and vice versa. The standard wired networking issues apply equally to wireless communications, including the importance of selecting a compatible topology, adherence to network architecture and protocol limitations, and of employing technologies that provide sufficient data transfer rates.

Of the networking technologies related to the wireless Web, personal area networks (PANs) and wireless local area networks (WLANs) are the most critical to understand. Both of these technologies provide the last leg of connectivity between the Internet or other networks and the personal devices that users rely on to access and create data.

From a business perspective, communications and networking technologies define the cost of circuit and component design, within the constraints of fulfilling customer needs. In the end, the added value that mobile communications technology has over wired communications is related to the affordability of and easy access to the features provided by these technologies.

5

Cellular Communications and Protocols

When one door closes another door opens;
But we often look so long and so regretfully upon the closed door
that we do not see the ones which open for us.

Alexander Graham Bell

INTRODUCTION

As illustrated in Part 1, the ultimate success of any business venture concerning the wireless Web depends on having a solid technology, leadership with the vision and business acumen to bring the potential of the technology to fruition, and a supportive or at least accepting sociopolitical environment. In at least one or two of these areas, the United States may have a second-mover advantage over the European and Asian companies and their prospective wireless Web customers.

At a minimum, U.S. executives now have a good idea of which questions to ask. After all, who's to say whether or not domestic customers will jump at the chance to buy a Coke from a vending machine, or buy wine, or pay rent using their cell phones? And even if they do, what type of information infrastructure and combinations of technologies will present customers with an irresistible mix of utility, security, responsiveness, and cost-effectiveness? After corporations pour huge amounts of capital into creating a high-speed, reliable, ubiquitous wireless communications infrastructure, where will the profits come from, and how will they be sustained? Are the descriptions of new wireless Web technologies that flood the technical papers and journals merely a reflection of a fad, or a lasting trend? Will the infatuation that teenagers in parts of Europe and Asia have with personal, hip, and inexpensive wireless devices carry on to adulthood? Will the loops and pockets for cell phones that are standard issue on virtually every backpack made for teens in Korea and Japan seem like some vestigial appendage to teens in the United States, or will they too embrace wireless communications? Will domestic wireless content providers, such as Disney, that supplies cartoons for Japan's I-Mode phone system, find the domestic market equally receptive to its products? Furthermore, will the U.S. consumers' passion for the PC short-circuit Web-enabled, smart phone services and instead drive the extension of high-speed Web access to underserved communities via fixed wireless technologies? Similarly, will consumer expectations, having been shaped by their experience on the multimedia-rich Web, be impossible to meet, given the relatively slow, predominantly text interfaces provided by Web-enabled phones?

In attempting to answer these and other questions about the wireless Web, the West European picture seems clearer than the domestic one. First, the huge political and technologic infrastructure advantage that Europe has over the United States is the GSM continentwide standard. The European Union scored a major political victory when it convinced Nokia, Ericsson, and the other major cellular players to collaborate on GSM as a second-generation digital standard. As a result, European businesspeople can buy a GSM phone in Italy, France, or Germany and bring it home to Finland. There, they can choose from several service and pricing plans offered by competing carriers. In contrast to the United States, European cellular carriers are barred from subsidizing phones by passing costs on to subscribers. As a result, rates are a true reflection of the level and nature of the service provided. For most European customers and the European wireless industry, this is a win-win situation. European customers can compare oranges with oranges, and cellular operators and cell phone manufacturers can focus on developing new features and improving the technology for all GSM phones.

Japan's NTT DoCoMo presents another perspective on the technologic trajectory of wireless Web communications. DoCoMo's I-Mode, which has virtually saturated the Japanese market, offers subscribers a constant online connection without the hassle and delay of dialing in. In addition to providing services that are apparently precisely in line with what Japanese consumers want and need, DoCoMo is in a league of its own technologically. Not only has NTT DoCoMo created the world's smallest, most sophisticated, feature-laden cellular handsets, it is also the first operator to introduce third-generation (3G) cellular using the same communications standard that will eventually be deployed throughout Europe.

In sharp contrast to the typical European or Japanese experience, a cellular subscriber in the Northeast region of the United States will probably have to buy a new mobile phone as well as sign up for a new wireless plan if he moves to the Pacific Northwest. It can be an expensive move, especially if he hasn't fulfilled his original plan's one- or two-year service obligation. He may end up paying a termination fee to the original carrier, as well as having to buy a new cellular or PCS phone. Even in the same region of the United States, customer choices may be limited. For example, a businesswoman in the Northeast considering Nextel PCS service is locked into a Motorola wireless phone. Her only option for a more feature-rich phone is to buy a more expensive Motorola model. Furthermore, if she decides to switch to another service, she'll probably have to buy a new PCS phone from another manufacturer. Even so, the FCC cites dictating cellular rates as evidence that consumers are benefiting from multiple competing standards for service.

Despite the technological prowess of NTT DoCoMo and the political savvy of Europe's wireless access providers, the United States and Canada have an opportunity to take the lead in the use of some niche technologies, such as wireless PDAs, and in the development of middleware or software that pulls everything together. In the context of the wireless Web, *middleware* is the software running on a network that provides connectivity between wireless devices and the wired network. Middleware encompasses applications that compress and decompress data, provide security, perform data and application synchronization, manage wireless devices from a distance, manage software and hardware inventories, store and forward messages, provide Web clipping, and provide database connectivity, for example, between a CE handheld and an Oracle database.

Even in the world of hardware providers, there are only so many Ciscos. In addition, many companies once regarded as domestic, such as Motorola, are really international players that use local talent and materials whenever politically or economically advantageous. It may be that U.S. companies are best equipped to profit from adding value to core technologies developed elsewhere and providing them to rapidly developing markets like China.

Whatever the ultimate role of the United States in the development of the wireless Web, it's clear that establishing a presence in this market is first about creating or otherwise acquiring and manipulating reliable technologies. Taking this perspective, this chapter builds upon and reinforces the basic communications and networking technologies discussed in the previous chapter regarding the context of cellular communications, so the underlying principles become practical and real. In addition, it explores key enabling technologies, including voice recognition and the Bluetooth personal network system, with a view toward the trajectory of wireless technologies as they relate to the wireless Web.

CELLULAR COMMUNICATIONS

Up to this point, the discussion of communications technology and networking has been applicable to most wired and wireless communications systems. To illustrate the practical relevance of the basic communications principles introduced in Chapter 4, such as multiplexing schemes, bandwidth requirements, and receiver sensitivity and selectivity to the more practical, commercial aspects of the wireless Web, this section focuses on the principal delivery vehicle for wireless Web content—the cellular telephone system.

The terms *cellular phone* and *cellular radio* are often used more or less synonymously with mobile wireless communications. However, cellular radio or telephone is just one aspect of wireless communications technology, and a distinction that has as much to do with marketing as it does with real technological differences. Wireless communications encompasses technologies like cordless phones, analog and digital cellular phones, PCS phones, Web-enabled phones, smart phones (which are Web-enabled, and provide a number of other features not found in ordinary cell phones), one-way, $1\frac{1}{2}$ way (acknowledgment of messages only), and two-way pagers, and wireless PDAs. Unless a distinction is warranted, all of these technologies will be referred to simply as cellular phone systems. As described below, the key issues in cellular systems, and where incompatibilities arise, lie in operating frequency allocation, the features and restrictions imposed by the different modulation types (which are in turn a function of licensing), the availability (or lack thereof) of a supporting network infrastructure, and how interference is dealt with.

Frequency Allocation

The greatest source of confusion for potential wireless subscribers in the United States is in establishing the difference between cellular and PCS services. This confusion apparently arises partially by accident, and in part through planning and a concerted marketing campaign by PCS providers. This contention between cellular and PCS services is reasonable, given that the spectrum for PCS services was ostensibly established by the FCC for the primary purpose of creating competition for cellular operators.

On the surface, the only significant technical difference between PCS and digital cellular services is in the assigned operating frequencies. Domestic cellular phone systems operate at about 800 MHz, whereas PCS systems typically operate from about 1.5 to 1.8 GHz. From an operational perspective, the PCS services offered by Sprint, Nextel, and other domestic PCS carriers follow the cellular model of fixed, networked base stations with connectivity to the public switched telephone network. Similarly, mobile units can move freely from cell to cell within the regions covered by the service provider.

From a practical business perspective, the differences between PCS and digital cellular have several ramifications. Given the frequency differences, the antenna structures for PCS use can be $\frac{1}{2}$ to $\frac{1}{3}$ the size of comparable antennas designed for cellular use. The upshot is that PCS antennas are usually more compact, which affects mobility as well as consumer demand. The increasingly popular two-way pagers, which also operate at the higher PCS frequencies, are able to use an internal antenna without losing effectiveness. The wireless Palm VII, in comparison, has a larger fold-up antenna, since its

DIGITAL CELLULAR OPERATING BANDS

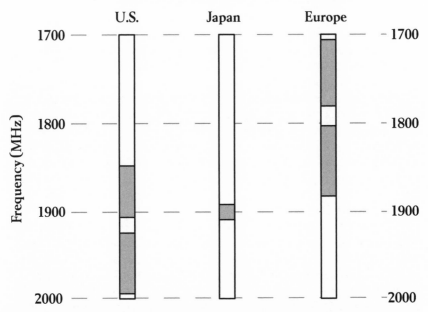

Figure 5-1. Primary digital cellular and PCS operating bands in the United States, Japan, and Europe. Because there is little overlapping in systems operating in the same or adjacent bands, cell phone manufacturers have to develop units capable of operating on muliple frequencies in order to provide global coverage for international business travelers. The option is for travelers to purchase separate phones for each area.

antenna length is comparable to that of an 800-MHz cellular phone. In addition, absorption and propagation at the higher PCS frequencies are very different, with some atmospheric and geographic conditions favoring a lower-frequency cellular signal, and others favoring a higher-frequency PCS signal. Interference issues are more challenging with PCS as well, especially since there are many services running on or near the PCS band. Finally, the higher PCS frequencies may be associated with greater health risks, compared to the lower cellular frequencies. Figure 5-1 shows the primary digital cellular and PCS operating bands in the United States, Japan, and Europe.

Modulation

Modulation, the process of varying the main or carrier frequency in accordance with the information to be transferred to a receiver, can be accomplished through a variety of methods. One approach is to create virtual channels—like the multiple, parallel tubes in the communications model from Chapter 4—so that hundreds of subscribers can share the same band of frequencies. Modulation methods are normally linked to operating frequencies and types of wireless services through FCC licensure. That is, there may be no technical reason why a particular type of modulation must be used for one service, and another service only a few MHz away must use another. These and other license constraints may have a historical, technologic, or political basis.

The modulation technique used in many second-generation (2G) cell phones in the United States falls under a general category called *spread spectrum*. As the name implies, the modulation technique spreads transmissions across a spectrum or range of frequencies (multiple, parallel tubes in the communications model) instead of transmitting over a single radio frequency (a single tube in the communications model). Although spread spectrum techniques are generally known today because of their use in cell phones and other modern wireless communications systems, they were actually developed in the late 1940s in the United States.

The two most common types of spread spectrum modulation techniques used in wireless communications are Direct Sequencing Spread Spectrum (DSSS) and Frequency Hopping Spread Spectrum (FHSS). DSSS is a wireless spread spectrum method that breaks each transmission into pieces, scatters them across a range of frequencies, and reconstructs the pieces at the receiving end. As in the multitube (spread spectrum) communications model described in Chapter 4, each piece of the message is marked with a code specifying a receiver, allowing pieces of messages intended for multiple recipients to travel in the same frequency band without directly interfering with each other.

FHSS is a spread spectrum method that "hops" its transmission across multiple channels instead of remaining on one signal frequency. By FCC rules, FHSS transmissions must hop or change frequencies after a specified maximum time. For example, wireless communications using the 2.4-GHz ISM (Industrial, Scientific, and Medical) band, which is shared by several services, including Bluetooth, must change frequency several times per second. Since a random number generator controls the frequency hopping sequence, FHSS messages are difficult to intercept. Not only must the intended recipients know the random number generator's sequence, they must also have the appropriate user ID.

An advantage of using spread spectrum modulation for cellular communications is that it deters eavesdroppers because the signals are encoded and difficult to intercept. Communications systems based on spread spectrum technology are uniquely suited for applications requiring privacy, signal covertness, interference rejection, selective addressing, and multiple access—all of which apply to wireless Web communications. Unlike the conventional techniques used to ensure message security, such as cryptography, spread spectrum communications can not only conceal the message but the sender's identity as well.

Spread spectrum modulation is used in wireless applications ranging from cell phones, satellite and ground-based communications to navigation and RADAR. For example, the GPS uses spread spectrum technology to allow users with GPS receivers to determine their location anywhere on the globe to within about 1 m. GPS satellites blanket the earth with spread spectrum radio signals, allowing handheld devices to determine position through triangulation of the signals. Software in a handheld GPS receiver can compute speed and direction, and a mapping program can use the position data to plot a businessman's position on the road to an important meeting, and even estimate how long it will take for him to arrive at the meeting. If it appears as though he's going to be late for the meeting, he can use his cellular phone to call ahead and notify the other participants.

Spread spectrum technology makes it possible for multiple signals to occupy the same channel or band of frequencies simultaneously with minimal mutual interference. Adding spread spectrum signals to a communications band already supporting signals has the effect of raising overall background noise. Returning to the communications model in Chapter 4, adding another user requires that an additional user ID marble be dropped down the Address Tube. In other words, the same communications channel now has to deal with one more subscriber, so every message is delayed by a small, virtually imperceptible amount. The result is a gradual decrease in communications efficiency for all subscribers using the channel.

An important feature of spread spectrum receivers is that they are relatively immune to both intentional and accidental interference. Practically speaking, this means that wireless networks in offices and factories can use spread spectrum modulation because the technique supports error-free network access even under electrically noisy conditions created by PCs, copy machines, industrial lighting, and the operation of heavy machinery. With increased noise and competing signals, a spread spectrum receiver may not respond as fast as normal, but at least there is usually a response. An added benefit of using spread spectrum with a wireless PDA or cell phone is relative insensitivity to fading, which is a reduction in received signal strength as a result of signal reflection, refraction, or absorption.

Cellular Networks

The first commercial cellular system, the Improved Mobile Telephone Service (IMTS), was created by AT&T in 1946. IMTS, perhaps better described as a repeater system instead of a cellular network, was the first mobile radio system to connect with the regular public phone network. It was based on a single high-power transmitter and a tall transmit and receive antenna (usually located on a hilltop) that provided a line-of-sight operating radius of over 80 km (50 mi). Since the VHF and UHF spectrum was virtually open at that time, IMTS used a communications channel with a huge frequency spread from 150 to 450 MHz. In order to provide two-way communications, the mobile units, which were based on heavy, power-consuming vacuum tube technology, had to provide several watts of power for their signals to reach the centrally located receiver antenna with sufficient field strength.

Because of the high power levels and the coverage provided by the central antennas, IMTS systems had to be located hundreds of miles apart to avoid interference. As a result, islands of mobile telephone access, usually located around population centers, were separated by long expanses without service. In addition, since each IMTS cell supported up to only 23 channels or simultaneous users, subscribers frequently had to wait extended periods of time in order to access the telephone network.

The modern cellular network, invented by Bell Laboratories and installed in the United States in 1982, improved upon the IMTS system in a number of important ways. As in the IMTS system, the service area is divided into local regions called *cells*, with each cell containing a more or less centrally located transmitting and receiving antenna. In addition, the same antenna structure can be used for both transmit and receive antenna, or a separate antenna structure can be used, separated by a short distance. However, instead of a single, high-powered transmitter, the modern cellular design is based on a network of low-powered transmitters and centrally located omnidirectional antennas, each providing a range of perhaps 10 km (6 mi). Cells are typically 10 to 20 km (6 to 12 mi) apart, separated from cells using the same frequency by a buffer of at least two cells to avoid same-frequency interference. Since the number of voice channels available per cell at any time is about 45, and there may be 100 or more cells in a metropolitan area, several thousand simultaneous calls ($45 \times 100 = 4500$) can be handled by a typical cellular network. Caller capacity is vastly improved over the original IMTS design.

Smaller cells means lower cell and handheld unit power requirements for reliable communications, and decreased battery drain and relaxed antenna requirements for handheld units. Of course, the power output of a cell phone doesn't automatically change dynamically with need, but the decreased power output requirement is reflected in the cell phone designs made possible by the smaller cell size. The downside of using low-power levels is the added expense associated with erecting and maintaining additional cells, especially since a typical cell installation can cost over $100,000, including hardware installation and securing rights to erect a cellular antenna.

A key feature of the modern cellular system, absent in the original IMTS design, is coverage overlap. City and metropolitan areawide coverage is accomplished despite the finite number of frequencies or channels available by assigning different frequencies to adjacent cells, and by activating cell transmitters in a way that tracks subscriber movements through the cellular network. As a handheld cellular unit moves from one cell to the next, the relative field strength of the signal from the handheld unit decreases in the first cell and increases in the other. A computer-based switching network monitors this relative change in signal strength, which varies with the square of the distance from each cell, and switches the message intended for the handheld unit to the transmitter in the second cell from the transmitter in the first cell. Because of the relatively small cell size and the time required for one cell to hand off a subscriber to another cell, most cellular systems have difficulty tracking a fast-moving mobile cell phone. Many cellular systems, especially those located in metropolitan areas where cells tend to be much smaller and more densely packed than those located in rural areas, are unable to track a subscriber moving through the network above about 115 kph (70 mph).

Of particular note is that each cell in a cellular network, which is composed of a transmitter and a receiver, is connected to every other cell as well as to the public telephone network. A Mobile Telephone Switching Office (MTSO) provides the connectivity to the public telephone network. The MTSO is what allows a businessman to call his office on his cell phone while he's stuck in traffic. It's also what allows his secretary to use her office phone to call him when there's a major problem that he has to deal with. Without a MTSO, cellular communication would be limited to other subscribers using cell phones and the same cell phone service. Connectivity through the MTSO provides the basis for a variety of other services as well, including accessing the Internet and roaming outside of the local calling area into other cellular networks. For example, a business traveler from Boston who is working in San Francisco can use her cell phone because her local MTSO communicates with her home network for authentication of her status as a registered user of the system—assuming, of course, that the cellular or PCS services are compatible.

Balanced Communications Systems

In the world of svelte cellular phones, pencil-thin PDAs, and shrinking two-way pagers, there is a practical need for mobile devices that use the minimum power necessary to establish reliable communications. It doesn't make sense, from an economic or engineering perspective, to build a handheld cell phone with a receiver that is more sensitive—and therefore more susceptible to noise—than is needed to cover the range supported by the handheld's transmitter output power. As illustrated in Figure 5-2, the transmitter output power and receiver sensitivity of a cellular communications system are optimum when coverage for sending and receiving messages is about the same. This is especially true at the fringes of cell range, as shown in the figure. At the fringe of the cell, both the cell and handheld subscriber units can receive each other's transmitted signals.

In contrast, a scenario in which a handheld unit's transmit power is not matched to its receiver sensitivity. Although the handheld unit's signal is strong enough for the cell to detect, the cell's transmitter is out of receive range for the handheld. In other words, a handheld unit is wasting energy on

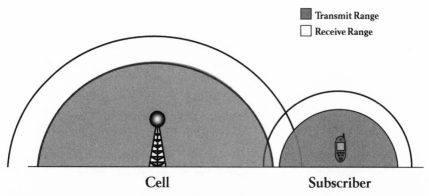

Figure 5-2. Balanced Communications. The optimum condition is when coverage for sending and receiving message is about the same, especially at the fringe of cell range.

transmitter power that could otherwise be used, for example, to extend standby time. In addition, by transmitting more power than necessary, the handheld unit contributes to the overall noise of the system, and may interfere with other mobile and fixed cell users. For subscribers concerned about the health risks of handheld "microwave ovens," the extra power simply presents a greater potential risk. Most handheld cellular and PCS units provide a little over $1/2$ W of output power. Mobile units, which rely on the car battery for power, typically produce 3 W, the legal limit allowed by the FCC. This added power is also usually complemented by a more sensitive receiver and a superior antenna system, thereby maintaining a balanced system.

Geographic Coverage

The Achilles heel of the U.S. cellular network, at least from the perspective of the traveling public, is the lack of nationwide cellular coverage. Unlike the situation in Western Europe, there is no single domestic cellular or PCS system that provides uninterrupted coverage from coast to coast. The intentional or designed-in gaps in coverage are no accident. From an economic perspective, these gaps may be justifiable, in that covering an uninhabited stretch of desert in Arizona may not have a reasonable return on investment, compared to covering Tucson. In this regard, the lack of nationwide coverage in the United States is in part due to wide variations in population densities. Europe, being more densely and uniformly populated than the United States, can expect a reasonable return on investment for virtually every cell on the continent. Since there are very few sparsely populated areas in Western Europe, mobile operators can reach more subscribers with a smaller investment in the cellular network.

In addition to intentional lapses in coverage, there are unintentional gaps as well. This is commonly a result of signal absorption from vegetation and reflection from cars and buildings, or because height or other restrictions necessitate the use of separate antennas for the base cell's transmit and receive signals. Separate antennas can result in uneven coverage on transmit and receive. The result of intentional and unintentional gaps is that, outside of areas with dense cellular coverage, for example, the major metropolitan areas and away from major highways, there are frequently dropped and poor quality calls.

In contrast to spotty and regional cellular and PCS coverage, pagers, including the more recently introduced two-way variety, provide more or less blanket coverage of the United States—at least for receiving messages. The increased coverage available for pagers is due primarily to the configuration of the pager cells. Each cell is composed of a powerful, centrally located transmitter that can cover a wide geographic area. Within each cell are several highly sensitive receivers that can respond to the 1-W two-way pager signal. In addition, each cell is linked to a network of other cells by both satellite and cable connections in order to provide national coverage.

Dealing with Interference

Cellular phones, like all other communications devices, are not only susceptible to signals from other devices but also generate signals that can interfere with other devices. For example, as every business traveler who flies knows, FAA regulations prohibit the use of cell phones and certain other electronic devices during takeoff and landing because of the potential of interference from these devices with the equipment on board the plane. Similarly, many hospitals ban the use of cell phones, especially near recovery areas, because of the potential for interference with sensitive life support and monitoring equipment. Cell phones are susceptible to interference from other phones, from microwave ovens, cordless phones, laptops and PCs, external disk drives and printers, and automobile ignition systems. Some of these sources can simply be avoided.

Although susceptibility to interface is less of a problem with digital receiver designs, a large percentage of cellular users in the United States are using older analog technology, which is more likely to be affected by high strength signals on adjacent frequencies. Digital cellular systems are less susceptible to interfering signals than are older analog receivers.

One of the major concerns over interference is regarding the 2.4-GHz spectrum, which is becoming saturated with signals from PCS phones, wireless LANs, Bluetooth, and even microwave ovens. Because of concerns about interference, as well as the simple need for more bandwidth, research into fourth-generation (4G) cellular communications is taking place at even higher frequencies where greater bandwidths are available. At higher frequencies, greater bandwidth is generally available for communications for technologic reasons and because no one has claimed or licensed the space from the FCC. The HyperLAN project, a European venture into 4G systems, uses the 5.3-GHz band once relegated to experimenters.

The higher microwave frequencies, which approach optical frequencies, are generally more challenging to work with compared to lower VHF and UHF frequencies. For example, generating power at the higher frequencies is more difficult, in part because electronic components are not as efficient at higher frequencies, and in part because when designing ultra-compact communications devices the higher frequencies represent uncharted territory for many communications engineers. Generating $\frac{1}{2}$ W of output power at 800 MHz is much less challenging than generating the same power at 2 or 4 GHz from the same size handheld unit.

WIRELESS WEB PROTOCOLS

Communications Protocols

A major component of the information-handling infrastructure of the wireless Web is the collection of communications protocols that establish an environment that can support services such as Web access. Before discussing the individual protocols, it's important to distinguish between packet switching and circuit switching. *Circuit switching* is the way the worldwide telephone system works, which is why it is often referred to as the Public Switched Telephone Network (PSTN). In circuit switching, a connection is made between sender and receiver for the duration of the conversation or data transfer. The circuit is free to be used by another party only when the switch is opened, regardless of when the communication was finished *Packet switching*, in contrast, sends packets of information from the sender to the receiver, leaving the communications channel open to other subscribers who are free to send packets through the system. The original message is parsed into small slices and put into packets that are individually addressed and numbered to the recipient, and each packet may take a different route to get to the recipient. Packet switching is important because it is the model upon which the wired Internet is based. Furthermore, packet switching on the wireless Web, first implemented in a big way by NTT DoCoMo for their I-Mode, allows an always-on condition since the communications channel isn't held captive by a single subscriber, and can receive a packet of information at any time.

Paradoxically, the evolution of wireless protocols in the United States is the reverse of that found in Europe. While Europe has evolved from a first-generation (G1) analog cellular system with five major, incompatible standards to a single, pan-European GSM standard, the United States has moved from a single G1 analog standard into three noncompatible digital standards, TDMA, CDMA, and GSM. There are literally dozens of other networks, especially in the areas of paging networks and specialized services that are not listed for the sake of clarity.

AMPS (Advanced Mobile Phone System) is the first-generation (1G) analog cellular system used throughout the United States. Analog cellular is almost ubiquitous across the United States. With a suitable modem and a laptop or PDA, analog cellular can be used for wireless data communications. Data throughput using analog cellular is slow. Subscribers typically experience about 2 KBps data throughput on the system, which operates in the 800-MHz band.

MOBITEX (Mobitex International) is a data-only two-way pager network developed by Ericsson and known in the United States as BellSouth Wireless Data. In addition to supporting RIM's two-way paging, this system is used by Palm and GoAmerica service providers and some wireless LANs, including those based on RIM's type II card for laptops. Mobitex operates at 400 and 800 MHz, with a data rate of 8 KBps. Mobitex uses a cellular network model, with each cell served by an intelligent base station. BellSouth provides coverage for about 93 percent of the United States.

A related service offered by Motient Corporation competes for wireless messaging in the United States. Motient, which supports wireless modems for PCs as well as wireless PDAs including those from RIM, offers wireless services in four general categories: terrestrial data, terrestrial voice and data, satellite-only data, and satellite point-to-multipoint voice communications.

D-AMPS (Digital-AMPS or Digital Cellular) is one of the two main types of second-generation (2G) digital wireless service in the United States. The other domestic digital service, PCS, uses small antennas and more closely spaced cells. D-AMPS, which is supported by two incompatible multiplexing schemes, provides increased channel capacity, caller ID, built-in pagers, and other features not available on analog cellular systems. Digital cellular radio signals are more difficult to intercept and decode, compared to analog cellular, providing a more secure communications channel. In the United States, D-AMPS is licensed to operate in the 800-MHz Band.

CDMA (Code Division Multiple Access) is a spread spectrum, second-generation (2G) communications service developed in the United States by Qualcomm. Although CDMA is a popular standard in the United States and South Korea, and is gaining market share in China (even though China postponed plans to build a mobile network based on CDMA), it was not embraced by Europe, in part because the European GMS standard provides superior sound. Voice is important; even in Japan and Finland, where digital services abound, cell phones are used primarily for voice communications. CDMA, which supports a data rate of 14.4 KBps, is technically superior to its main competitor, TDMA, in terms of bandwidth efficiency. CDMA can support more calls in a given bandwidth, compared to TDMA. In the United States, CDMA operates in the 800-MHz and 1.9-GHz bands. The CDMA wireless communications protocol has many parallels with the communications model developed in Chapter 4.

NA-TDMA (North American—Time Division Multiple Access), the first digital standard tested in the United States, is one of the three competing second-generation cellular standards in North and South America. This standard supports data throughput of up to 19.2 KBps, but typical speeds are around 8 KBps. TDMA, which is used by Nextel's PCS service, operates on the same bandwidth as CDMA cellular, but the two protocols are incompatible with each other. Whereas CDMA uses spread spectrum technology to assign each user a code within the spectrum, TDMA divides the frequency into time slots and gives users access to a time slot at regular intervals. Although Nextel is built around TDMA, it uses a proprietary network. TDMA is the largest network in the United States, and second in the world, behind GSM. In the United States, NA-TDMA operates in the 800-MHz and 1.9-GHz bands.

CDPD (Cellular Digital Packet Data) is a wireless communications protocol used primarily in second-generation (2G) wireless data communication systems. Each device in a CDPD network has a unique network address and remains connected as long as the cell phone or wireless PDA is on; broken connections are automatically and transparently resumed. CDPD has a maximum speed of 19.2 KBps, as defined by the FCC, which is adequate for graphics-free Web surfing and email. CDPD is a popular standard for a PCMCIA wireless modem cards that allow any laptop to connect to the wireless Web through a patchwork system that provides about 50 percent coverage in the United States.

GSM (Global System for Telecommunications), a variant of TDMA that uses time-division technology, is extremely popular in Europe, where it has essentially decimated the CDMA system. GSM is used in over 130 countries, representing over 70 percent of the wireless subscribers worldwide. Even so, the domestic representation of GSM is less than 10 percent . The typical GSM data throughput is about 16 KBps. GSM is a PCS network that operates at 1.9 GHz in the United States and 900 MHz or 1.9 GHz throughout most of the rest of the world. Wireless phone manufacturers are more than happy to offer a solution to the frequent flying executive who needs to maintain phone communications throughout the United States or the world in the form of multimode phones that are capable of switching between analog and various modes of digital communications dynamically.

I-MODE (Internet Mode) is NTT DoCoMo's second-generation (2G) wireless communications protocol used throughout Japan. I-Mode, which has a maximum speed of 28.8 KBps, is based on the Internet Protocol (IP and a subset of HTML. The Internet Protocol, a component of TCP/IP, is the chief method of transporting data across the Internet. I-Mode, which operates in the 1.9-MHz band, is based on a packet-switched infrastructure that supports the "always-on" wireless connectivity that I-Mode is famous for. Because I-Mode is so far ahead of any other wireless Web implementation, it's often regarded as 2.5G.

GPRS (General Packet Radio Services) is the planned interim (2.5G) high-speed digital cellular upgrade to Europe's GSM network. One of the features of GPRS is that the packet-switched infrastructure supports the ability for cellular subscribers to maintain a fast, always-on connection to the wireless Internet. After GPRS, which represents the evolutionary endpoint of the GSM technology, the countries in Western Europe are planning to deploy wide-band CDMA for third-generation (3G) services. Although GPRS software can be installed as a software upgrade to existing GSM networks, it doesn't improve the network's capacity significantly. In addition, GPRS is unlikely to be able to achieve download speeds of much above 100 KBps. GPRS is positioned as an interim strategy that is expected to last from 18 to 24 months, during which time the infrastructure for G3 will be put into place.

EDGE (Enhanced Data rates for Global Evolution), like GPRS, is an intermediate (2.5G) solution to increasing the throughput on the wireless Web. EDGE can boost data speeds on both GSM and TDMA networks to more than 300 KBps, up to 2 MBps in some cases. Like GPRS, however, EDGE doesn't increase network capacity significantly, meaning it is likely to be an intermediate technology for many operators. EDGE, like GPRS, represents a nondisruptive way to upgrade existing GSM networks without diminishing the revenue stream.

CDMA 2000 (Code Division Multiple Access 2000) is a third-generation (G3) wireless technology derived from second-generation CDMA. Developed by Qualcomm, CDMA 2000 can be laid on top of an existing CDMA network. The first release of CDMA 2000 will supposedly boost download rates to 100 KBps, while the next stage will support speeds of more than 300 KBps. CDMA 2000 is projected to eventually support data streams of up to 2 MBps.

W-CDMA (Wide-Band Code Division Multiple Access), a rival to CDMA 2000, is a third-generation (3G) wireless communications protocol derived from CDMA. W-CDMA is Japan's cornerstone for their 3G initiative starting in Tokyo and will become available nationally over a three-year rollout period. W-CDMA will initially deliver content at download speeds of up to 300 KBps, with capabilities to 2 MBps. W-CDMA is backed by NTT DoCoMo, Nokia, and Ericsson, among others. It is expected that China will eventually move to W-CDMA for at least part of its cellular communications solution. W-CDMA is often referred to in Europe as UMTS.

UMTS (Universal Mobile Telecommunications Systems), a third-generation (3G) network protocol built with W-CDMA technology, is expected to become the first global mobile phone standard to have high-speed capabilities. Europeans with UMTS cell phones will be able to surf the Web and enjoy services that take advantage of being online all the time just as users of Japan's I-Mode have done since 1999. Although initial data throughput will be around 300 KBps, access speeds near 2 MBps will eventually be supported.

TD-SCDMA (Time Division-Synchronous Code Division Multiple Access) is China's homegrown standard for third-generation (3G) cellular. Often referred to as 2.9G cellular because it isn't quite up to the technical specifications of other 3G proposed standards, TD-SCDMA is being developed in conjunction with Siemens. The Chinese Academy of Telecommunications Technology (CAT), Alcatel, and Ericsson are also involved in developing the standard. Even though TD-SCDMA is not quite 3G technology, because it is inexpensive, it is thought to be suitable for poorer, remote areas of China that won't have a need for 3G for several years. TD-SCDMA is prominent not because of the technology proper, but because the standard enjoys the support of the Chinese government. The U.S. company Qualcomm claims that TD-SCDMA uses components of its patented CDMA technology, and that they are entitled to licensing fees. China is apparently motivated to create its own standard in order to avoid paying royalties to Qualcomm and others. China may eventually use W-CDMA for 3G service in the big cities, avoiding at least some of the Qualcomm licensing issues.

IMT-2000 (International Mobile Telecommunications for 2000) is a next-generation, global wireless service initiative proposed by the ITU-T (International Telecommunications Union—Telecommunications Sector). This third-generation (G3) standard, which is more of a concept for fourth-generation (G4) wireless communications than a standard, defines a 128-KBps data rate for mobile applications, 384 KBps for handheld devices, and 2 MBps for fixed wireless LANs. The standard includes frequency allocations for mobile satellite services, generally referred to as the GMPCS (Global Mobile Personal Communications by Satellite). Terrestrial cellular services will operate in the 2-GHz band.

Generations

Some domestic companies are moving from 2G, which was designed primarily to support voice, directly to 3G, which is designed to carry multimedia, bypassing the 2.5G temporary patch. For example, for AT&T to move to 2.5G based on TDMA would require the company to install new equipment in all of its 10,000 cell sites across the United States. With a projected life span of only two or three years, a 2.5G initiative would simply be too expensive for the expected ROI. The risk, of course, is that 3G may take several years to materialize, and competing companies may use this window of opportunity to develop their own 2.5G solutions, some of which may be superior to AT&T's 2G system.

Special Protocols

Bluetooth. The highly publicized Bluetooth protocol, a common set of specifications for short-range RF wireless communications network, is supported by approximately 2000 companies, from IBM, Microsoft, and Hewlett Packard to Dell and Palm. Because of uncertainty in the eventual success of Bluetooth, many of these companies support competing standards as well. Bluetooth defines the hardware and software required to provide the 10-m (30-ft) operating radius in the 2.4-GHz band with a maximum throughput of 720 KBps. The technology, which uses a low-power, two-way radio link that is built into a microchip, is designed for transmitting and receiving small amounts of data. Initial applications include linking cell phones and cordless headsets, linking PDAs with cell phones, linking smart cards still tucked in a customer's wallet with a cash register at checkout lines, and automatically collecting tolls from cars passing through toll booths.

Bluetooth is viewed as a way to replace the cables to printers, scanners, mice, keyboards, and other peripherals to desktop PCs. In this regard, Bluetooth is a replacement for IR connectivity. Whereas IR is directional or line of sight, Bluetooth's RF signal is omnidirectional. In addition, whereas IR is one-to-one, Bluetooth provides a one-to-many connection for up to eight voice and data communications devices.

Bluetooth supports two modes, Private and Promiscuous. While in the Private mode, a Bluetooth device will respond to signals from only specified devices. A PDA would normally be configured in Private mode, for example, allowing only the owner to access his or her address book. In the Promiscuous mode, a Bluetooth device, such as a printer, can receive input from any other Bluetooth device. One application of Bluetooth technology is to support automatic, private access to a PDA-based address book from a subscriber's cell phone without any effort on the subscriber's part. The user enters the name of the person to be contacted and the number is retrieved from the PDA, which could be in the subscriber's briefcase. The PDA may also log the file in the PDA's database, noting the time and length of the call and the person contacted.

Although the success of Bluetooth isn't guaranteed, the supporting companies, including Dell, IBM, Motorola, Qualcomm, Ford Motor Company, and British Airways, are pouring resources into the standard. For example, Microsoft is working with the chip manufacturer Intel to integrate Bluetooth more closely with the Windows operating system. Similarly, Motorola offers a Bluetooth car kit, with Bluetooth features available to domestic and foreign car companies. IBM released one of the first widely available Bluetooth devices in 2000, a PCMCIA card for laptops.

Another automotive Bluetooth initiative, spearheaded by Motorola, is to equip vehicles with a Telematics Control Unit (TCU) that is kept in the trunk of a car. Each TCU provides cellular phone service, GPS, Web-based mapping, as well as the usual mobile office amenities such as address book and calendar. While the unit sits securely mounted in the trunk, a cordless Bluetooth phone handset controls the unit. Obvious extensions to the system under development by Motorola are to provide Bluetooth connectivity to gas station pumps for ordering and paying for gas, as a garage door opener, and to control home lighting and alarm status on entry and exit.

A major concern with Bluetooth is that its 128-bit encryption system may not be sufficient to prevent attack by viruses or, more significantly, theft. For example, with the right equipment, a thief could stand at the end of a checkout line at a grocery store and capture everyone's charge information as

Bluetooth-enabled charge cards or cell phones transmit their financial information to the Bluetooth-enabled cash register. Another limitation is the reliance on a variety of batteries in multiple devices—any of which could fail because of an expired battery.

Wi-Fi. Although not a direct competitor to Bluetooth, the Wireless Fidelity (Wi-Fi) protocol, also known as the IEEE 802.11b High Rate Standard, is yet another component-to-component wireless communications protocol that has major industrial backers. Wi-Fi is backed by the Wireless Ethernet Compatibility Alliance, which includes Lucent, Cisco, and 3Com. Wi-Fi is positioned to become the standard for high-speed wireless LANs, with features like encryption for security. A new generation of chips is making Wi-Fi more cost-effective than competing, nonstandardized wireless network systems.

Any Wi-Fi certified device, from a personal computer to a stereo system, should work seamlessly with every other Wi-Fi certified device. Whereas Bluetooth seems to be aimed more at personal devices, Wi-Fi is projected to provide wireless connectivity for business travelers in airports and in major hotels. However, like Bluetooth, Wi-Fi will also allow anyone with the proper hardware to connect between laptop and desktop at speeds of 11 MBps—over an order of magnitude greater than the speed supported by Bluetooth.

SWAP. Like Wi-Fi, SWAP (Shared Wireless Access Protocol) is a low-cost, high-speed wireless networking protocol that supports the HomeRF networking system. With a maximum speed of 10 MBps, the protocol supports streaming multimedia on multiple devices and with multiple networks. SWAP is backed by Intel, Motorola, Siemens, and Proxim, and is positioned as a direct competitor to Wi-Fi.

UPNP and **JINI.** In the move to connect all appliances in the home with wired and wireless communications to the Internet, allowing everything to be controlled and monitored from anywhere, two additional competing standards have evolved. UPNP (Universal Plug and Play) from Microsoft and JINI from Sun Microsystems, Inc. JINI is the standard proposed for wired and wireless connection of appliances to the Internet, backed by Sun Microsystems, Inc., and based on their JAVA language. Given the uncertainty of the eventual winner, a consortium of leading consumer electronics companies have formed the Home Audio Video Interoperability Organization (HAVi) to develop a technology for entertainment systems that works with either JINI or UPNP. Although Bluetooth, Wi-Fi, JINI, and UPNP have overlapping aims, Wi-Fi and Bluetooth are not compatible with each other, nor are they compatible with JINI or UPNP.

High-Level Protocols and Languages

The following are a sampling of the top language technologies being applied to developing and presenting content on the wireless Web, often through the use of a microbrowser. A *microbrowser* is a software application designed to run on handheld wireless devices and to interpret and display documents written in languages such as WML and HDML. Equivalents to a micro-browser on the wired Web are Netscape Navigator and Internet Explorer.

These languages sit on top of the communications protocols previously discussed that provide an infrastructure upon which voice and data communications can occur. These languages address the actual content that subscribers see when they interact with the wireless Web. These Web implementation languages can be considered applications or environments that run on top of the protocol layer of the wireless Web, just as the HTML, Java, and JavaScript languages work on the wired Web. See Figure 5-3 for the lineage of these languages.

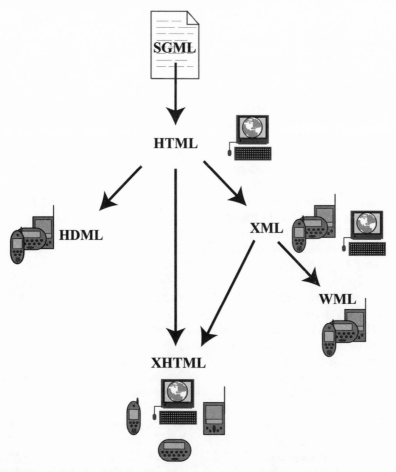

Figure 5-3. The lineage of languages for the wired and wireless Webs. WML is XML-based. The globe represents the wired Web.

SGML (Structured General Markup Language) is not a wireless language or protocol, but it is the parent from which most wired and wireless languages are derived, as shown in Figure 5-3.

HTML (Hypertext Markup Language) is the language of the wired Web and, with some small modifications, of NTT DoCoMo's I-Mode. HTML is used to create Web pages, often in combination with applets written in Java or some other language to provide improved security, dynamic graphics, and other content. In addition to generic HTML, there are a variety of flavors or minor variations of HTML, such as Compact-HTML used by Windows CE handhelds.

The problem with HTML, from a wired and wireless Web perspective, is that the data are buried within the HTML code. For example, if the goal is to present the following formatted statement over the Web:

The quick brown **fox** *bit* the lazy **dog**.

Then the HTML equivalent would appear in the form:

```
<HTML>
   The quick brown <BOLD>fox</BOLD> <I>bit</I> the
lazy <BOLD> dog</BOLD>.
</HTML>
```

As a result, it's difficult to extract and repurpose the data for other uses, such as support for transaction-based processes over Web-enabled cell phones. As illustrated in Figure 5-4, for an enterprise with all data stored in an HTML format, the content must be reformatted for each type of device supported, from cell phones with postage stamp-size displays to larger RIM Blackberry, Palm, and PocketPC displays. That is, if there are five types of devices supported from a central HTML-based archive, then every change in the central content ripples through the system, requiring recoding of the HTML for each of the five devices. The more different types of devices that must be supported, the more fragile the system, and the more maintenance overhead involved.

HDML (Handheld Device Markup Language) is a proprietary language for coding Web sites so the content can be downloaded quickly onto wireless systems. HDML, a modification of standard HTML for use on wireless devices, is the basis for WML. Some older microbrowsers can only access HDML-written Web sites. HDML allows cellular subscribers to access the Internet and send and receive email.

WML (Wireless Markup Language) is a language for implementing user interfaces on wireless devices. WML, which is analogous to and based on HDML, is optimized to create Web sites that are compatible WAP. WML, a core part of WAP, is designed for specifying user interface behavior and content on portable wireless devices. Unlike HDML, WML supports scripting.

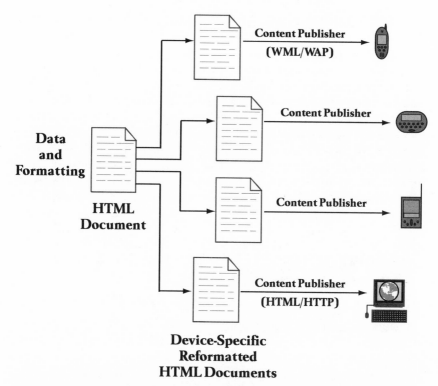

Figure 5-4. An HTML-based wired and wireless content distribution system. Since content and data display are coupled, HTML content must be reformatted for each type of device to be supported. Changing the source content usually requires reformatting the HTML code for each device. Similarly, supporting a new device requires reformatting the content as well as redefining how the content is displayed.

Because WML is based on XML, there are a variety of commercially available tools that can be used to generate and manipulate WML code, compressing an application's time to market.

A variety of translation tools are available for moving content from the wired to the wireless Web. For example, IBM's WebSphere Transcoding Publisher dynamically translates HTML and XML content originally developed for the multimedia-rich wired Web into WML for display on wireless devices. Web sites coded in WML can be accessed via WAP gateways, which are servers that compress data into a form compatible with Web-enabled cell phones.

WMLScript (Web markup language script) is a lightweight scripting language for the wireless Web that looks and performs something like JavaScript on the wired Web. WMLScript allows programmers to check the validity of user-supplied data, access device-specific features, and generate a message.

XML (Extensible Markup Language) is a markup language for the Web that supports the definition, transmission, validation, and interpretation of data on a variety of hardware and software environments without specifically coding for each environment. In other words, XML allows a Web designer to create a program once, without the need to create a separate version for every model of wireless PDA and cellular phone on the market.

XML was introduced in part because HTML, the language of the wired Web, doesn't distinguish between data and the presentation of data, and only deals with the appearance of information. That is, the wired Web is replete with information that is trapped in HTML forms. Although there are search engines that can locate some of this data, for the most part, it is unusable by other applications. XML is popular in the wired as well as the wireless Web development shops because it is self-describing. An XML message contains the data being passed to another system—a wireless PDA, for example—as well as a universal description of that data. This data about data or metadata can be used for formatting on the particular device used to view the data.

Continuing with the example above:

The quick brown **fox** *bit* the lazy **dog**.

Would appear as XML in the form:

```
<PHRASE>
   The <SPEED>quick</SPEED> <COLOR>brown</COLOR>
<ANIMAL>fox </ANIMAL> <ACTION>bit</ACTION> the
<SPEED>lazy</SPEED> <ANIMAL>dog</ANIMAL>.
</PHRASE>
```

Although unformatted, the XML document has structure and tags that can be used to infer meaning. For example, the XML document could be queried to determine that it contains a phrase that references two animals, a "fox" and a "dog," and two speeds, "quick" and "lazy." The formatting for the display devices is handled by XSL, described below. XML is also extensible, meaning that developers can define new tags (codes used in formatting or identifying data), as well as define how the tagged content should be used by the application running on a smart phone or wireless PDA. For example, a tag might specify that a text string contain numeric data. XML tags can be combined with HTML, providing increased flexibility when working with data on the wired and wireless Web. The formal combination of HTML and XML is called XHTML, which is poised to become the standard implementation language on the wired Web. XHTML allows documents to be created in HTML and for mathematical equations to be in the form of XML.

XML excels at data aggregation and syndication tasks, where *aggregation* is the process of collecting data from disparate sources, and *syndication* is the process of distributing data to disparate channels, such as wireless PDAs and cell phones. Even when every subscriber is using the same hardware and software, XML can be useful by providing user-specific interfaces. For example, a customer could be presented with a graphically rich Web storefront, whereas a manager could receive a no-frills, information-rich ordering status display. For these and other reasons, XML is quickly becoming a standard on the Web, wired or not.

The main deterrent to using XML at this point of wireless Web infrastructure development is that the performance of XML on some 2G wireless networks can be less than adequate. The popularity and utility of XML should improve rapidly as bandwidth improvements are made in the wireless infrastructure. Paradoxically, although XML was developed by an engineer with Sun Microsystems in 1996, Microsoft, Sun's major competitor, is using a version of XML known as Biztalk as the center of its Internet strategy.

XSL (Extensible Stylesheet Language) is an extension of XML that allows transformation of XML-based data into HTML and other presentation formats. By using XSL, the presentation format can vary from the underlying data structure. XML, together with XSL Translation (XSLT), separates the content from formatting, allowing one XML content document to support multiple style formats. For example, the content in the XML statement above can be formatted for several wireless devices through the use of XSL code that defines the document structure for each device.

A device that supports bold and italic text output would have an XSL document in the form:

```
FORMAT "ANIMAL" = BOLD
FORMAT "ACTION" = ITALICS
```

However, if a second device doesn't support bold but does support color, then emphasis on the two animals could be provided by using red text instead of the default black text. Using the same XML document as a source, the XSL would take the form:

```
FORMAT "ANIMAL" = COLOR: RED
FORMAT "ACTION" = ITALICS
```

As illustrated in Figure 5-5, support for multiple wired and wireless devices is simplified by an XML/XSL environment, compared to the multiple interface model required by a native HTML environment.

WAP (Wireless Application Protocol) is a collection of standards that developers and hardware manufacturers follow to provide a standard environment for wireless applications. Phone.com of Redmond City, California, is the impetus behind the development of WAP, as well as the design of the browser that appears on WAP phones. WAP is the backbone protocol that lets users connect to the Internet across any digital wireless network and through any

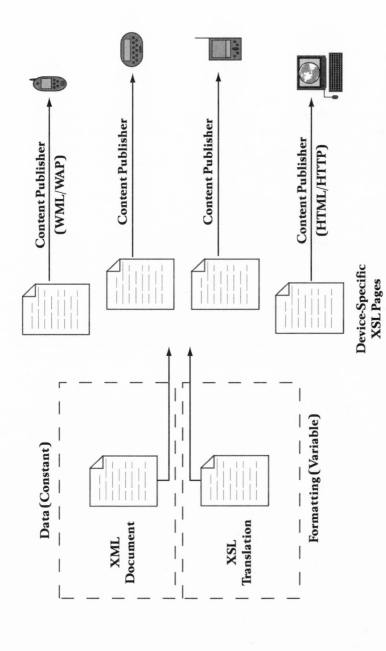

Figure 5-5. An XML/XSL-based wired and wireless content distribution system. Because the data (in XML) is decoupled from the display information, one XML content documents and multiple XSL style sheets can support multiple devices without modifying the content. The content provider converts device-specific XSL pages to serve the language and protocol for particular devices: HTML/HTTP for the wired Web and WML/WAP for Web-enabled phones, for example. Compared to an HTML document, system maintenance is reduced and new devices are more easily added.

wireless device, application, or service provider. In order to get content from a Web server on the Internet to a mobile device running a WAP browser, a WAP gateway is necessary. A WAP gateway forms the protocol and format conversion to transmit content to a mobile device such as a wireless PDA.

The challenge for companies developing wireless Web content that is WAP compliant is that WAP is an evolving standard. Microbrowser developers and hardware manufacturers have to make provisions for new features while maintaining backward compatibility with existing cell phones. For example, Push Access Protocol (PAP) was first introduced in WAP 1.2. This feature, not available on WAP 1.1, provides a standard, programmable way of pushing data, such as stock quotes, to a WAP-enabled cell phone. When Nokia released the source code with their WAP browser, it became easier for developers to create services customized for their needs.

Handling legacy cell phones is another challenge, because pre-WAP—enabled microbrowsers only understand HDML, the language from which WML was derived, and don't recognize WMLScript. One solution is to provide a gateway that automatically translates WML into HDML. However, in this approach, the advanced features of WML not found in HDML are lost and unavailable to subscribers without current WAP microbrowsers.

While developers in the United States have to make provisions for users with pre-WAP microbrowsers, European developers face the opposite problem. Since most European cell phones support some version of the WAP standard, Web sites written in the older HDML language need to be translated to WML by a gateway before they can be interpreted on WAP-enabled wireless devices.

The WAP protocol model, contains the transport layer, security layer, a means of application delivery, and finally, at the top level, some means of developing content for users. Whereas the wired Web uses TCP/IP as the basic transport protocol, WAP is based on the network protocol, such as GSM or CDMA, as well something called the Wireless Datagram Protocol. This protocol presents a consistent data format to the higher layers of the WAP protocol, giving developers independence from the underlying wireless network hardware and software.

At the next level up, Wireless Transport Layer (WTL) Security handles security features of WAP. Up one more layer, WSP (Wireless Session Protocol) and WTP (Wireless Transaction Protocol) provide an environment for transactions and for linking wireless applications to various services. At the highest level of the WAP protocol is content development or wireless application environment, which contains definitions of the user interfaces on various handheld devices. Whereas the wired Web supports HTML and JavaScript for content development at this level, WAP accepts WML and the parallel to JavaScript, WMLScript, the programming and display languages in the WAP environment. That is, JavaScript is to WMLScript as HTML is to WML.

In theory, WAP is an open, network independent, global specification intended to allow cellular subscribers to access and interact with information and services on the Web. WAP has a lot going for it. For example, WAP works across all three cell phone technologies in the United States, allowing domestic content providers the luxury of not having to create specific messages for different displays.

In practice, WAP has some severe limitations. For example, WAP has had a slow start because handsets with WAP-compatible microbrowsers were initially not available, services have been slow in coming, and there are different interpretations of the WAP standard, causing incompatibility problems on some cellular devices. Because of these incompatibility problems, WAP has severe competition at the low end of the market from Short Message Services, which works with most digital phones. SMS is a protocol used to send short text messages to non-WAP cellular phones. It's popular in Nordic countries and in Western Europe because it can run on older-generation phones, it is relatively inexpensive, and it supports secure payment for mobile electronic commerce. In 2000, about a third of all online trades in Singapore were made through SMS-based Internet connections. New versions of WAP are being developed and released, but each release requires a new handset. Another threat to the lifeline of WAP is that 3G networks may eventually have enough throughput to handle the fully wired Internet — that is, native HTML without the need for WAP or any other cellular-specific protocol or environment.

China, the largest potential wireless market worldwide, is ahead of the other Asian markets in introducing WAP. However, like other WAP installations, the network is slow and features are limited. Motorola is pushing GPRS in China as a way to provide high-speed WAP services. A practical example of applied WAP technology is DHL in Stockholm's package tracing service, wherein a customer calls the DHL service via a cell phone and enters the number of the package to be traced. The service returns a list of dates and locations for the package, whether or not the package has been delivered, and, if it has been delivered, the name of the person who signed for the package.

Other Approaches

In addition to the above languages, there are a variety of tools that have been announced for developing wireless applications. For example, Sun Microsystems introduced J2ME (Java 2 Micro Edition, also known as JavaLite) as a development platform for Web-enabled cell phones that is a potential competitor to WAP. J2ME, which has been embraced by RIM and other hardware providers, represents a major departure from the PC approach to computing because it is an abstraction of the hardware and operating system. In other words, instead of the PC-era client-server architecture, J2ME is synonymous with a sessionless, distributed online viewing and browsing architecture. In this regard, J2ME supports a virtual machine that is more a programming environment than an operating system such as Palm OS or Windows CE. These and similar operating systems support session-based interactions, meaning that the communications connection is active from the beginning to the end of each interaction.

Even if a company doesn't use a tool to rewrite its content for the wireless Web, wired Web content can still be accessed by a technique called Web Clipping, screen scraping, transcoding, or morphing. Web Clipping involves reading the contents of a Web site, stripping the graphics, links, and multimedia, and then displaying the text on a wireless device. Web Clippers tend to be site specific, in that they make some allowances for the individual Web sites, so text formatting is optimum for reading and interacting with the site. Web Clipping was popularized by Palm Computing to support its wireless PDA, the Palm VII. By offering Web-site–specific clipping applications for free downloading from its Web site, Palm was able to provide users of its wireless PDA with access to the most popular services supported by the wireless Web.

In many ways, clipping or screen scraping is a throwback to the 1980s when vendors used a similar approach to move data from mainframe applications to the then-new desktop PC. The problem with the approach back then, and today, is that when there are changes made to the screen display— to the Web site in this case—the scraper must be modified to recognize the change and the nature of the new data. In addition, because the scraping process tends to be device specific, a different scraping algorithm has to be developed for each wireless device. For example, the scraping or clipping applications developed for the Palm VII don't work for wireless phones that sport postage stamp-size screens. In other words, simple screen scraping is usually viewed as a short-term fix that doesn't scale.

Second-generation screen scraping provides the ability to dynamically follow changes in the source HTML and reflect these changes in the appropriate manner in a variety of handheld environments. For example, one approach is to take the original HTML code and convert it to an intermediate form, such as XML and XSL that can more easily serve a variety of wireless handheld devices. For example, Netmorph, Inc., provides a middleware solution to moving from the wired to the wireless Web that involves converting the standard HTML feeding a Web site to XML and XSL, which maps to a variety of handheld devices. Changes in the HTML code that feeds the wired Web site are automatically reflected in the XML. One of the features of the Netmorph model is that, once the conversion to XML is complete, the wired and wireless are separate and independent. For example, the wired Web site can go down and not affect service on the wireless handheld devices.

DISCUSSION

The development of every wireless communications system represents an engineering effort. Unlike pure scientific exploration, the goal is to create a means of providing consistent communications—a technology—that represents the tension between form, function, and affordability (see Figure 5-6). For example, the affordability of a Web-enabled cellular phone includes the direct or subsidized handset price; the service contract (which can include prepaid service, one-rate service, with or without extra roaming charges); the cost of accessories, such as a headset, belt clip, spare battery, charger for home or office; as well as incidental operating costs, such as a replacement battery every year. From the cellular operator's perspective, affordability includes the cost of cell installation, power, insurance, maintenance, management, as well as day-to-day operations. There is also the cost of acquiring customers, such as marketing and advertising, and keeping customers happy through customer service. Infrastructure costs ranging from renting tower space to laying cables also affect affordability.

In the realm of function, from the customer's perspective, wireless communications technology is evaluated in terms of services provided, such as e-mail, voice mail, text messaging and paging, mobility (which is related to battery life), privacy, roaming capabilities, coverage area, and the intuitiveness

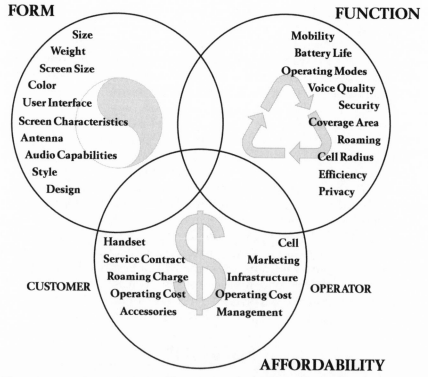

Figure 5-6. Developing successful wireless technologies requires adequately addressing the tension between form, function, and affordability, from both the customer and operator perspectives.

and ease of learning the user interface (which includes the graphics interface, voice-enabled interface, and keypad or stylus). From the cellular operator's perspective, function includes spectrum efficiency, network security, deployment time, and cell radius.

The third element in the triad—form—is reflected in the physical parameters of a cell phone, such as the weight, size, shape, and color. Form also includes subjective traits, such as "style" and "coolness," which, although often difficult to quantify, can be recognized immediately by subscribers. A cell phone's display screen size and placement, number and arrangement of buttons, and size of the external antenna all contribute to the form of a cell phone or other wireless device.

The technology involved with wireless communications is reflected in the value subscribers and operators place on a particular mix of these three traits. Consider the failure of the original Iridium satellite communications system, with its brick-size handheld unit, and the lackluster appeal of the feature-packed and overly complicated PDAs that predated the Palm Pilot. Both cases demonstrate how failure to adequately address form, function, and affordability can make the difference between global success and catastrophic failure.

It's obvious that the functionality made possible by technology is the basis for the initial activity on the wireless Web. However, as the technologies that appear to have the most promise begin to standardize, the emphasis within the area of functionality must shift from raw capabilities to manageability issues. These include the provision for security, and the ability to integrate or at least coexist with other technologies used in an enterprise or the subscriber's home. Similarly, within the realm of affordability, the cost of maintenance over the life of the product becomes a primary focus. During the standardization process, form has to support changes in function and support increased affordability, by decreasing manufacturing costs, for example, and to keep pace with the competition and customer expectations.

The current success of cell phones, two-way pagers, and wireless PDAs illustrates the dynamic tension depicted in Figure 5-6. With the industry's plan to roll out generation after generation of standards, subscribers who want or need the latest features will have to buy a new phone every 18 to 24 months, paralleling the constant upgrade market established for laptops and desktop PCs. As long as developers can provide the technology with the optimum mix of features in the right form at a reasonable price, there may not be much resistance from consumers to the constant upgrade pressure. For example, if the experience of NTT DoCoMo transfers to the United States, then subscriber churn rate, or rate at which subscribers leave for other carriers each year, should decrease significantly. Domestic wireless carriers experience a churn rate of about 30 percent, which is significant, considering that it costs about $300 to attract and add a new subscriber. However, just providing Web access isn't enough to capture subscribers. There is the issue of rising expectation, with companies leapfrogging each other in features and performance in an effort to win over subscribers. For example, NTT DoCoMo, which was operating at capacity within a year of its I-Mode offering, had no choice but to move to a new generation of wireless technologies.

Looking ahead, the limiting factor in propelling the wireless Web into everyday reality is establishing a standard, secure, affordable, universally accessible, high-speed infrastructure to support Web-enabled devices. Paradoxically, it may be that wireless Web infrastructure in the United States and much of Europe ends up primarily being the last-mile communications between subscribers and national high-speed networks. The wireless Web is melding with all forms of wired Web access.

The next innovations in wireless Web ecommerce will likely take advantage of other wireless technologies, such as GPS, combining them in new and useful ways. For example, although it's possible to locate a caller within a few hundred feet with cellular technology, GPS is more exact. Using an integrated approach that involves GPS and local cellular, nearby stores can offer invitations, in the form of sales notices, to customers strolling by. Similarly, smart cards, which consist of memory and a CPU embedded in a plastic card, will eventually become wireless, complementing cell phones as a form of digital currency.

Chapter 6 continues the discussion on technologies that will have a direct impact on the development of the wireless Web. In particular, it explores the emergent, enabling technologies that have the potential to transform wireless devices into conduits for pervasive Web access.

EXECUTIVE SUMMARY

The genesis of the modern cellular system involved dividing service areas into small cells so that radio frequencies could be reused, resulting in increased call capacity without significantly increasing the bandwidth requirements. The key issues in cellular systems, and where the incompatibilities arise, are in operating frequency allocation, the features supported by the different types of modulation, the nature and availability of the underlying network infrastructure, and how interference is dealt with.

The communications concept of switching is also central to cellular systems, especially the distinction between circuit and packet switching. In circuit switching, a connection is made between sender and receiver for the duration of the conversation or data transfer. The circuit is free to be used by another party only when the switch is opened, regardless of when the communication was finished. Packet switching, in contrast, sends packets of information from the sender to the receiver, leaving the communications channel open to other subscribers. Packet switching is what allows the "always-on" connection between wireless devices and the cellular network.

The most important wireless protocols are AMPS, D-AMPS, CDMA, MOBITEX, NA-TDMA, CDPD, GSM, I-MODE, GPRS, EDGE, CDMA 2000, W-CDMA, UMTS, TD-SCDMA, and IMT-2000. In addition to these general wireless communications protocols, there are specialized wireless protocols, including Bluetooth, Wi-Fi, UPNP, and JINI that specify short-range wireless communications networks.

High-level protocols and languages specific to the wired and wireless Web include HDML, WML, XML, and WAP. WAP is a stripped-down alternative to the standard protocol used on the wired Web that has a good chance at becoming the standard for Web-enabled phones despite its limitations. With XML and a related scripting language, XSL, a single Web site can be constructed that is readable by a variety of devices, regardless of their screen size, local memory, processing power, or data input/output features. JavaLite or J2ME, which allows the creation of an appliance-oriented, sessionless, virtual machine as opposed to an operating system, represents a radical departure from the standard client-server, session-based architecture used on the wired Web.

In addition to authoring content specifically for wireless devices, another approach is to leverage existing Web content by using Web Clipping technology, which removes multimedia and other high-bandwidth content from wired Web pages and makes the content available to handheld users. Simple clipping or screen scraping offers a quick fix to the move to wireless devices from the Web, but the approach isn't scalable and tends to have a high maintenance requirement. Second-generation technologies use a variety of techniques allowing changes in the original Web content to be automatically reflected on all wireless devices without manual intervention.

The development of successful wireless communications systems is an engineering effort that recognizes the tension between the form, function, and affordability of a wireless device.

6

Enabling Technologies

Learn from the mistakes of others—
you can never live long enough to make them all yourself.
                                                    John Luther

INTRODUCTION

There's much more to communications than simply establishing an information conduit between a sender and a receiver. After all, two empty cans properly connected by a taut string can provide reliable and inexpensive
communications. However, such a system isn't very practical in most situations, such as busy public areas, and it doesn't scale very well. What's worse,
the point-to-point channel doesn't connect to the wireless Web or the public
phone network. In other words, although a can-and-string system provides
affordable communications, the form and function of this simplistic technology do not provide much added value to users over the predominant legacy
system—yelling.

Improving the way customers communicate, conduct commerce, and
transact business—using metrics such as speed, ease of use, efficiency, and
effectiveness—requires more than establishing a connection, even if it is
immediately affordable to everyone. A communications system has to provide situation- and user-appropriate form and function. That is, it has to either
support the current process for accomplishing some task that the users are
engaged in, or suggest a process that can help users achieve their goals more
effectively and efficiently.

This chapter continues the discussion of the technologies that will have a
direct impact on the development of the wireless Web. In particular, the following material explores the emergent, enabling, or synergistic technologies

that have the greatest potential to transform wireless devices into conduits for pervasive Web access. This chapter explores the technologies that can take the current cell phone system in the United States, (equivalent to a can-and-string system as far as communications with the wireless Web are concerned), and transform it into an indispensable tool that propels businesses and subscribers into the future.

EMERGENT ENABLING TECHNOLOGIES

Thanks to a continuous stream of enabling technologies, followed by a process that has evolved to put these technologies into attractive, affordable packages, cellular technology is progressing at a dizzying pace. For example, since the form factor—or packaging size—is critical for providing pervasive communications, the rate of miniaturization of handheld and even wearable wireless devices has superceded even that of laptop computers and digital cameras. Cell phones—at least those in the laboratory and the limited-run prototypes available to the well-heeled early adopters—are to the point of the clip-on communicators depicted in *Star Trek*, in the form of digital wearable jewelry, sometimes referred to as Digital Wearables. Some of the many challenges of providing even more compact access to the wireless Web includes developing hands-free methods of requesting and interacting with data and innovative methods of powering communications devices so that they can maintain always-on connectivity.

These and other challenges are being met with the aid of emergent technologies in the areas of voice recognition and speech synthesis, as well as advances in portable power technologies. Another emergent, enabling technology is the cellular communications infrastructure, especially in the area of fixed wireless communications. Fixed wireless, using both terrestrial and satellite technology, promises to provide Web connectivity to residential subscribers denied access to the wired Web because of geographic, wired infrastructure, or economic constraints.

For example, thanks to fixed wireless, entire countries may be able to leapfrog from the nineteenth century, bypassing the wired legacy systems of the twentieth century, directly into twenty-first century wireless communications. In Tanzania and Ghana, where each country's wired infrastructure is less extensive than that of a small U.S. town, wireless local loop technology makes wireless pay phones and pocket pagers possible in even the remotest areas. Fixed wireless technology has a place in the most congested, densely populated cities of the world as well. For many commercial subscribers in the domestic urban sprawl, fixed wireless represents high-speed, high-bandwidth connectivity to the Internet at a price-point that can't be matched by traditional wired services.

The most prominent enabling technologies on the horizon include terrestrial and satellite fixed wireless; a variety of user interface technologies, including Emotionally Intelligent Interfaces, voice recognition, and speech synthesis; voice portal technologies; portable power; and a variety of privacy and security tools. These technologies are described in more detail in the following paragraphs.

Terrestrial Fixed Wireless

Terrestrial or land-based fixed wireless, especially in the "last-mile" circuit, is becoming increasingly technologically and economically feasible because of advances in low-power miniature cells and other wireless network technologies, and the significant business opportunities the related service offers. In many parts of the United States and Europe, terrestrial fixed wireless competes directly with DSL and cable modems for high-speed Web access, especially when these services, although heavily promoted, fail to materialize as viable options. In many cases, it's simply a question of who can get to customers first, and wireless has the upper hand when it comes to set-up time.

In the United States, service providers such as AT&T, Sprint, and World-Com have tremendous economic incentives to bypass the regional telecom companies. By using fixed wireless installations, they can provide customers with long-distance service without having to pay the regional telecoms' high access charges for last-mile access. In other words, they can charge customers more for long-distance service and still provide the customer with a less expensive alternative to local wired service. In addition to potential cost savings, fixed wireless offers high-speed Web access to customers who either haven't elected to use DSL or cable modem because of cost, or because they live in rural areas or in cities that don't offer high-speed wired Web connectivity. In some rural areas of the United States, for example, there simply isn't enough of a potential subscriber base for local telecoms to offer DSL service. Economics aside, often the technology simply won't support a critical mass of subscribers. For example, because of signal loss over standard telephone lines, DSL cannot service subscribers more than about 6 km (4 mi) from a telephone switching station.

When set-up time and cost are primary factors, fixed wireless—or, more specifically, terrestrial fixed wireless—has an advantage over wired services. Fixed wireless can be installed quickly for large numbers of subscribers without major physical changes to the information infrastructure, such as digging up streets to lay cable for DSL or cable modem subscribers. Installing the infrastructure for a residential fixed wireless network can be as simple as attaching a series of microcell radios, each only a little larger than this book, to the public light fixtures in a community. The light fixtures provide a line-of-sight platform for antennas, as well as ready access to power. One company that uses microcell technology is Metricom, which offers 28.8-KBps wireless service to both mobile and fixed subscribers. To use the service, subscribers simply install inexpensive and unobtrusive fixed wireless units on the sides of their homes, within sight of one of the microcells.

There are other fixed wireless configurations as well. For example, Teligent uses a single, omnidirectional antenna, providing 128 KBps- to 640-KBps service to residential neighborhoods. Sprint's SpeedChoice service is based on a broadcast antenna mounted on the highest location available, providing a coverage area of about 55 km (35 mi) radius per antenna. Speed-Choice is unique in that, while downloads occur over the fast wireless connections, uplinks occur over ordinary 56-KBps analog modems. Most other services use a single cellular unit at the residential site for both sending and receiving data.

In the fixed wireless arena, seemingly minor technical factors, such as operating frequency, can have a huge impact on the economics of network configuration and potential subscriber base. For example, AT&T uses the same radio spectrum it licenses for its PCS services for its fixed wireless services. At this frequency, signals can travel through or around buildings, trees, and other structures without excessive signal loss. Therefore, line-of-sight connectivity between a cell installation and a subscriber isn't a necessity. However, Sprint and WorldCom offer fixed wireless services that operate at much higher microwave frequencies, where signals don't bounce around trees and in between buildings, but propagate in straight lines. As such, they require line-of-sight communications between subscriber installations and large, expensive, omnidirectional antenna clusters mounted on huge towers. Because of the line-of-sight requirements, these fixed wireless services are most effective in urban areas without skyscrapers to obscure signal paths. Similarly, TeraBeam offers a speed of 1 GBps over the last mile in line-of-sight communications over the IR band, which is not regulated by the FCC.

In terms of physical infrastructure, AT&T has the advantage of over 10,000 cellular towers—each capable of supporting about 5000 subscribers—scattered across the United States. Through the use of directional antennas and without the need to hand off subscribers as they move from one cell to the next, adding a fixed wireless subscriber has a minor impact on overall network performance, compared to adding mobile cellular phones. The AT&T fixed wireless system can use the available frequencies more efficiently, providing support for both fixed and mobile wireless subscribers. Given this infrastructure, and because AT&T mobile and fixed services operate on the same band, it is in a unique position to provide integrated fixed and mobile wireless services. This provides customers with the option of owning only one phone. At home, the unit operates like a cordless phone, with at-home calling rates applied. Away from home, it operates as a mobile cellular phone, with a different billing structure.

Commercial fixed wireless systems often represent the most economically viable means of providing high-speed Internet access to corporations operating in office buildings located in major metropolitan areas, especially when the technology is coupled with wireless LAN technology inside the building. In the United States, less than 5 percent of all urban office buildings are wired for Internet access.

The major players in the commercial fixed wireless arena, namely Nextlink Communications, Winstar Communications, Teligent, and Advanced Radio Telecom, were the most successful bidders in the U.S. commercial fixed wireless spectrum auction. Although each of these companies provides services that operate in the 30-GHz band, they use different technologies to achieve the same goals.

The two basic types of commercial fixed wireless service are *point-to-point* and *point-to-multipoint*. Recall from Chapter 4 that two characteristics of antennas are gain and directivity, and that antenna designs can be highly directional or less so, as requirements dictate. Point-to-point fixed wireless uses highly directional (and therefore high-gain) pairs of antennas to connect the communications network in one building with that of another. Since the system isn't shared with any other sites, the full bandwidth of communications—over 150 MBps—is available to the subscribing company.

Triton Network Systems uses a modified point-to-point configuration, in the form of a wireless ring network that requires two antennas on each building, each providing connectivity to another building. If one antenna in the network fails due to lightning or a power outage, the system can remain operational because of the built-in redundancies in the data path.

The point-to-multipoint design uses central, moderately directional antenna clusters, which are connected to the Internet. Subscribing companies use highly directional dish antennas to communicate with the central, Internet-connected hub. Since several companies share the available bandwidth through the central hub, data rates are considerably slower than point-to-point can offer, but still greater than that of DSL or cable modem. Regardless of the wireless networking configuration, one of the greatest limitations of fixed wireless systems in major metropolitan areas is acquiring the right to install antennas and radio equipment on rooftops and the sides of buildings. Not only are there structural, power, and height issues, but local ordinances regarding aesthetics, insurance, and safety can take months or even years to resolve.

Satellite-Based Fixed Wireless

Satellite technology is perhaps the clearest example of how significant science fiction has been in defining the dreams of innovators and entrepreneurs, and, eventually, the realities of everyone's lives.

Arthur C. Clarke conceived the notion of a satellite-based communications system based on three geosynchronous satellites acting as extraterrestrial relays in an article he wrote for *Wireless Magazine* in 1945. Clarke's insight, which obviously became part of the collective vision for the scientists and engineers who grew up reading his stories, came decades before the technology was invented that was capable of creating the system he described.

Although satellite communications systems are at least an order of complexity above terrestrial systems, at the most basic level, they can be thought of simply as cells in the sky. Instead of a centrally located transmitter and receiver located on a tower, these orbiting cells are positioned thousands of kilometers above the earth, in a variety of orbits, providing communications to fixed and, in some cases, mobile and even handheld units. Like terrestrial cells, orbiting cells require connectivity among each other and with the public telephone network. The connectivity can occur with direct satellite-to-satellite wireless communications or through communications with ground-based networks, including wired networks. Of course, connectivity to the public telephone network requires a link to ground-based stations.

Like terrestrial fixed wireless, orbiting cells can provide a viable alternative to wired Web access. The specific advantages of orbiting cellular communications over terrestrial cells—increased bandwidth; wide coverage area; self-contained, rapidly deployed communications; and low cost per site—are detailed below.

Increased Bandwidth. The optimum operating window for ground-to-satellite communications is generally considered to be between 1 and 4 GHz. At these higher operating frequencies, there is greater potential bandwidth available for modulating signals compared to, say, an 800-MHz terrestrial cellular system. For example, assume that, because of circuit and antenna design constraints, communications channels are limited to the main or carrier frequency ±1 percent. At 800 MHz, this corresponds to an available bandwidth of ±8 MHz or 16 MHz. At 4 GHz, ±1 percent corresponds to ±40 MHz or 80 MHz—or five times the bandwidth available at 800 MHz.

Wide Coverage Area. Whereas coverage in a terrestrial cell might be limited to 10 km (6.2 mi), an orbiting cell can provide a cell size—usually referred to as a footprint—approximating the size of the planet, depending on the orbit. Orbiting cells are typically in one of three orbits: Geostationary Earth Orbit (GEO), Low Earth Orbit (LEO), or Medium Earth Orbit (MEO). The orbit not only affects the footprint, but also the signal delay or latency, availability of communications, and terrestrial antenna and power requirements.

A satellite or orbiting cell in a Geostationary Earth Orbit has a footprint of about one-third of the globe, allowing virtually full coverage of the planet with only three satellites (some areas near the north and south poles may be unserviceable, depending on the season). Satellites in geostationary orbits appear stationary in the sky because their orbits lie in the plane of the equator, at an altitude of about 36,000 km (22,000 mi), completing one orbit every 24 h. Since each satellite moves in the same direction as the Earth's rotation, they remain in a fixed position over the equator, providing a fixed target for terrestrial dish antennas. The first geosynchronous communications satellite was placed into service in 1963.

The challenge in working with GEO systems is that there is a delay, or latency, involved in the communications loop. Even though the radio waves to and from a ground station to a GEO satellite travel at the speed of light (300 million m/s), because of the distance involved, this trip takes about half a second. With voice communications, this delay is perceived as an annoying echo. Data transmissions are similarly affected, but the delay isn't usually as detrimental to the quality of communications. Because of the latency problem, geosynchronous communications satellites aren't viewed as a replacement for terrestrial cellular voice service. For comparative purposes, the first generation of two-way pagers provided communications with a latency of between 30 and 90 s, compared to 2 s for data transferred over G2 cell phones using terrestrial networks. The initial wireless Palm network provided a barely tolerable 5- to -15s latency per transaction.

To achieve the quality of communications of terrestrial cells systems, satellites following medium and low earth orbits are more suitable than satellites in geosynchronous orbits. Lower orbits are associated with much shorter latency times and smaller footprints (cell size). As in terrestrial systems, smaller cell size requires more closely spaced cell sites. In theory, the closer the satellite is to the terrestrial station or handheld unit, the stronger the signal from the satellite, and the smaller the possible size of the handheld unit.

Because LEO-based communications satellites have the lowest orbits, their footprints are also the smallest. LEO-based communications systems require large numbers of satellites, including spares, and a correspondingly greater cost. LEO- and MEO-based satellite communications work like traditional cellular systems, with a slight twist. As the subscriber's signal decreases in one cell and increases in an adjacent cell, the cells communicate and hand the subscriber off from one cell to the next. However, instead of the subscriber traveling from cell to cell, the subscriber is motionless. From the subscriber's perspective, the cells are moving. LEO communications satellites hand off subscribers every 10 to 20 min versus every 2 to 4 h for MEO satellite communications systems.

There are several commercial ventures into satellite-based communications systems. A notable MEO project is the ICO system from ICO Global Communications (www.ico.com). The ICO system (so named because the satellites follow an Intermediate Circular Orbit) is based on 10 satellites and TDMA technology. It's designed to integrate mobile satellite communications with the terrestrial mobile networks running GSM, D-AMPS, and other protocols. ICO is designed to support voice, fax, and messaging, with a data throughput of initially only 2.4 KBps, and an ultimate capacity in the hundreds of KBps range.

Major LEO initiatives include the resurrected Iridium system, Global-Star, and Teledesic (www.teledesic.com). The Iridium LEO-based system, built over five years at a cost of $4 billion and with a monthly maintenance cost of over $10 million, is based on 66 LEO satellites, with a goal of supporting primarily voice through heavy but luggable handset units. GlobalStar, like ICO and Iridium, is designed to support voice, fax, and messaging services. The system is based on 48 satellites, interlinked through a ground communications network, complementing the terrestrial cellular phone service with a 7.2-KBps data channel. Since one of GlobalStar's backers is Qualcomm, it's not surprising that the satellite system supports Qualcomm's CDMA standard.

The Teledesic network, originally backed by Bill Gates and Craig McCaw, is designed as the "Internet in the sky," with a data throughput of over 64 MBps on the downlink and 2 MBps on the uplink. With 288 primary LEO satellites and 12 spares, the system is designed to extend the terrestrial fiber network to anywhere on the planet. The Teledesic design supports a variety of protocols, including TDMA. Eventually, the Teledesic system is supposed to provide capacity in the hundreds of MBps range.

As evidenced by the fate of Iridium LLC, there are challenges ahead for satellite-based communications systems that aim to provide Internet access to the world. The failure of the original Iridium project is blamed for ICO's failure to secure funding and its subsequent filing for bankruptcy, for example. However, while GlobalStar's fate is less certain, ICO and Teledesic were both reinvigorated with a $1 billion investment through the mechanism of a holding company, ICO-Teledesic Global, that controls the satellite assets of Craig McCaw, chairman of both ICO and Teledesic. In addition to these high-profile satellite systems, there are a variety of other high-bandwidth cellular communications projects at different levels of planning and development, including Cyberstar, Astrolink, Spaceway, and Skybridge.

Self-Contained, Rapidly Deployed Communications. A local terrestrial satellite station requires only power, a satellite dish, and portable communications hardware, making satellite communications ideal for emergencies in remote locations. These simple requirements make for rapid installations as well. Often, the greatest impediment for providing communications to an underserved area isn't technical, but revolves around fulfilling local regulatory requirements in a timely manner.

Even though satellites are global devices, when a ground station is established, the local regulations and politics have to be recognized. For example, there are issues of frequency allocation and coordination with local services to consider, licensing, connections to the local telephone network and the Internet, as well as respect for sovereign rights and interests. Obviously, satellite communications systems have military and civilian applications.

Low Cost Per Site. The economics of satellite communications are such that it's often the least expensive method of providing a high-bandwidth channel between points separated by more than a few hundred kilometers. The distance covered by terrestrial microwave hops is limited by the curvature of the earth. A hop of 1700 km (1000 mi) for example, might require a network of 20 terrestrial microwave dishes with land-based repeater hardware. The same distance might be covered by a single satellite hop. Because the rental of satellite channels is readily affordable and there is no network maintenance overhead to deal with, satellite communications can quickly become a viable option to a traditional terrestrial network.

Returning to the discussion of communications fundamentals in Chapter 4, the microwave frequencies used in satellite communications demonstrate several important characteristics involving propagation and absorption. For example, microwave communications to and from satellites are subject to atmospheric absorption, the effects of rain, refraction, or bending of the waves as they pass through the atmosphere, scattering, diffraction, and multipath propagation. Microwave signals are absorbed by vegetation and even water vapor in the air. Water absorption of microwave radiation peaks at 22 GHz, making this frequency band unusable for terrestrial wireless or terrestrial-to-satellite communications. However, this frequency band can be used for intersatellite links, which don't involve the signal passing through the atmosphere. Multipath propagation occurs when the signal from a satellite is split among several paths, either because of disturbances in the atmosphere, reflections off of an airplane passing overhead, or the presence of a fixed structure, such as a nearby building. The result is that the signal interferes with itself, potentially rendering the data useless by the time it arrives at the ground station.

USER INTERFACE TECHNOLOGY

The user interface, where the cell phone subscriber or wireless PDA user meets the wireless Web, is the point at which form and function either coalesce to provide value or collide and create confusion. User interface technologies are important because a good user interface can make a mediocre technology usable, and a great user interface can make the same technology a pleasure to use. When teamed with an exceptional technology, a great user interface can propel the combination to the status of the "next new thing."

The user interface is the veneer that covers or reshapes the intricacies of the communications device and the associated infrastructure from users while allowing them to focus their attention on what's being presented. While all user interfaces share the trait of communicating with the user, they vary significantly in form and function. When a typical wired Web user talks about a user interface, she's usually referring to the quality, quantity, and arrangement of the graphics, buttons, and menus on her computer screen. However, the wireless Palm Pilot series with stylus pointing devices and the RIM Blackberry with its miniature keypad have user interfaces that rely much less on what's displayed on the screen and more on the size and shape of the physical units.

Of course, the task is much more involved than a simple cosmetic change, simply putting lipstick on a pig. The underlying functionality must be robust enough to support the user interface. For example, latency profoundly affects interface design. The Microsoft Windows hourglass would be inappropriate for the customer sitting in traffic, waiting to determine where she should make a turn.

User Interface Components

Except for the recent popularity of voice recognition and speech synthesis as components of a user interface, most of the user interface work with PCs has been graphical in nature, and, except for games, with much less emphasis on the tactical, auditory aspects. Even the simplest user interface is a complex, multitiered structure that supports a dialogue or communications channel between the user and the device. The interdependent interface components can be categorized as Physical, Graphical, Logical, Emotional, Intelligent, and Emotionally Intelligent. The highlights of these components and the technologies relevant to the wireless Web are described below.

Physical Interface. The Physical Interface component communicates a user's physical actions *to* her cell phone or wireless PDA and provides feedback *from* her device. Data input mechanisms range from a hardware or software keypad, miniature trackball, stylus, microphone, joystick, touch screen, digitizer pad, video or still camera, data glove, data suit, retinal imager, or fingerprint recognition device. Feedback can come from LCD panels, haptic (force feedback) controls, or audio, including music and synthetic speech, and even odor.

The Physical Interface largely defines the form, and therefore limits the functionality of a wireless device. A cumbersome, overly complex physical interface will ruin the user experience, regardless of the functionality it provides. As illustrated in Figure 6-1, as the foundation of the user interface hierarchy, the Physical Interface is highly relevant in the design of wireless Web-enabled devices. Consider the relevance of the Palm Pilot's stylus in the elegance of the overall interface design. The stylus provides an intuitive, immediately understood point and click tool that most users adapt to within minutes. Similarly, RIM's Blackberry physical interface incorporates a thumbwheel and miniature keypad that allows one-hand operation.

Graphical User Interface. The Graphical User Interface component (GUI) is the collection of windows, icons, menus, buttons, and other controls drawn on a screen that map the user's actions to the physical layer below. On the wired Web, the GUI is often viewed as synonymous with Microsoft Windows, the Macintosh OS, and the Web browsers they support. For wireless devices such as cell phones, WAP and the related microbrowser environments serve the same purpose, although they do so in a much simpler way.

All of these PC-based GUI systems are based on metaphors. With the exception of games, the predominant desktop metaphor is that of a desktop, which is usually traversed with the aid of a mouse and a large, ergonomically correct keyboard. As far as the wired Web is concerned, interface designers are continually making tradeoffs between interface bandwidth and interactivity potential, given the practical constraints of infrastructure bandwidth. Some bandwidth-demanding technologies, such as streaming video, simply can't be used for the general domestic public until a high-speed infrastructure is established.

A common metaphor for Web-enabled cell phone interface designers is the card, and cards are arranged in one or more decks. In addition, a card can be one of several types. Choice cards allow subscribers to select from a list of choices, Display cards display data, and Entry cards present data entry fields to the subscriber. Although the metaphor is reminiscent of Apple Computer's HyperCard environment, the visual component of the interface is more similar to a text-only DOS or mainframe environment.

Although these concerns of the wired Web world continue to challenge designers, at least as far as interface design is concerned, the wireless Web has changed everything. The desktop metaphor, with its trash can and seemingly infinite layers of folders within folders simply won't do for a Web-enabled cell phone. One area of development is that of defining new interface metaphors that allow and encourage speed and versatility, as opposed to an empty-calorie diet of eye candy. The original Palm Pilot and the RIM Blackberry wireless PDA are often-cited examples of how a simple, elegant design metaphor, in this case that of a traditional paper-based organizer, can be extended to an electronic format without losing functionality or adding unnecessary complexity in the translation process.

With the increased focus on voice as an interface component, the role of the GUI in handheld devices is less prominent. Working with voice (a Physical Interface component, as described above) as an interface is challenging, especially when most of the work during the 1980s and 1990s in interface design focused on the graphical aspects of the user interface, as described below. Whereas graphical designers are concerned with the role of metaphors and color schemes and the aesthetics of layout and icons, voice interface designers work in a space defined by human limitations (as in short-term memory), linguistic clarity, accommodation, fulfillment, user support, predictability, interpretation, suitable tempo, precision, forgiveness, and responsiveness. Some of these concepts have parallels in the GUI world, but many are foreign, and will require interface designers to study the differences. Understanding the importance of the similarities and differences in the two modalities is especially critical in multimodal interface designs, where a GUI, voice recognition, and speech synthesis are combined.

Logical Interface. The Logical Interface component deals with the rules, guidelines, and standards of interface behavior, such as how an interface should display the results of a calculation. The Logical Interface helps define user expectations. For example, in proper logical interface design, pressing the "1" key consistently enters a "1" on the display panel. On a subtler level, if hitting the "submit" soft button (the function of a soft button on a cell phone is determined by the application) while logged onto a stock trading site initiates a trade but pressing the same button, relabeled, five minutes later cancels the trade order, this behavior would violate the logic of the interface design. The technologies involved in Logical interface design have more to do with the rules, guidelines, and standards of interface behavior than with hardware or software design per se.

Because of the limited screen real estate available for a robust GUI on a cell phone, the Logical Interface component is critical to minimizing possible frustration when accessing the Web and other services. For example, in purchasing an item through the Web, the text-only interface on a small cell phone display must provide the means of entering charge card information in a logical, efficient manner. That is, if an error is made in entering the charge card number, the subscriber must be presented with a logical method of correcting the error, and preferably one that doesn't also require that she re-enter other information, such as her name and mailing address. Even reasonable customers will walk away from an eCommerce transaction when the interaction isn't logical and supportive of their needs. Entering the same data through the GUI available on a standard computer monitor isn't nearly at the level of logical complexity as the smaller cell phone or PDA screen. Moving from field to field is accomplished by pointing and clicking or using the TAB key. Similarly, editing any of the information can be done, regardless of the sequence in which the information is entered.

Emotional Interface. The Emotional Interface component is intended to elicit emotions in the user. As game developers have demonstrated, an Emotional Interface can be fun. Games highlight the basic components of an Emotional Interface: there must be some element of risk, the prospect of a physical or virtual reward, a degree of uncertainty, and the process of interaction; and/or the end point of the game must elicit some form of emotion in the player. This component of the user interface is important for wireless interface developers to master, given that NTT DoCoMo's I-Mode is popular with teens primarily because of its games and emotive content.

Intelligent Interface. The Intelligent Interface component is primarily concerned with providing the overall interface with adaptability and a variety of pattern recognition techniques. Intelligence, after all, is simply the ability to adapt—that is, to change with experience. Pattern recognition technologies relevant to the wireless Web include *speech recognition* (the ability to convert the spoken word into machine-readable text), *machine translation* (automated conversion of text from one language to another), *natural language processing* (NLP) (interpreting the meaning of text within a given language), and *intelligent agents* (a broad range of intelligent programs that perform specified tasks on behalf of customers).

Emotionally Intelligent Interface. The Emotionally Intelligent Interface (EII) component is designed to modify user behavior by forming a bond, such as trust, with the user. A fully emotionally intelligent interface would not only express emotions but would know how to manage those expressions and how to use its emotions to modify user behavior. For a positive bond between the user and his or her cell phone, the EII component should approximate a helpful customer support professional. In other words, it should be respectful, helpful, empathetic, socially adept, truthful, unambiguous, anticipatory, persuasive, responsive, and emotive.

Obviously, the technologies available for Web-enabled cell phones have a long way to go before they can approximate the ideal EII. Since EIIs are concerned with influencing emotions in users, some form of pattern recognition is needed to recognize what emotions are likely to be generated in a given situation. New developments in the area of Emotionally Intelligent Interface designs, which rely on software agents and graphically rich, human appearing Bots, are changing the wired Web.

Bots can speak and emote appropriately to support the qualities found in a person-to-person interaction, including trust, an emotional bond. A Bot or software robot can carry on a humanlike conversation with a customer through the instantaneous exchange of text messages and one-way (from Bot to customer) transfer of images that correspond to the tone or content of the text messages. The images are typically that of a real or synthetic person's face, but could be other characters as well, thanks to technologies such as LifeF/X's stand-ins, which take a single image of a person and animate it in a lifelike way, using local computational ability. In this thin-client system, bandwidth requirements are minimized since rendering occurs locally, unlike streaming video of a real person. The downside, at least until G3 phones are generally available, is that few cell phones have the local processing power necessary for real-time video capture and compression. This is likely to change as soon as video processing capabilities become commonplace on wireless PDAs and cell phones.

While Bots and synthetic actors represent the near horizon of interface design on the wired Web, especially using thin client technology, the current incarnation of the wireless Web must emphasize speed and versatility as opposed to graphics. Even so, while most of the world awaits the arrival of G3-level speeds on the wireless Web, there is sufficient bandwidth for interfaces based on voice recognition. Initially, these will be faceless, nameless voices; but as bandwidth capabilities increase, they will be supplemented with the faces of synthetic actors, adding to the emotionally intelligent interface component.

Applications

Every device embodies variations of the six user interface components in different ways, with some taking on more significance than others. For example, for an ordinary (non-Web–enabled) toaster, the Physical and Logical interface components are the most significant. Most users expect a toaster to operate by applying heat to a slice of bread after they've placed a slice on the rack and lowered the rack by pressing the on-off switch. The Logical component comes into play regarding the degree of doneness. Users expect a logical, direct correlation between the light-to-dark setting on the toaster to the output of the toaster. The other four interface components are insignificant in most toaster designs.

Similarly, the six user interface components apply in varying degrees to devices designed for wired and wireless Web access. Assuming a standard desktop PC for wired Web access and a Web-enabled cellular phone for wireless access, the greatest discrepancies in user interface component mix is in the Physical and Graphical User Interface components. At least in the current incarnation of Web-enabled phones, the relevance of the GUI is limited by screen real estate. There is only so much that can be done, from a GUI, with a few lines of text. Even the graphical, color screens available to NTT DoCoMo's I-Mode customers are less important to the overall device user interface, relative to Physical Interface components. The physical form factor—including device size, weight, color, keypad layout, screen size and placement—defines the subscriber's experience more than the graphics on the screen.

The other large discrepancy between handheld wireless and wired Web access interface components is in the Emotional Component. Assuming the I-Mode experience translates to other Web-enabled phone systems, one of the major draws for Web access is the fun factor, especially in the teen market. Cartoons, games, and jokes are the most popular uses of the I-Mode, highlighting the relevance of the Emotional Component of the user interface on device design.

Within the realm of user interface technology, it's important to note that the particular mix of interface components helps define the personality of the interface and, by extension, of the cell phone or wireless PDA. All interfaces, whether as part of a cell phone or wireless vending machine, have personalities. The major personality traits of dominance, submissiveness, conscientiousness, emotional stability, and openness can be applied to the user interface of a particular device, such as a wireless PDA.

Wearable Computers and Communications. Thought by some to be the ultimate in user interface design, wearable communications and computing are supported by advances such as the development of flexible integrated circuits that can be wrapped around bracelets, including image sensors and displays. Although cellular phones, wireless PDAs, and two-way pagers are now pocketable objects, there is a move in the industry to create wireless, wearable computers and electronics that do everything from entertain to assist at work. Prototype wearable communications systems have been around for years, and a few commercial versions of wearable computing have surfaced, all sporting wireless connectivity.

For the consumer market, Philips and Levi Strauss developed the ICD+, a jacket with a GSM, voice-controlled cell phone, MP3 player for playing music downloaded from the Web, a headset, and a remote control. Making a call involves simply flipping up the collar; the volume controls are in the sleeves. The ICD+ jacket uses a personal area network or PAN, woven into the fabric of the jacket to serve as the backbone of the network. The ICD+ jacket isn't the only such wearable device. Nike has integrated MP3 players into their sportswear line, and Motorola and Swatch Group have developed telephone wristwatches.

Other wireless personal communications systems have been developed with government agencies in mind. However, what these systems lacked was an established standard for communications. For example, prototype systems have been developed for the military in which soldiers wearing biosensors and personal LANs communicate their status to a central cell. Dead or alive status is verified by each soldier's wireless EKG. In this way, the commanding officers know when to risk retrieval of a downed soldier in the field. Similarly, prototype vests have been developed for the U.S. military that determine the severity of wounded in the field, based on locations and size of entry and exit holes in the vests. A soldier with an entry wound in the lower right chest would probably warrant rescue and triage, whereas one with an entrance and exit hole in his left chest (i.e., through the heart) would probably be assigned to a low ROI for a rescue mission.

Prototypes of wearable computers and PANs and several consumer-oriented systems are commercially viable today. For example the POLAR (www.polar.com) heart monitoring watch gathers pulse information that can be downloaded into a PC for analysis of the user's training. A similar system exists for bicycles in the form of a wireless device that tracks cadence, torque, heart rate, and other variables for later analysis on a PC.

In the commercial area, wearable computers have a more significant impact, especially where ergonomics, efficiency, and throughput are driving factors. For example, Symbol Technologies manufactures a wearable scanning and computing system that is used by virtually all UPS warehouse workers to tag packages for tracking. Their WSS 1000 unit, which resembles something out of *Star Wars*, attaches to the user's forearm and uses a laser scanner attached to a finger or the back of the hand. The PDA-sized main unit has an LCD display and alphanumeric keypad as well.

Bandwidth Compression. Supporting interactivity requires a minimal level of bandwidth, loosely corresponding to the various generations of the wireless communications infrastructure. In the evolution of wireless communications, first-generation (G1) pagers represent the lowest level of interactivity. Conversely, person-to-person, live videophone communications on late G3 infrastructures provide the highest level of interactivity, with visual and auditory cues available for all parties in the discussion. Between these two extremes are a variety of computer- and human-mediated modalities, each dependent on a certain level of technologic support, and each capable of providing a different level of interactivity. Note that the increases in interactivity for email and paging are relatively small from one generation to the next, since subscribers can only type or read email messages so fast, regardless of how quickly the underlying infrastructure can handle the data.

For example, consider a computer-mediated Voice Portal, a form of voice-only conversation between a human subscriber and a computer that serves as a portal to the Web. A Voice Portal recognizes the patterns of the subscriber's voice and synthesizes speech, and requires at least G2.5-level bandwidth. Even with all of the support technology involved in establishing communications between a subscriber and the Web, a Voice Portal only provides interactivity approaching the level associated with a person-to-person conversation over a cell phone.

A wireless VideoPhone seems in many ways like something out of science fiction, especially when the combination of voice and video over a wired modem or DSL connection is still problematic at best. A Bot Portal is a synthetic version of a VideoPhone conversation. It's equivalent to a Voice Portal with a computer-generated, animated face that can be displayed on the cell phone's LCD panel, providing a level of interactivity equivalent to that of a live person-to-person phone conversation. With ever-increasing bandwidth provided by post-G3 infrastructures, Voice and Bot Portals will approach the level of interactivity provided by live VideoPhone conversations.

Given the bandwidth requirements of live VideoPhone communications, the first commercially successful application of Bot Portal technology will likely be as a compression utility for VideoPhones. That is, Bot technology can be used to provide emotional, photo-realistic animated images of the speakers without the need to send streaming video over a wireless channel.

Companies such as LifeF/X (www.lifefx.com) are developing technologies that take a single photo of a subscriber and, using that image as a basis, create a virtual actor or stand-in that can be reproduced on the receiver's end. Instead of using the entire 2-MBps bandwidth of a communications channel to send the image of a talking head to a recipient, a still image, with emotional cues and the sender's voice, is sent. The thin-client signal may require a bandwidth of only 20 KBps for transmission, and no additional bandwidth when it is reconstituted on the receiver's cell phone. The reconstituted image is an animated stand-in of the actual speaker, complete with lip syncing and gross head movements. In addition, it will be possible to use a still image from an archive—one showing the sender in a business suit, for example—to use at inopportune moments, such as when a businessman is just rolling out of bed or is having a bad hair day. While this compression technology and the Bot Portals they support aren't yet applicable for images of the view at the top of a ski lift, they will be sufficient to create faces on a watch-sized screen. Stand-in compression technology will be especially appealing, as there will certainly be economic incentives to avoid the high-bandwidth requirements of streaming video.

The above are but a sampling of the enabling technologies that have the greatest likelihood of influencing the trajectory of wireless Web computing on a global scale. The most compelling of the enabling technologies on the near horizon, voice recognition and speech synthesis, are described in more detail below.

Voice Enabled Interfaces (VEIs)

Voice recognition, the ability of a device to translate the spoken word into machine-readable text or commands, is almost to the point that it can be applied to wireless devices with confidence. Similarly, speech synthesis, the generation of understandable speech from machine-readable text, has been a viable commodity for decades. Only recently, however, have advances in speech synthesis made it applicable to accessing the wireless Web. While synthesized speech technology in the 1970s produced mechanical-sounding output, with choppy speech and improper intonation, modern synthesizers can produce more human-sounding speech with user-configurable speaker qualities, such as the age and sex of the virtual speaker. Even when the voice inflection produced in these synthesis programs isn't perfect, the speech is virtually always understandable.

In many respects, voice recognition teamed with speech synthesis a VEI is the most natural user interface for a cell phone, primarily because it doesn't require the subscriber to change his or her existing modes of interaction. Virtually every businessperson is accustomed to talking on a cell phone, and, except for a few PDA aficionados, interfacing with a cell phone through a miniature keypad or plastic stylus doesn't come as second nature. In addition, talking on a cell phone is generally socially acceptable, especially in a business setting. There isn't the need to don a special headset with a heads-up display or anything out of the ordinary in order to use the technology. Furthermore, there is no stylus or other device necessary to operate a VEI.

In many instances, a VEI may be the only practical option in environments that demand hands-free and eyes-free information access. For example, businesspeople driving through heavy traffic or walking down a crowded street have to be aware of their surroundings. Accessing data in hands-busy environments is an obvious fit for VEIs, as long as subscribers can walk and talk at the same time.

The trajectory of VEI is overwhelmingly positive. Both Voice Recognition and Speech Synthesis software are commodity items on desktop and laptop PCs, despite the presence of keyboards and mice that may make VEIs seem superfluous. However, given the information input and output constraints of a Web-enabled cell phone, voice recognition suddenly takes on a new relevance. In fairness, many PC users have shunned voice recognition for its inaccuracies and difficulty in correcting errors once they've been made. After a half-hour or more of training, even the best PC-based voice recognition systems still make one error every 10 to 20 words.

Fortunately, voice recognition technology is improving constantly. The global voice recognition developers, IBM, the financially troubled Lernout & Hauspie, and Philips, have made great strides in the past decade, including the ability to work with virtually unlimited vocabularies and some degree of speaker independence. In addition, newcomers, such as Motorola, are developing systems expressly for wireless communications, free of the legacy constraints of PC-based voice recognition systems. These and other voice recognition software developers are working with thin-client technologies such as the ASP model of application distribution that negate the need for high-speed, computationally intensive local processing on a cell phone. In the ASP model of VEI, the cell phone acts like a wireless microphone, with the voice recognition software running on a remote server.

A concern with cell phone—based voice recognition systems—assuming that recognition accuracy continues to improve with each generation of speech recognition technology—is that of audio quality and bandwidth. The voice recognition engines developed for PCs use more of the audio spectrum than most cell phones support. That is, PC-based voice recognition systems use the information content in speech above the frequencies normally carried by phones to differentiate between similar sounding words. The challenge is that the voices of passersby, traffic, and other environmental noises also tend to occur at higher frequencies, and these noises can render a voice recognition system useless.

Another hurdle, and one that may take years to address, is that voice recognition and synthesis have been mainly English language—based technologies. Although there are systems developed for the mainstream European languages, such as German, these systems tend not to be as robust as their English language counterparts. This discrepancy is in part because the current generation of voice recognition engines has been developed assuming nuances and structures inherent in the English language. Not only is the language model of sentence structure that can be applied to English significantly different from, for example, the structure of Korean, but the sounds used in the two spoken languages do not have a one-to-one correlation. For example, in the Korean language (Hangul), numbers from 0 to 99 use Korean phonemes. However, for numbers greater than 99, a mixture of Chinese and Korean is generally used. Similarly, the question:

"Do you speak English?"

is structured in German as:

"Speak you English?"

with the verb at the beginning of the question.

Every language, especially English, has similar nuances, and these must be represented in the language model used by a VEI system. The result is that it's not a simple question of remapping sounds to create a new VEI in another language. For voice recognition and synthesis to serve as a global interface to cell phones, the voice recognition software developers will have to develop recognition and synthesis technologies optimized for dozens of different languages and their regional variations as well.

The language models used in voice recognition engines are domain and user specific. That is, a language model for recognizing questions about directions to specific places on a map is different from one that supports questions about the stock market. Similarly, most subscribers have stereotypical ways of asking questions, and use phrases that are peculiar to their peer group. An engineer might reasonably be expected to use different words and phrases when interacting with an inventory system compared to, for example, an attorney. Similarly, a subscriber in the Midwest may have a vernacular that is considerably different from that of a subscriber native to the South.

In speech synthesis systems, the challenge is in creating more naturally sounding speech with context-appropriate emphasis on the proper words. As in speech recognition, the appropriate sounds can be generated when there is sufficient information on the working context as well as the nature of the listener.

Voice Portals

The most promising application of VEI technology to cellular communications is in creating Voice Portals. As noted earlier, the motivation behind Voice Portals is to use voice recognition and synthesis to obviate the limitations of interacting with the Web through a visually limited interface of a Web-enabled cell phone. Instead of entering a URL, subscribers dial a phone number. Using voice commands, subscribers select from a list of features, just as they would use a typical voice mail system. After selecting a topic or working context using voice commands, subscribers can request specific information. The system then performs the appropriate search and reads the results back to the subscriber using voice synthesis. In other words, a Voice Portal represents the marriage of VEI technology with a search engine and connectivity to the Web. It's also important to note that VEI technology can be used in multimodal interfaces in which voice recognition is used for input. Text information, with or without synthesized speech, is provided as output, just as most voice recognition systems are used on PCs.

To explore how a Voice Portal might operate in a typical business setting, assume that the subscriber is a businesswoman en route to Boston's Logan airport, and that the time is 7:05 P.M., and the date is Oct 7. From the back seat of the cab, she dials the airport's automated reservation system with her cell phone and, when the automated operator answers, she asks:

"When is the next flight to Dallas?"

At this point, she has established a communications link between her phone and the cell, from the local cell to the MTSO, which provides connectivity to the public phone network and to the airline reservation system's VEI Service. Continuing with the process within the VEI Service, her voice query is first cleaned and filtered by the Signals Preprocessor to remove road noise picked up from the cab and other potentially interfering signals. Next, the Speech Recognition (SR) Engine handles her query, in audio form.

The SR Engine first attempts to map each of her spoken words to sound definitions in its library. For example, the top four matches for her spoken "Dallas" might be "Dulles," "Dallas," "Denver," and "Denmark," in that order. In other words, the Phonetic Matcher assigns certainty factor to each word it processes, and, in the example, (incorrectly) assigns the greatest certainty to "Dulles" because "Dulles" sounds closest to the businesswoman's spoken "Dallas" (see Figure 6-1). Early voice recognition systems stopped here, and often confused similarly sounding words, such as "hat" for "cat" or "hot" for "cot." However, as this case illustrates, voice recognition systems based on simple phonetic matching—especially those with vocabularies of more than a few dozen words—provide recognition accuracies only in the range of 60 to 70 percent. This level of accuracy is not acceptable to most business travelers.

Voice recognition systems with active vocabularies of only a dozen words or so can provide nearly perfect recognition, even with noisy environments and speakers with pronounced accents. If the only single-syllable word in the vocabulary is "cat," then the possibility of other, similar sounding words being recognized as "hat" is very small.

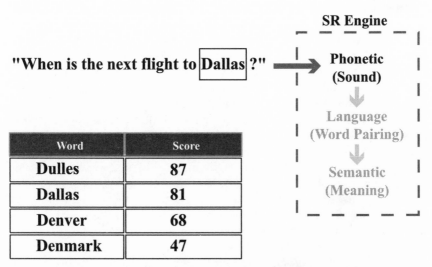

Figure 6-1. The Phonetic Matcher component of a speech recognition engine assigns a certainty factor or probability to each of the words in its vocabulary that matches a spoken word. In this example, "Dulles" has the closest match to the spoken word "Dallas," based solely on the similarity of their audio waveforms.

The next phase of processing within a modern SR Engine uses a Language Model that examines probabilities of word pairs (in some systems, word triads, or three-word sequences are examined). In this example, the Language Model in Figure 6-2, which is specific to flight reservations but generic to all subscribers, assigns a greater likelihood to the word pair "next flight" than to a similarly sounding word pair, such as "best flight." The Language Model is critical in situations where the Phonetic Matcher assigns a greater score to less likely word sequences, such as "next night" or "best night." In other words, the Language Model can override a match suggested by the Phonetic Matcher if the differences in the scores involved are great enough.

At the level of phonetic matching, recognition accuracies on the order of 80 to 90 percent are usually possible, which translates to roughly one or two recognition errors per 10 words, which may be acceptable in some situations. Even so, there are techniques, such as training, that can be used to increase the recognition accuracy by a few percentage points especially if there is a large working vocabulary of several hundred words. In this example, the processing in the Phonetic Matcher and Language Model has been based on *generic* subscriber data. That is, the pronunciations used by the Phonetic Matcher represent the average of pronunciations from male, female, young, old, southern, northern, and western speakers. Similarly, the Language Model is generic, in that it doesn't represent how a particular subscriber tends to speak. For increased accuracy, the Speech Recognition needs to be trained to recognize

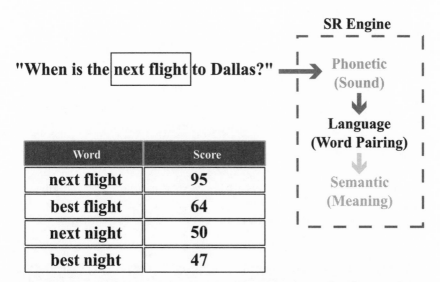

Word	Score
next flight	95
best flight	64
next night	50
best night	47

Figure 6-2. The Language Model component of a speech recognition engine assigns a probability to word pairs in order to increase the accuracy of recognition. In this example, in the context of a travel reservation system, the word pair "next night" has a greater probability than "best night."

the exact pronunciations of the businesswoman, and to have the Language Model represent probabilities of word pairs in her speech patterns.

The last phase in this simplified view of the SR Engine, Semantic Processing, attempts to determine the semantics or meanings of the words recognized thus far, for the purpose of using the text as a basis for computer operations. For example, "Dallas" is recognized as a place or destination, and "next flight" is recognized as a time constraint. These and similar determinations are sent to the Text Formatter, which presents a Query Generator with information in a format that can be used to generate a search statement to the Search Engine.

Assuming that the Speech Recognition Engine is 100 percent accurate, "When is the next flight to Dallas" eventually becomes transformed into a machine-readable query that looks something like:

```
Select *.* from flight_table where
departure = "Boston" and
destination = "Dallas" and
date >= "Oct 7" and
time >= "7:05 pm"
```

where "flight_table" is a table of flight information that is maintained in the reservation system's database, and the departure, destination, date, and time constraints are applied to the search. Assuming everything works perfectly, the Search Engine produces a result something like:

```
Delta #756
Dallas
October 7
7:05 pm
```

The Results Formatter of the VEI Service rearranges the output into rough linear text:

```
"October 7, Dallas, 7:05 pm, Delta #756"
```

and the Sentence Generator creates a less cryptic and more user friendly:

```
"The next flight to Dallas is at 8:00 pm tonight on
Delta #756"
```

which is presented to the Speech Synthesizer. The synthesizer creates the human-like speech equivalent of the Sentence Generator's output, and this speech is sent back through the public telephone system to the cell and then to the businesswoman's cell phone. Alternatively, or in addition to the synthetic speech, the textual information could be sent to the businesswoman's cell phone.

Note that this is a very simplified discussion of the complex information handling and processing technologies that make Voice Portals possible. For example, not considered is the communication of the businesswoman's location from the cell to the MTSO for processing by the automated reservation system, or the automated answering system that greets her after she connects to the system initially. In addition, the potential for providing text along with synthesized speech output isn't discussed. Assuming the cell phone is capable of displaying several lines of text, then it could capture the information, creating a record that could be stored by the subscriber for later reference. This type of multimodal interface is especially helpful when there isn't a piece of paper around to transcribe the information provided through synthetic speech, for example.

The challenge in creating a workable Voice Portal, from an interface design perspective, is that of providing enough choices while not overwhelming the subscriber, and of organizing the content so that sophisticated subscribers can bypass lists and go directly to what they want. One of the main limitations of Voice Portals is that the data is presented sequentially, and the amount of information (such as the contents of a menu of choices) that can be remembered is limited by the subscriber's short-term memory. Most people have trouble remembering lists offering over seven or eight choices, especially if they're hearing the choices for the first time. It's like going to a restaurant and listening to the list of specials. Most diners ask the waiter to repeat the choices at least once. As noted above, the addition of a text output option, as part of a voice-enabled multimodal user interface environment can circumvent the memory problem by presenting long lists as scrollable text. This option can be offered either in parallel with synthesized speech or instead of speech. In a parallel system, subscribers have the option of ignoring the text, but have it as a backup if they forget or don't hear an item from a list because of external noise or because of their short-term memory limitations.

As in a voice mail system, once users know the extension of the party they're trying to reach, they should be able to bypass all of the introductory information put there to orient a first-time or infrequent visitor to the service. Another challenge in creating Voice Portals is providing the level of personalization that subscribers are accustomed to on the wired Web. If the subscriber isn't interested in sports, for example, then he shouldn't have to endure listening to sports options in the future.

Although significant attention is being given to the theoretical accuracy of voice recognition systems, the adequacy of recognition is really a practical issue. For example, for someone desperately in search of information about an order, a voice recognition system with 95 percent accuracy seems like perfection compared to the alternative—a message that says please call back in the morning.

The prognosis for the eventual success of Voice Portals as a means of accessing the wireless Web is excellent, as exemplified by the early offerings in this field. For example, first-generation Voice Portals provide stock quotes, traffic updates, movie listings, news headlines, and weather using a combination of digitally prerecorded messages and synthesized speech.

The problem with the first-generation Voice Portals is that the recognition and synthesis processes are imperfect. Recognition accuracies hover around 90 to 95 percent, and the synthetic speech doesn't sound quite human, even when the intonations are correct. Wireless communications require a high degree of accuracy from the voice recognition component of Voice Portals. All else being equal, a wired phone system will provide better quality audio for voice recognition processing than will a wireless phone. Predominantly wired communications systems, in general, provide lower noise levels than do systems that rely primarily on wireless communications.

A more complex issue for voice recognition developers is how to efficiently and affordably create language models for the wide variety of contexts for which Voice Portals are likely to be used. Creating a language model can be a costly, time-intensive endeavor that depends foremost on acquiring samples of in-context speech that can be analyzed for patterns. In medicine, for example, extensive language models for voice recognition systems must be developed for each specialty—that is, separate models for Radiology, Cardiology, and Internal Medicine, for example—in order to create systems that provide reasonable recognition accuracy. This degree of specialization isn't surprising, given that, just as with human operators, when the context is known, it's easier for the operator to understand the meaning of otherwise ambiguous questions.

To appreciate the significance of the language model, consider, for example, the potential ambiguities in the question:

"Who is on *first?*"

Assuming a sports context, specifically one pertaining to baseball, "first" would probably be equated to "first base." Thus, a sports language model would translate the query into:

"Who is on *first base?*"

However, a language model for a medical scheduling system would categorize "first" as synonymous with "first call," or:

"Who is *taking first call?*"

where "Who" refers to the physician to be called at night in the event of a medical emergency.

PORTABLE POWER

More than any other factor, battery size and capacity limit handheld wireless device form, function, and affordability. For example, even though the Palm VII wireless handheld computer relies on a communications infrastructure capable of always-on connectivity, the designers decided not to implement that feature. In exchange for requiring subscribers to actively request information updates, the Palm boasts a battery life measured in days. In exchange for this battery life, customers have to log in each time they want an update on the weather or stock prices, or to check if they have email.

In contrast, the OmniSky wireless modem, designed for the Palm V series, provides excellent always-on connectivity, but the battery life is only about six hours. Furthermore, the Palm VII is designed to use the bulkier AAA batteries, compared to the thin, internal battery pack used in the OmniSky. As a result, a Palm VII user can usually find replacement batteries anywhere in the world. However, the OmniSky user has to remember to carry the special charger with him, and he's not going to find emergency replacement batteries at his corner convenience store.

There is nothing innately inferior about using an encapsulated battery for power, other than being unable to buy a replacement on short notice. For example, RIM's Blackberry 957 wireless PDA/pager, which uses a built-in rechargeable lithium ion battery, boasts a typical battery life of several weeks. Blackberry, which uses the same wireless network as the Palm VII, provides always-on connectivity, notifying the user of new mail or alerts keyed to events such as changes in stock price. RIM solved the problem of short battery life in part by using creativity in their engineering. The Blackberry's holster has a magnet that switches the LCD off when the Blackberry unit is placed in it.

The battery accounts for at least half of the weight and often up to a quarter of the cost and volume of a typical handheld cellular phone. Despite all of the advertisements with pink bunnies marching forever because of improved battery designs, battery technology has lagged far behind advances in computer technology. While computers are following Moore's law, doubling the transistor density on a chip every 18 months, the improvements in basic battery chemistries are advancing at single-digit rates.

As in the case of computer chips, because batteries are normally hidden from view, advances in battery technology aren't always readily apparent. What is obvious are the results of the technology, in terms of cost, size, weight, power output, and battery life. Of course, with added size and weight come increased reliability and greater output capacity.

Because factors such as battery life can make or break a product, the challenge presented to a wireless device developer is selecting a battery design that minimizes size, weight, and cost while maximizing output capacity. An early draw for the Palm Pilot, for example, was its ability to work for a month on two AAA alkaline batteries, especially for users accustomed to one hour of battery life from their laptop. Similarly, one of the attractions of RIM's Blackberry wireless PDA—in addition to the stylish design that includes a hidden antenna—is a three- to four-week battery life from a single two-hour charge. One of the battery-saving design elements of the Bluetooth standard is that Bluetooth devices go into a power-saving sleep mode when there's nothing to communicate.

The most popular chemistries used in rechargeable batteries (although a battery is a collection of electrochemical storage cells, the terms *battery* and *cell* are often incorrectly used interchangeably) for cell phones are nickel cadmium, lithium ion, and nickel metal hydride. Each chemistry is associated with a certain energy density, maximum recharge rate, peak discharge current (for transmit operations), charge retention, and cost.

The cost of a battery includes not only the initial purchase price but also the operating cost amortized over the life of the battery, which may include hundreds of discharge-recharge cycles. Nickel cadmium batteries can be recharged more times than nickel metal hydride or lithium ion batteries before failure, for example. Energy density is important in providing the greatest amount of energy in the smallest volume possible, which directly affects form and mobility. A high maximum recharge rate is important when the subscriber has only a few minutes to recharge the phone between meetings or before a flight. Most cell phone batteries can be recharged in less than two hours. A high peak discharge current is crucial to support short, high-intensity current requirements, such as when a cellular phone or wireless PDA is in transmit mode. Charge retention is a measure of the self-discharge rate of a battery. A battery with low charge retention has to be recharged frequently even if it hasn't been used. Lithium ion and nickel metal hydride batteries have better charge retention than nickel cadmium batteries.

Because battery chemistries have such different characteristics, batteries can be combined to provide characteristics that would be impossible or too expensive with a single battery type. For example, RIM's 950 two-way pocket pager/PDA uses two batteries—an internal, rechargeable lithium ion battery and a disposable AA battery. The AA battery, which has a low peak discharge rate, supports the low-current receive mode. The lithium ion battery, which has a high peak discharge rate, is used for powering the transmitter for sending email messages.

In general, lithium ion batteries are lighter than nickel cadmium or nickel metal hydride batteries, and also provide greater energy density than either of these two popular chemistries. Nickel cadmium batteries tend to be less expensive than either lithium ion or nickel metal hydride batteries. Not only do nickel cadmium batteries have a lower initial price but they can also be discharged and recharged hundreds of time with minimal loss in capacity. A typical lithium ion battery used in a cell phone can be recharged perhaps 300 times, compared to about 500 for a comparable nickel metal hydride battery or 600 times for a nickel cadmium battery. Batteries based on nickel cadmium chemistries can exhibit a memory effect in which they prematurely fail to deliver current even though a partial charge remains.

Lithium polymer batteries, which rely on a solid plastic electrolyte instead of a liquid like that used in lithium ion units, can be very thin and light and shaped or molded to fit virtually any handheld cellular device. Lithium polymer batteries offer performance similar to lithium ion batteries, but at a lighter weight and greater cost. In general, batteries based on lithium chemistries provide the best shelf life, capacity, energy density, and discharge characteristics of any battery type. However, lithium is relatively unstable. Lithium is volatile in the presence of water, and because lithium is toxic to the environment, federal regulations limit the amount that can be contained in a battery. Like the battery chemistries popular in the 1980s that used mercury to extend battery life, discarded lithium batteries poison the environment.

Although new materials, such as lithium polymer and enhanced titanium are being used to extend battery life a few minutes, the most promising technologies on the horizon make use of old materials in a new way. For example, fuel cells that make electricity by mixing oxygen and hydrogen using a process invented in the mid-1800s, are being repackaged in a way that may make the technology economically viable. These zinc-air batteries are being marketed as environmentally friendly, high-energy–density disposable batteries that cost about one-sixth as much as a comparable rechargeable lithium ion battery. Zinc-air batteries are relatively free of the heavy metals found in lithium ion and nickel metal hydride batteries.

The demand for increased energy densities and lower profile cases has been a motivation behind the popularity of encapsulated battery pack designs found in virtually every cell phone and in many wireless PDAs. Encapsulated battery packs are extremely compact, available in a variety of interchangeable sizes and capacities, and are relatively impervious to shock, vibration, moisture, and other environmental factors. In addition to providing for mechanical stability, encapsulation reduces the number of terminals exposed to possible corrosion. The downside, as noted earlier with the OmniSky modem, is that emergency power can be impossible to find if a battery pack fails or a businesswoman forgets to take the charger with her on a long business trip.

Another promising approach is to advance battery technology indirectly by focusing on the battery's controlling circuitry. These so-called smart batteries use embedded microprocessor chips to control their charge and discharge rates, thereby extending battery life. This technology has been applied successfully in laptop computer battery designs.

SECURITY AND PRIVACY TECHNOLOGIES

Before grocery store clerks can be expected to habitually ask customers "cash, check, or cellular?" the issues of wireless security and privacy must be addressed. Analog cellular—the most common wireless phone technology in the United States—is plagued with security holes. Since analog cellular signals occupy a fixed frequency, anyone with a modified UHF receiver or scanner can hear and record entire conversations. Like the human-operated radio links of the 1970s and 1980s, literally hundreds of people could be listening to a subscriber's conversations, including eCommerce transactions where credit card and other personal information is exchanged. In addition, the serial number used by analog cellular phones for subscriber authentication can be recorded as well, allowing someone to steal air time by using the purloined number. Because cellular serial number theft isn't normally noticed until the subscriber's bill arrives at the end of the month, a thief can use a number for weeks with impunity, and then switch to the new serial number, thereby avoiding detection.

One of the advantages of digital cellular over the older analog technology is improved security. Instead of using a single, nonvarying frequency, digital cellular relies on encoded spread spectrum signals that are much more difficult to intercept and decode. Even so, with the right equipment, digital cellular signals can be intercepted and their contents examined. Digital cellular does provide a higher level of deterrence, however. Instead of a $500 receiver and a laptop that could be used to monitor analog cellular, a $5000 receiver and a laptop are required to interrupt and decode digital cellular. While this added expense excludes most casual busybodies from digital cellular conversations, the added cost to private investigators and corporate spies may be insignificant.

Security issues aren't limited to mobile wireless technology. Fixed wireless networks represent a major security risk as well. On the wired Web, Secure Socket Layer (SSL) is the dominant security protocol for monetary transactions and communications. Information being transmitted is encrypted, and only when the user's Web browser and the computer server on the other end that is running the Web site have the same key can they communicate. Both Netscape and Internet Explorer and most wired Web sites that accept charge card information over the Internet support SSL. It's important to note that SSL is wedded to the client-server architecture of the current wired Web.

Anyone with a laptop equipped with an inexpensive wireless modem can potentially access a commercial or private wireless LAN without ever setting foot on private property. Unless a wireless network has been properly configured with the appropriate security software, a hacker can drive into a company's parking lot, log on to the company's wireless LAN, and, within less than 20 minutes, download the contents of the entire server. If the hacker has malicious intents, he could either erase the server's hard drive or modify critical information, and then install a virus on the server. Either way, the company is effectively shut down, at least as far as fixed wireless communication is concerned.

The solution to providing adequate security isn't to abandon wireless network technology, but to develop the technologies necessary to provide reasonable security. To this end, the security technologies that have been developed applicable to the wireless Web include a variety of password protection schemes, supplemented with biometric security technologies, antivirus utilities for PDAs and Web-enabled cell phones, and encryption technologies for handhelds. A promising approach entails keeping wireless devices separate from personal identifying data stored on special smart cards.

Antiviral Utilities

The world's first cell phone virus, Timofonica, surfaced in June of 2000. The worm virus, written to infect phones on Timofonica, Spain's largest wireless network, sends email to everyone in the subscriber's Microsoft Outlook address book. It also sends short text messages to random Telefonica phone numbers, spamming the network. Fortunately for subscribers, the virus was stopped before it had a chance to propagate through the telephone network. The first virus to hit PDAs, a Palm-specific virus called Phage, made its debut only three months later, in September of 2000. Although Phage is relatively innocuous as viruses go, it is proof that viruses can in fact attack handheld devices.

In anticipation of the inevitable wave of virus attacks on wireless handheld devices, a number of companies have developed antivirus utilities designed specifically for wireless PDAs. Until wireless devices have sufficient memory and bandwidth connectivity to the Web, the main threat from a virus is to use a handheld wireless device as a carrier. In other words, a handheld wireless device can become infected with email attachments and files that don't damage the device, but are passed along to a PC and the network to which it is connected when the device is synced. Following this line of reasoning, McAfee offers a product, VirusScan Wireless, that is designed to keep Palm OS, PocketPC, Windows CE, and Symbian EPOC handheld devices from transmitting viruses while they are being synchronized with a desktop system. That is, their product executes on the desktop, assuming wireless devices won't be downloading applications through slow-speed wireless connections.

Eventually, however, bandwidth limitations will be relaxed, and wireless PDA owners can be expected to operate free from the tethers of a syncing station. Web-enabled cell phones, for example, aren't designed to periodically sync with a desktop PC. Recognizing that it's possible (or at least the possibility presents a challenge and a degree of notoriety) for a programmer to develop viruses that can propagate in the small amount of RAM and local processing available on G2 cell phones, most antivirus utility vendors are at least appealing to subscribers' sense of uncertainty by offering utilities that execute on their handhelds, not on the desktop. Examples of first-generation products introduced for wireless-Web–enabled

PDAs and cell phones are InoculateIT for Windows CE devices by Computer Associates, F-SecureCorp's Anti-Virus for EPOC for devices compatible with the Symbian EPOC standard, and a Palm-only antivirus utility from Symantec Corp.

Biometrics

Simple password protection schemes have several major security holes. Since passwords are frequently lost or forgotten, many wired Web users pick a password that they can easily remember: the phone number of a friend or the name of one of their children, for example. Even when network operators require passwords to take the form of a "nonsensical" mix of digits and letters, passwords are usually easily guessed. Birthdays fit the alphanumeric mix requirement, for example. For wireless Web users, the problem with password schemes is that it's a hassle to remember and then enter, with a keypad or stylus, yet another personal identification number. The advantage of a wireless device's instant gratification can be negated by a tortuous security interface.

One approach that is being developed to speed and simplify user authentication for wireless device subscribers is to rely on biometrics, or individual-specific characteristics that can either be recognized by the wireless device or the network to which it is connected. A variety of biometric technologies, including fingerprint, face, voice, retinal, and even DNA pattern recognition are in various stages of development. All of these technologies have been used with some success on desktop PCs, especially fingerprint recognition, which is inexpensive and, for most information, secure and reliable. Fingerprint recognition works by comparing whirls and swirls of a user's fingerprint to the patterns stored in memory. The two technologies used in fingerprint recognition are *optical* and *capacitive*. Optical recognition takes a photograph of the fingerprint, whereas capacitive fingerprint recognition indirectly measures the thin layer of saline fluid that resides between the living and dead skin on a user's fingertip. Optical recognition has a smaller form factor, meaning that it can be more easily used with handheld devices. However, optical fingerprint recognition doesn't work well if the user has changes in his or her skin condition, such as dirt or scarring.

Regardless of which type of recognition technology is employed, a user with the same or very similar fingerprint causes the equivalent of a password to be generated by the wireless device, which authenticates the subscriber to the network. Authentication—proving that people are who they say they are—is virtually impossible with password-only schemes, since a password can be stolen. In operation, fingerprint recognition is unobtrusive and quick. The user simply places a finger on a transparent plate and the image capture hardware on the other side of the plate takes a digital photograph of patterns on the fingertip. Validating a cell-phone charge with a fingerprint seems natural, since the device is already in the subscriber's hands. A number of manufacturers, such as SONY and Motorola, offer optical fingerprint identification units that can be used with wireless laptop computer systems.

The challenge with wireless devices is to provide the components required for biometric identification in a small form factor and without compromising functionality or battery life. Given these constraints, the biometric technology most likely to be applied to Web-enabled cell phones will rely on some form of image recognition. Since live video capture and transmission is viewed as one of the "killer apps" of G3 cell phones, these phones with high-bandwidth connections to the Web will have image capture capabilities built in, and these sensors should be able to serve a dual function of fingerprint recognition.

Encryption

Encryption is the use of a key or code to generate a seemingly unintelligible message that can only be deciphered by someone with knowledge of the key and the algorithm used to scramble the original message. Thanks to practical needs of governments and the military at times of war, encryption is one of the oldest information technologies, dating back thousands of years. The two basic types of encryption, *symmetric* and *asymmetric*, are described below.

Symmetric Encryption. Most encryption technologies are symmetric, in that either the encryption and decryption keys are identical, or one key is derived from the other. For example, a simple rotational encryption scheme adds or subtracts a value for every character in a message. To illustrate the technologies involved in encryption, assume that a sender wants to send the message:

THEWIRELESSWEB

Using a simple rotational scheme, each letter of the message is replaced with a letter that is 7 places later in the alphabet. Since there are 26 letters in the alphabet, the process starts over at 26. In other words, "Z," the 26th letter, becomes "G," the 7th letter of the alphabet. Mathematically, this symmetrical encoding scheme is represented as:

$$\text{Encoded} = [\text{Original} + 7] \bmod 26$$

where mod stands for modulo, the remainder after division by 26.

Using this method, which lends itself to the decoder rings that are occasionally offered in cereal boxes, the original message becomes:

AOLDPYLSLZZDLI

As long as the recipient knows the encoding algorithm and the key (in this case 7), she can quickly and easily decrypt the message. In this example, a decoder ring, like the mathematical relationship between encoding and decoding, is bidirectional. This simple letter substitution scheme is quick and relatively easy to set up. However, it also provides only a modicum of security against a hacker. Because the mod operator in this example limits the encoded letter to a value of between 1 and 26, there are only 25 possible keys.

A more secure symmetrical encryption approach, and one used by most governments and corporations to send secure communications over the Internet or other networks, is to use a multidigit key, such as 7-14-2-12.

Mathematically, the encoding scheme is represented as:

$$\text{Encoded}_1 = [\text{Original}_1 + 7] \bmod 26$$
$$\text{Encoded}_2 = [\text{Original}_2 + 14] \bmod 26$$
$$\text{Encoded}_3 = [\text{Original}_3 + 2] \bmod 26$$
$$\text{Encoded}_4 = [\text{Original}_4 + 12] \bmod 26$$

In this example, the key is fixed-length, with the encoding pattern repeating every fifth character. With the input of:

THEWIRELESSWEB

Using the multidigit key 7-14-2-12, the encrypted message would read:

AVGIPFGXLGUILP

Sequential rotational encryption can be visualized through the use of multiple decoder/encoder rings. Note in these examples that encoding is performed by adding values, but they can be subtracted as well. That is, the encoding-decoding relationship can be reversed.

The greater the key length, measured in bits, the more complicated and time consuming the cracking process will be. The possible number of keys of a particular length is 2 to the power of the key length. For example, there are 2^8 or 256 possible eight-bit keys. The most common symmetric encryption algorithm is the 56-bit Digital Encryption Standard (2^{56} = 72,057,594,037,927,936). Because of national security, the largest exportable key length is 40 bits, which provides for over 1 trillion possible 40-bit keys.

Many current multidigit encryption schemes use a key size up to 128 bits, making decryption resource intensive for unauthorized recipients of encrypted messages. The current standard for data encryption used by the U.S. government, established in 2000 through the U.S. National Institute of Standard's Advanced Encryption Standard effort, is based on a variable-length key size of up to 256 bits.

However, there are schemes that undermine the security of even longer, variable length encoding sequences. For example, certain characters (such as "E") appear more often than others (such as "Q") in text, and these relative frequencies can be used to crack the encoding scheme. This type of attack works best with longer text messages, but won't help someone trying to crack numerical data. In some instances, the easiest way to break a code is to simply steal the key from the intended recipients by snooping around their hard drive or intercepting their email.

Even when the encryption technologies work flawlessly, there are practical, process-oriented challenges associated with using symmetric encoding schemes. The most significant challenges are the need to exchange keys, poor scaling, and the difficulties of establishing secure communications with heretofore unknown parties. Symmetric encoding requires that the sender and intended receiver first communicate, through some secure mechanism, the keys they intend to use for encryption and decryption. In other words, the parties have to establish some secure communications channel first so that they can have secure communications later. This need to exchange keys can be a major problem, especially when the sender and recipient are geographically distant and there is a need to change keys periodically. The courier wearing a trench coat and carrying the key in an aluminum Zero briefcase is one approach, but this mechanism is inconvenient and expensive.

The scaling issue becomes apparent when there is more than one pair of individuals exchanging information. If a company has 2000 employees, each accessing the corporate network from mobile phones and wireless PDAs, then someone in the company has to maintain a database of 2000 keys, one pair for each employee. Providing each employee with the same key wouldn't do—that would allow employees to decrypt messages intended for other employees. In addition, if secure employee-to-employee communications are supported through the company email system, then each pair of potential contacts requires a separate pair of keys, and each of these keys has to be maintained and stored by the individual employees.

This is a typical *n-squared* problem, in that a company with n users requires up to $n^2/2$ unique keys, including the key each employee holds for himself so that he can encrypt confidential data for his own use. For 2000 employees ($n = 2000$) this translates to:

$$\text{Unique Keys} = n^2/2$$
$$= 2000^2/2$$
$$= 2,000,0000$$

In other words, in order to provide 2000 employees with secure interpersonal communications requires a key management system with up to 2,000,000 unique keys.

Systems with large numbers of users also present major challenges because it's difficult for someone to keep track of all of the people involved, much less their keys. In a large organization, or one that does business with a large number of outside parties (an online brokerage house with thousands of wireless accounts, for example) there is frequently the need to establish secure communications with heretofore-unknown parties. Again, some secure method of information exchange has to initiate the process. Several online trading services simply use the mail to send a key or password to subscribers, while others use unencrypted email. One problem with these methods is employees or subscribers who pose as the intended recipient in order to obtain confidential information. Obviously, the method used to initiate secure communications depends on the nature of the communications, and the value of the information at risk.

Asymmetric Encryption. In addition to symmetric operations, encryption can also be based on an asymmetric approach, in which the password is different for encryption and decryption. The most common form of asymmetric encryption, developed by Whitfield Diffie and Martin Helman, is Public Key Encryption. While this is the most widely used system for encryption on the Internet, there are technologies especially suited to the wireless Web, such as Elliptic Curve Cryptography, as well as technologies that may prove equally valuable in the future, such as Quantum Cryptography.

Public Key Encryption. A prominent technology that has been applied to the challenge of distributing keys to wired and wireless Web users is Public Key Encryption (PKE). This technology, which is best known as the ubiquitous RSA security that provides the backbone of the security protection for most eCommerce, is based on a pair of keys generated by a single algorithm. One key is public, known or at least knowable to everyone, and one key is private, known only to the sender. The private key, which is never shared with recipients or transmitted, is used to decrypt information that's been encrypted by someone using the public key. In other words, encoding is done using a generally available public key and decoding is done using a private key available only to the intended recipient. Using a physical padlock as a comparison, PKE is equivalent to requiring one key to lock a padlock and another key to open it. The actual encoding and decoding can use a variety of schemes, such as the symmetrical rotational encryption described earlier.

In the PKE technique, each person has both a public key and a private key. Someone sending a message to a recipient uses an algorithm that creates a "session" key from the recipient's public key. The session key is the key value specific to a given message from a particular sender to a particular recipient. The session key for another message to a different recipient would likely be different, because it is a function of the recipient's public key. Only the recipient can decode the message, using her private key. The public key, as well as the session key, is generated from the private key. The recipient calculates the session key using his private and public keys, which is equal to the sender's session key.

That is, the session key is the same value for a particular pair of senders and recipients, even though they are calculated using different formulas.

With knowledge of the public key and the session key, it's possible for anyone to calculate the private key. However, the solution to the mathematical relationship between the public and session keys is an exponential function of large prime numbers (a prime number is a whole number, such as 7 or 37, that can only be divided without a remainder by itself and 1).

For the mathematically curious, the relationship between the session, public, and private keys takes the general form:

$$\text{Session Key} = \text{Public Key}^x \bmod n$$

where x is unknown and n is a very large prime number. As a result, it is extremely time consuming to attempt to solve for the session key, even on the fastest mainframe computers.

The greatest significance of PKE in the wireless Web is its use in establishing a Public Key Infrastructure (PKI), which is minimally a pervasive security infrastructure implemented and delivered using public-key technologies. One purpose of a PKI is to provide a mechanism to verify that specific public and private keys belong to a particular subscriber. This certification is issued by a Certification Authority (CA), such as a cellular provider or online trading service, which verifies identities and associates these identities with private and public keys. In other words, a certificate binds a public key to the name of the entity that holds the corresponding private key. Of note is that the patent on RSA encryption expired in September 2000, paving the way for lower-cost, even more widespread use of this industry-standard security technology.

Certification Authority services are an essential component of any PKI system because they are the entities that directly issue, renew, and revoke certificates. Without a CA infrastructure to manage certificates and provide seamless authentication, the entire PKE process would be unwieldy and impractical for most businesses. It's important to note that, unlike SSL, which is wedded to client-server architecture and sessions, PKI can be used with a variety of alternative architectures.

Elliptic Curve Cryptography (ECC). ECC is a digital signature system that provides the same functionality as RSA, but does so more efficiently. With ECC, it is possible to create a stronger cryptography system using a shorter key size. Since performing computational operations on the smaller key is more efficient, ECC is more suited for a computationally constrained platform, such as a cell phone or wireless PDA. For example, whereas the processing of a digitally signed transaction might take up to half a minute on a Palm device using RSA, an application using ECC would likely take a little more than a second.

Quantum Cryptography. One of the most promising asymmetric encryption technologies is Quantum Cryptography, which is based on quantum mechanics. This branch of theoretical physics explains the behavior of subatomic particles in terms of energy states and the wavelike properties of matter. Quantum Cryptography relies on a quantum entanglement process employing pairs of "entangled" photons that can generate a completely random sequence of 0s and 1s distributed exclusively to two users at remote locations. This random sequence of digits serves as the key that can be used to scramble the message into an apparently random sequence of letters. The power of Quantum Cryptography is that any attempt by an eavesdropper to intercept the sequence alters the message in a detectable way, alerting the recipient that the communications channel has been compromised.

WIM Cards

In practice, it isn't reasonable for subscribers to use their Captain Marvel decoder rings to encrypt the email they send over wireless PDAs or cell phones. A more practical, user-friendly approach is to issue a smart card to subscribers with all of their authentication information stored in machine-readable form. Smart cards, in the form of credit card-size devices containing a microprocessor chip, have been in use in Europe since the mid-1970s. In comparison, smart cards have had limited success in the United States, with several failed attempts in the health care industry. A more recent attempt, the American Express Blue Card, first released in 1999, is a smart card designed to be used with a personal card reader that connects to a PC. Merchants never get an account number, but do receive an authorization code. The customer's credit card number never appears in the company's database, and is therefore secure from hackers. PC-based card readers proved too cumbersome for casual users who want to infrequently purchase small-ticket items through the Web.

In Europe, smart cards, called WIMs (Wireless Identity Modules) use Public Key Encryption technology to address the greatest security threat for wireless devices: theft and loss. Some GSM-compatible handsets have a slot to fit the credit-card size WIM card, rendering the phone useless without the card. Subscriber data stored on the card is used rather than the telephone internal serial number. Each WIM card contains a microchip that stores an algorithm that encrypts voice and data transmission and identifies the subscriber to the mobile network as an authentic caller. The widespread knowledge that stealing a cell phone without the corresponding WIM card leaves the phone numberless and without a serial number is a deterrent to theft. This protection assumes that the WIM cards are stored separately from the wireless device. WIM cards using PKI are compatible with cell phones using WAP 1.2, and are also equipped with internal SIMs (Subscriber Identification Modules).

SIMs are fingernail-size cards that contain information the service provider uses to identify the phone and register it on the network as a native device. By changing SIMs on a GSM phone, it's possible to use a single phone for both the United States and Europe without paying roaming charges in either region.

The disadvantage of this approach is the hassle of having to open the back of a phone and swap the SIM, which can be damaged or lost in the process.

The Bottom Line

When it comes to security and privacy technology, there are no perfect solutions. Antiviral programs have been around for decades, mainly because new virus technologies are being developed every day. As soon as someone learns how to detect and disable a virus, it seems that there is another virus introduced over the Internet. Similarly, even the best biometric security system can be defeated by someone with enough motivation. For example, it's possible to follow someone to a restaurant and secure the wineglass she used and obtain a copy of her fingerprints. Printed on a suitable film, the image of the fingerprint can be used to fool a fingerprint detection device. Finally, even the best encryption technologies can be cracked, given enough time. Fortunately, time is usually the issue because a message that is two or three weeks old may have no practical value to the eavesdropper. For most subscribers, the technologies available today and on the horizon provide enough of a deterrent to discourage hackers and corporate spies.

WIRELESS WONDERS WRAP-UP

This chapter ends Part 2, "Wireless Wonders," which discussed the more technical aspect of the Wireless Web. The technologic high points are the developments in the areas of wireless and wired infrastructures, and the use of new device technologies, from voice recognition to new battery technologies that will support the increasingly large power requirements. The trajectory of communications technologies suggests that there are certain must-have technologies that will be crucial in developing next-generation wireless Web interfaces, which may be device dependent. For example, cellular phones will benefit from speech recognition and synthesis, at least as far as accessing Web content is concerned. For person-to-person communications, it's likely that live video or still image transfer will be the killer application of the future. Technologic advances in the areas of image capture and display technologies, such as Light Emitting Polymer (LEP) screens that consume less power than LCD screens and don't require backlighting, will certainly impact this capability.

In the area of image display, larger color displays are forecasted for cellular phones. Heads-up displays, which are head-mounted virtual screens, have yet to prove practical, especially for mobile and otherwise moving users. Advances in display chips, especially in the area of high density, low power, color displays, will probably impact wireless PDAs more than cell phones.

In the area of image capture, the technologic challenges include supporting the required resolution and frames per second through new lens designs, compression algorithms, image storage technologies, while keeping power requirements within reasonable limits. In addition to supporting person-to-person communications, imaging technology will make other technologies, such as fingerprint, face, and gesture recognition reliable security measures. In the long term, as videophones become standard issue, synthetic actors and Bots will be applied as well, using thin-client applications that minimize bandwidth requirements while providing personal service. For the immediate future, within the G2-G3 infrastructure, the most promising user interface developments are in the area of Voice Enabled Interfaces, including Voice Portal technology.

Part 3, "Convergence," explores the future of the wireless Web from economic, technologic, and sociopolitical perspectives. The goal is to provide guidelines for businesses in the process of—or at least contemplating—establishing a presence on, and fully utilizing, the wireless Web.

EXECUTIVE SUMMARY

With the exception of fixed wireless communications, wireless connectivity is synonymous with a compact form-factor that allows portability. Achieving a level of portability and miniaturization supportive of pervasive communications with the wireless Web depends on developing hands-free methods of working with Web data, providing a secure and private communications environment, and providing the energy—in the form of new battery technology—to power it all.

The most prominent emergent technologies to address these needs include a variety of pattern recognition technologies, including voice and image recognition, voice synthesis, new battery designs, new interface technologies—including emotionally intelligent interfaces—and systems that these technologies tie together, such as Voice and Bot Portals.

Fixed wireless services, while dependent on the wireless Web for connectivity, resemble those of the wired Web for most subscribers. Terrestrial fixed wireless competes directly with DSL and cable modem companies for subscribers, especially subscribers in outlying areas. Similarly, satellite fixed wireless service provides affordable, high-bandwidth, wide area coverage and services not possible through other means. Several satellite projects on the horizon have the potential to redefine how the world accesses and communicates through the wireless Web.

Advances in user interface technology specific to wireless operations on the Web will provide greater access to the wired Web. In the hierarchical interface model, the six basic interface components are Physical, Graphical User, Logical, Emotional, Intelligent, and Emotionally Intelligent. The application of these components or technologies ranges from introducing more of a fun-factor to wireless communications, following the NTT DoCoMo model, to creating wearable communications. The most promising user interface technologies include Voice Enabled Interfaces (VEIs) that make use of voice recognition and speech synthesis techniques.

In order for a complex communications network to work properly, not only must the battery technology catch up with advances in communications but subscribers' security and privacy must be assured. Technologies include antiviral utilities for Web-enabled handhelds, biometric technologies for authenticating subscriber identity, and a variety of encryption techniques to ensure private messaging.

In particular, lightweight Elliptic Curve Cryptography (ECC) technology, when combined with a well-designed Certification Authority (CA), is a major enabling technology for wireless Web eCommerce. Unlike SSL, which is used on the wired Web and is wedded to the session-based client-server architecture of the wired Web, ECC and the CA technologies can be used with the sessionless architectures proposed for the wirelesss Web.

Part Three
CONVERGENCE

7

Realizing the Potential

He that will not apply new remedies must expect new evils,
for time is the greatest innovator.

Francis Bacon

INTRODUCTION

It's common practice for high school physics students in the United States to be introduced to the concept of the interconnectedness and persistence of matter by an insightful teacher who reminds them that they're breathing some of the same air molecules that Aristotle, Caesar, and Napoleon breathed centuries ago. However, but for the written record and what is passed down by an oral tradition, the teachings, conversations, and actions of these and other great figures in history are lost to the ether, never to be recounted fully again. Although some of the hydrogen and oxygen molecules breathed by current high school students in the United States and abroad will inevitably be inhaled by their counterparts a thousand years from now, there is also a good chance that at least some of their personal email conversations and other electronic communications and transactions will be available as well—even if the students don't gain the significance of ancient Greek philosophers or charismatic world leaders. There will certainly be a record of public transactions—utility bills, tax records, birth and death dates, and the like—but these data are unlikely to add profoundly to the culture or general knowledge of future generations. It is the personal details of the life of Aristotle that are intriguing—his beliefs and teachings—not that he managed to pay his property tax on time.

Achieving a modicum of immortality through technology has been a goal of humankind since before recorded history. Whether through the use of red ochre in a prehistoric burial ritual, embalming and embedding a pharaoh in a pyramid or other monument, commissioning a portrait, writing a book, or, more recently, via a tape recorder or some type of camera, a key issue is the availability of a technology that provides a persistent memory. How many executives have missed an opportunity to record one of their experiences because they didn't have a camera handy, or failed to capture a profound thought on paper or in a digital recorder before it slipped into the abyss of forgetfulness?

At a time when technologies from paper and pen to miniature cell phones and pocket-size digital cameras are ubiquitous, the issue shifts from the availability of technology to one of conscious effort. Even though the technology of recording conversations and transactions is affordable and common in most developed countries, other than special occasions—birthdays, graduations, and weddings—few people take the time to record many significant aspects of their lives. Granted, not everything that everyone does is worth recording. However, for those who are actually doing something significant with their lives, it's rare for them to take the time to maintain a relatively detailed diary, complete photo album of their activities, or otherwise create a record of life from their perspective. Most productive professionals are focused on achieving their goals, and what they record is usually associated with some requirement established by the government to ensure adequate payment of taxes.

In addition to government records, much of what is recorded for each citizen is the result of their business transactions—which is also related to taxable purchases. For example, every month private cellular subscribers in the United States receive a detailed phone bill, which, although often barely understandable, usually contains a record of phone numbers, times, communications charges, and the associated state and federal taxes. Even though these records typically lack any reference to the topics discussed or who was involved in the conversation, the phone company generates the records automatically, without any conscious effort on the part of the subscriber. On occasion, these records are relied on for the "public good," as evidence in criminal investigations, for example. From the subscriber's perspective, however, the type and granularity of the data reported are often insufficient, especially when a conversation deals with a critical business transaction. As noted in Chapter 1, one of the first attractions for using the telephone for transacting business was the lack of a record of the transaction. Without a written record of the conversation, any agreement made over the phone could always be contested later.

As the popularity of email increases, more knowledge workers are unconsciously creating an archive of their personal and corporate lives. Corporations, as well as consumer-oriented ISPs such as AOL, commonly archive personal and company email for years. Some corporations are beginning to realize the value in archiving employee emails, because they may contain important contact information that may otherwise disappear when the employee leaves for another company. From the employees' perspective, however, the potentially thousands of memos, many containing records of insights and strategies that may be of use to them in their future careers, are lost to them. Although there are legal issues of intellectual property ownership and work for hire, the fact remains that the information remains sealed away from the creator, and, unless the information is mined by the employer, from society as well. In addition, in a decade or two, when the company that the employee worked for is sold or acquired, and the information system is replaced with a different one, the fate of the legacy data, perhaps preserved on media no longer compatible with anything on the market, is probably the trash bin.

Even consultants who fastidiously maintain records of their business and personal emails and other electronically generated correspondence have trouble keeping their records accessible and usable as computer technology advances. Since the introduction of the desktop microcomputer, media, formats, and operating systems have evolved through dozens of incompatible generations. Paradoxically, the best archive for computer-generated data has remained paper printouts, which are difficult to search, maintain, index, and make good use of.

From the perspective of growing a matrix of private, corporate, and public information, the Internet, especially with the Web interface, is beginning to change everything. The Internet defines the communications standard that digital communications systems are increasingly relying on to transfer voice and data to and from a universe of devices. But in and of itself, the Internet and the enabling IP standard are no different than the networks used for decades by the phone companies. The difference is the memory function provided by the Web. Not only can emails and documents traverse the Internet but the contents of these documents and the record of the gross transactions can also be recorded on the Web for a variety of future uses—many of which have yet to be conceived.

Consider a world in which every toddler, regardless of income level, is provided with a rugged Web-enabled tablet that can be scribbled on with a tethered stylus that works like a piece of chalk on a chalkboard. With time, the tablet, or its replacement, serves as the child's working medium for preschool. She not only accesses illustrated books to read and to be read to through the tablet but she also performs her homework on the tablet. Later, in high school, she completes her homework assignment on the wireless tablet using voice recognition software. Her teacher, parents, and national accrediting agencies access and comment on her work through their own Web-enabled wireless tablets and desktop computers. In college, she uses an even thinner and lighter flexible tablet to record her laboratory experiments in a material sciences class. At her first job out of school, she uses a heads-up display and a voice recognition system to design engine components for a major aeronautical company, using notes that she posted to the Web when she was in the material sciences class—perhaps with a small royalty paid to her alma mater for the service. When she has her first child, her physician uses his wireless bedside tablet to record the child's weight and vital signs, starting its lifelong Web-based electronic medical record, and also simultaneously adding the details of the event into the mother's Web-based electronic medical record.

Though the data acquisition and creation hardware and the nature of the human interface will change over time, the constant in this future scenario is the interface to the Web, and its use as a standardized, lifelong repository for information. A life record of every subscriber's activities, medical history, education, business and private dealings, all recorded with a variety of Web-enabled devices and appropriately filtered, can provide data that will have value to the authors, their healthcare professionals, their employers, and the government. For example, with Web-enabled data acquisition hardware sewn into clothes and embedded in utensils and sports accessories, diet, exercise, interpersonal contact, and other "personal" information can be gathered for analysis, without interrupting or even informing the person.

The downside, for those concerned with privacy, is the ability of the government and businesses to profile citizens. Political affiliations and religious beliefs can be inferred from records of reading material purchased from an eBookstore or from a short story written by a student in Freshman English, or other information ostensibly gathered for a student's or society's benefits. Clearly, everyone must be given some degree of control over the windows to their information, disclosing some areas only as they see fit, unless they are compelled to do so by the government.

Although Finland and Japan may be different, U.S. society, technology, and business aren't yet prepared to execute this future scenario, but the trends to this potential path are becoming increasingly evident. For example, U.S. parents planning back-to-school purchases for their teenagers have to contend with more than clothes and new binders. Electronic organizers and communications devices are now required accessories. Expensive athletic shoes don't count for much anymore; students without a cell phone, PDA, or interactive pager just aren't with it.

From business and technologic perspectives, creating a worldwide wireless Web infrastructure is a project that dwarfs the building of the Pyramids in Egypt, in terms of both significance and difficulty. At some point in the future, when there are universal communications protocols and devices, those who elect to will enjoy instantaneous, recallable conversations on a global basis. In this future communications utopia, the free exchange and recording of ideas expressed in digital form will occur regardless of language or culture—thanks to translation technology—in an ever-expanding variety of ways.

This chapter begins Part 3, "Convergence." As the title suggests, this and the following two chapters discuss the convergence of the complex social, political, economic, and technologic forces relevant to the growth and development of the wireless Web, within the context of creating a pervasive computing environment. It explores the opportunities for advancing the technology, the change agents involved, and the characteristics of the complex change process. This chapter also identifies the applications of wireless Web technology most likely to succeed, from the perspective of what can reasonably be achieved in the near term, with an eye to future possibilities.

PERVASIVE COMPUTING

For most customers, the attraction of a pervasive computing environment—the anytime, anywhere, context-specific, personalized user experience involving the capture, production, or transfer of information—is the potential for computer and communications technologies to simplify their lives and to save them time. Pervasive computing includes both wired and wireless connectivity, with goals of supporting the early adopters who simply must have the latest, thinnest, fastest technologies, providing for the information capture and retrieval needs of everyday business, and offering news, entertainment, and communications capabilities to subscribers.

Communication and computing are becoming pervasive in part because the two technologies are becoming increasingly interdependent, increasingly reliable, and therefore invisible. After all, what constitutes a computer and what constitutes a communications device today? Most wristwatches, portable and cell phones, pagers, televisions, radios, and even bicycle odometers contain computer chips, but most people don't think of these devices as computers. Similarly, many laptop computers are configured to send and receive faxes, email, voice, and even video, but they aren't generally thought of as primarily communications devices. The majority of communications technologies simply fit into the process of everyday business and personal life, and, unless they fail unexpectedly, they become part of the framework, and fade out of conscious existence.

In sharp contrast with the concept of pervasive computing is invasive computing, where users make a conscious effort to boot a desktop PC, contend with formatting disks, and loading utilities so they can finally pull out a keyboard and a mouse and get down to work. According to current projections, on a worldwide scale, pervasive computing will soon overshadow invasive computing. For example, the number of Web-enabled handheld devices in use worldwide will equal the number of Web-enabled desktop PCs by the year 2003. Although pervasive computing involves the use of both wired and wireless connectivity, the shift to predominantly wireless handheld devices will change the way companies conduct eCommerce and provide services to their customers.

Steve Jobs' vision for the original Macintosh as an information appliance—the embodiment of pervasive computing—that presents users with the complexity and intrusiveness of an ordinary toaster has never quite materialized. However, the possibility exists on the immediate horizon for the dream to be realized, albeit in the form of an Internet appliance based on a virtual machine architecture instead of a traditional PC architecture. The current generation of Web-enabled cell phones and wireless PDAs suggests that the one thing these Internet appliances will have in common is lack of uniformity. In addition, unlike current session-based wired Web transactions, these appliances will support transient sessions and then the sessions will go away. In this dynamic relationship, applications are to JAVA virtual machines as URLs are to wired Web browsers. Similarly, instead of portals such as Yahoo that aggregate content, wireless portals will aggregate applications. Alternatively, the static PC era client-server architecture could migrate to the wireless Web, in the form of Windows CE and Palm OS, for example.

Regardless of the outcome of the OS versus the virtual machine battle, assuming the current trend continues, not only is the traditional desktop PC destined to be outnumbered by Web-enabled handsets and cell phones but it will also be overshadowed by TV set-top boxes and Web-enabled games as well. Although each of these devices typically includes more computing power than the original Apple computer, they aren't perceived as computers per se. They're devices that provide communications and entertainment and happen to use computer technology.

In the move to a pervasive computing environment, with time, the distinction between the Internet and other networks will fade. In one sense, this is purely a result of local conditioning, in that what customers in the United States have come to see and experience as the Web doesn't fully translate in a wireless phone experience. However, in countries like Japan and Korea, where the wireless voice services are nearly saturated, creation of a pervasive computing environment through the addition of Web connectivity to the existing wireless communications infrastructure is a natural extension of subscriber services. Not only does Web connectivity provide more value to cellular phone subscribers but it also represents a way for communications companies to boost revenues.

Wireless penetration rates and the extent of pervasive computing are higher in South Korea and Hong Kong than they are in Japan, even though Japan has the most advanced wireless Internet service on the planet. China, in comparison, has virtually the lowest penetration of wireless services of any developed country. However, because of its population, China is the largest wireless carrier in Asia. The Chinese government is backing wireless telecommunications companies because wireless may be the fastest, least expensive way to get the greatest number of citizens online since much of the country lacks traditional wired phone circuitry.

Despite the reliance on desktop computer systems and a less than optimum communications infrastructure, the United States is positioned to create truly pervasive computing environments within the next few years. The reasoning behind this prediction lies in the convergence of several factors, described below.

Convergence

In the United States, the move toward a pervasive computing environment is poised to accelerate because of a convergence of enabling technologic, sociologic, business, and political factors. For example, consider the technologic components of this convergence, starting with the evolution and differentiation of the microcomputer. What started as a dream that materialized as an Apple computer in a garage in Silicon Valley first evolved into the large, powerful desktop microcomputer. Only then did the evolutionary path include luggable, portable, and eventually handheld devices. In an evolutionary path that included successes such as the Apple II, the IBM-PC, and later the Palm, Simbian, RIM, and Windows CE handhelds, there are notable dead ends. Although the Apple Newton, PC-Jr and first luggable Macintosh, and CE handhelds missed their marks, laptop and handheld computing is now a mature technology. Although it would have been inconceivable only a few years ago, the RIM wireless PDA sports a 386 microprocessor operating at a faster clock frequency than the original desktop 386-based PCs.

Another component of the technologic convergence is the cell phone. Like the desktop microcomputer, the evolutionary path of the cell phone includes large, barely luggable devices with poor user interfaces and questionable reliability. Along with the metamorphosis of the cell phone hardware, the nature of the information that the cell phone is designed to transfer has changed as well. Increasingly, the distinction between voice and data is blurring, especially given Web-enabled cell phones capable of supporting voice-to-voice, voice-to-synthesized speech, text-to-text, and text-to-synthesized speech communications.

The convergence of voice and data also redefines what constitutes a computer, and where the telephone, a communications device, becomes a computing device. Today, the cell phone is a ubiquitous business tool and, for many teenagers, a fashion statement. Cell phone sales offices are now as common as Starbucks outlets in many major cities, and many regional service providers offer phone fronts in colors that match school or business colors.

Another component of the technologic convergence that has coevolved with battery-powered laptop and handheld computers is the thin, lightweight, LCD screen. A lightweight handheld unit would be virtually impossible without this lightweight, battery-powered, portable display technology.

Application architectures have also evolved, first from applications designed for the mainframe-centric, IT—department—controlled monoliths to applications designed to run on the more democratic client-server architectures, as well as peer-to-peer architectures, popularized by the Napster (www.Napster.com) site. Most recently, architectures favor the thin-client wired and wireless application service provider model (ASP and WASP, respectively). A WASP makes it possible for a subscriber with a Web-enabled cell phone with minimum local processing power and memory to perform complex search functions, interact with databases, and initiate transactions—all because the processing and memory are provided by a server. As a result of this convergence in trends in application architectures and hardware platforms, pervasive computing is becoming more of a conclusion than a possibility. For companies that add a wireless Web touch point to their business, there is considerable prospect of gain.

The conditions, technologies, and business opportunities that make the wireless Web attractive to content developers, service providers, and their potential subscribers include the emergence of new content delivery devices. For example, eBooks are projected to account for 10 percent of book sales by 2005 according to Barnes and Noble and other major book sellers. The proliferation of the Internet IP standard for communications, a global decline in computer and communications hardware costs, as well as faster, less expensive network technologies are significant attractors as well.

For domestic companies, there is the lure of the apparent success of wireless in Europe and Asia. There is also the prospect of significant domestic market potential, given the projections for huge increases in domestic wireless activity. Part of the reasoning behind this projected increase in activity is the result of new payment models that include one-rate plans, free nonwork-hour wireless communications, and wireless service plans that don't require the call recipient to pay for the airtime. Similarly, a shift in subscriber demographics to a more mobile workforce with a pent-up demand for just-in-time information, the handheld device proliferation, and decreased relevance of voice for telecom profits all point to the wireless Web as a solution for invigorating business in the communications space.

In addition to the pressure of constant technologic improvement, such as the constantly increasing wireless infrastructure speeds, there are several nonquantifiable factors involved in the push to the wireless Web. For example, there are corporate and national egos involved in taming the wireless frontier. There is nothing new about companies and countries doing everything possible to take the lead in a technology. For example, just as the United States has taken pride in the technology that flows out of Silicon Valley, Japan has taken as national policy a stance to become the leader in the Internet world by 2005.

The Long View

Given the convergence of factors that favor the success of the wireless Web, what are the best-case scenarios for the players involved? For example, assuming that companies in the United States manage to establish an affordable, ubiquitous, high-speed communications infrastructure, what are the rewards? Should the United States focus on middleware applications and let the infrastructure evolve on its own, free from foreign or domestic governmental intervention?

The primary reason Europe is thought to be ahead of the United States in telecommunications and accessing the wireless Web through cell phones and other devices is because of the standardization of the GSM protocol. And yet, the countries of the EU and the millions of NTT DoCoMo users in Japan have a minimal presence on the wired Web. Could it be that the ubiquitous nature of the wireless Web is oversold, at least in terms of the need for national coverage? After all, who cares—other than a frequent flying business executive—if a single cell phone works in Boston, San Francisco, and Tokyo? For the vast majority of customers, the extent of a network's national coverage doesn't really matter, as long as it works in their metropolitan area.

Is this a myopic business view of early adopters of technologies such as thin laptops, wireless PDAs, and Web-enabled phones as to what the United States has to do to compete successfully with European and Asian wireless companies? On the other extreme, will there be a backlash from the general consumer population if ubiquitous Web access, sold initially as a means of providing communalitywide communications, including education and student-teacher communications opportunities, is eventually perceived as Orwellian?

Given the international intent not to miss out on the next big thing—as many domestic and international corporations did in not realizing the potential of the wired Web until the likes of Yahoo and Amazon were already entrenched—many international corporations are moving ahead. In some cases they are moving with the same sense of misguided abandon that characterized the wired Web in its early growth spurts. However, as described later, this needn't be the case, since there are clear indications of what types of services will benefit from wireless Web access, and which types won't.

Although it may not fit the image that U.S. technology corporations promote, the domestic standing in the wireless Web has more in common with China than it does with the more technologically developed countries in the EU, Japan, or Korea. Like China, the United States is perceived as an enormous potential market for technologies developed offshore. Telecom giants and device manufacturers in Europe and the Pacific Rim countries are desperately attempting to control or at least become major players in the potentially lucrative U.S. market, despite their knowledge that the United States has a political structure designed to protect domestic business interests.

It remains to be seen if there is a way for U.S. corporations to leverage their R&D costs by exporting their middleware technologies, even if only in the form of licensing arrangements, to less technologically advanced markets in Asia, Canada, and South America. It's also possible that middleware technologies, such as voice recognition and synthesis, may dissolve the lead enjoyed by the first mover international wireless developers that rely on graphical devices and related infrastructures.

OPPORTUNITIES FOR CHANGE

The primary opportunities for change from either primarily wired desktop Web access or no Web access to Web-enabled wireless connectivity are summarized in Figure 7-1. These opportunities evolve around immediately satisfying a demand for timely, accurate, location- and user-specific information. For example, virtually every salesperson in a mobile sales force needs to access critical information at her customer's site, from her car, and from her office. However, in today's competitive market, she can't take the time to drive to a central office whenever she has to access corporate or public information on the Web. Location and time independent access to information is especially critical when there is a constant need to access time-sensitive information, such as the price of a stock, the status of a patient, data needed to close a business deal, or stock on hand to fulfill a customer's order.

The always-on capabilities provided by some Web-enabled wireless systems, and the push applications that they can support, provide enhanced functions that have application in time-sensitive situations. For example, notifications of changes in a patient's status, an alert that a stock value has increased or decreased by a predetermined amount, or a customer's need for immediate assistance are all examples of the value that an information push service can provide to its customers. For occupations that favor user-directed information as opposed to service-initiated information transfer, wireless pull technologies can provide instant access to specific, just-in-time information sources.

Opportunities for Change

Demand for any time, any place access to critical information

Demand for constant real-time communication

Demand for frequent access to time-sensitive information

Extension of wired eCommerce applications

Market for push/pull value added information

Need to exceed customer expectations

Potential value of serving location-based information

Support for transaction-oriented business processes

Figure 7-1. The primary opportunities for change from a primarily wired Web access toward Web-enabled wireless connectivity.

Handheld wireless access to the Web is especially relevant to transaction-based business processes, whether a businesswoman is purchasing a ticket to an entertainment event, trading stocks, or transferring funds from one of her bank accounts to another. In this regard, the extension of wired-Web eCommerce applications to the wireless arena can be supported, changing the dynamics of online shopping. For example, with a Web-enabled PDA, it would be possible for a customer in a retail outlet to search for the best price on the Web, and order the product for next-day home delivery from the site with the lowest price.

Consider how the partnership of AirClic, Inc. (www.Airclic.com), Motorola, Symbol Technologies, and Ericsson's Connect Things has the potential to fundamentally change the nature of retail shopping. If this or a similar project succeeds, customers will be able to browse through a retail outlet and scan an item they're interested in purchasing, using a combination of wireless and bar-code technology. Within seconds, a shopping bot will go out over the wireless Web and locate the same item. The customer will then have the option of experiencing immediate gratification or saving 30 or 40 percent off of the sticker price by waiting for the item to be delivered by FedEx the next morning. For wireless-enabled customers, browsing will take on a completely new meaning.

Perhaps the greatest opportunity for change supported by wireless Web access is by providing a company with the means of not simply satisfying, but exceeding, customer expectations. For example, consider the value of wireless communications to a businessman who is equipped with a wireless PDA. He can unobtrusively signal a limousine service while he's still in a meeting, notifying the service that the meeting is running shorter or longer than expected, and rescheduling the pickup time appropriately. Similarly, consider the value of wireless connectivity to the customers of a copier repair service. Customers in need of service can contact the repairman assigned to their account through a Web site and, in real-time, receive a notice from the repairman with his estimated time of arrival, as well as any updates on earlier or later arrival times. For the business traveler, wireless communications can make the difference between a pleasant trip and a night in a cheap hotel. A businesswoman who receives a page or email notification from the airlines that her flight has been changed, can use her wireless communications device to view or hear options for earlier or later available flights she would prefer to take—including seat assignments. For the business traveler, this service provides incredible value over the alternative of discovering that a flight has been cancelled after rushing to the airport.

IDENTIFYING WHAT NEEDS TO BE WIRELESS

Thanks to affordable technology, replacing a cable with a wireless connection is usually trivial. However, the challenge for a company moving into the wireless Web space is to identify which of their services actually need to be wireless, and of these, which will provide the greatest traction or ROI. One approach to making this determination is to use the *metric of transparency*. That is, adding a wireless touch point makes sense when the behavior change required of the customer—whether at work or on the road—is as little as possible. For example, requiring employees to log in to a voice portal with their cell phones may not be reasonable if they are working at their desks most of the time and have wired Web connectivity through a desktop PC.

An important factor in assessing the transparency of the introduction of wireless Web connectivity is the effect on the current process, in terms of additional steps or the modification of existing steps. That is, if the addition of a wireless touch point simply adds another step to a process that involves parallel data sources, such as the wired Web, then it will likely be poorly received. For example, equipping clinicians in a hospital with wireless tablets for them to record patient findings, but then requiring them to use a desktop PC in order to place medication orders probably won't be acceptable. It would be better to delay the introduction of wireless Web technology into the patient care process until all of the computer interactions that are required in a typical patient encounter and follow-up are available from a single device. Without a critical mass of applications on the wireless platform, the addition of a wireless device simply adds an additional layer of complexity to the existing system. The "you can't get there from here" problem shouldn't appear on a wireless Web touch point.

In some cases, the potential benefits of adding wireless Web access to an environment, from a customer value perspective, are obvious. For example, college campuses seem like a natural fit with wireless Web communications, with everyone concerned with accessing, managing, messaging, and creating intellectual property. College campuses in the United States were among the first businesses to have wired Web access, often in computer centers and, in many cases, in dorms as well. However, with frequent student movement from class to class and around campus, and the affordability of laptops and wireless hardware, untethered Web access is a practical adjunct to wired connectivity. For example, the University of Oregon in Eugene established an infrastructure that allows students with laptops and wireless modem cards to access educational content on the Web at 11 MBps.

In other cases, wireless Web connectivity makes sense when it can support an existing process or technology by providing added convenience or simplifying access for customers who don't want or don't need to know about desktop computers, modems, ISPs, and the like. For example, consider the applicability of wireless monitoring devices in the home health monitoring industry. Home monitoring is becoming increasingly popular, and a number of studies have shown that home monitoring not only works from a clinical perspective but it also can save money. For example, a home scale that measures changes in weight or a blood pressure cuff that dials in and deposits the information in a hospital database can save the patient the hassle and expense of having to get to a clinic. It also saves the healthcare system the cost of sending a nurse or physicians assistant to the home to perform a routine lab test. However, the setup is a problem, with modem connections, cables, and difficulties that most elderly—those most in need of home monitoring—don't handle very well.

One obvious application for wireless Web connectivity is personal health monitors that are currently connected to the wired Web. For example, there are asthma monitors that record air flow parameters for asthmatics, and then use a wired modem to upload the data to the Web, where it can be accessed at any time by patients and their clinicians. With the very young and older patients without ready access to a modem line or busy executives without time to download the data after each measurement, there is the likelihood that acute asthma attacks will be missed. Similarly, there are wired blood-testing systems for diabetics that measure levels of glucose, cholesterol, and triglycerides. The results can be sent to a PC and, from there, uploaded to the patient's personal Web page, which can be monitored by a clinician. However, for most wired devices, getting the information to the Web is a multistep process, and the time involved is prohibitive for patients who need to test their blood glucose several times a day. Instantaneous uploading of data and feedback that wireless would provide would ensure compliance.

Consider the potential benefits of a wireless home monitoring system for an elderly man with a heart condition and diabetes who is living alone in an assisted-living complex. The man, who finds it impractical to make frequent clinic visits, is equipped with several Bluetooth devices and wireless Web connectivity through his cell phone. Although only three devices are used in this example (a Bluetooth-enabled Med Watch, Scale, and Pill Box) others could be added as well, up to a total of eight devices. For example, a Bluetooth-enabled pacemaker, a self-inflating blood pressure and pulse rate monitor, or a bar-code scanner for diet tracking and analysis could be added to the patient's arsenal of devices.

Every morning and night, the patient can step on the scale, which stores his weight in local memory and sends the data through his cell phone to his Web-based medical record. A sudden increase of more than 1 kg (2.2 lb), which is associated with heart failure in a patient with known coronary disease, alerts the patient's clinician through the Web site and his PDA or cell phone. Similarly, a Bluetooth-enabled Pill Box could remind the patient to take his medications, including how many and what type of pills to take, and require that he verify that the medications were taken. Lack of patient compliance with medication prescriptions is one of the major costs associated with modern health care in the United States. Patients who don't follow their prescriptions require more and more frequent clinician visits, in part because inadequate and irregular dosing may compromise the effectiveness of medications.

The Med Watch, a fictitious device that resembles several medical devices under development, in this case a wrist-mounted glucose monitor, provides the patient with a real-time readout of her blood glucose level and transmits this data to her medical record. It's possible to add multiple functionality to devices, such as a bar-code reader to the Med Watch, allowing the patient to scan in codes on food packages and medication labels to track, for example, protein or calcium intake.

Once patient information is posted on the Web, it can be examined automatically by a rule-based transaction monitor that looks for trends and abnormally high or low values, similar to the alert systems designed to assist stock traders. The patient's clinician can also review the data, using a wireless handheld device that allows her to make notes in the patient's Web-based medical record. Similarly, since the data are on the Web, a variety of interested third parties can review the data and the data acquisition process in action. For example, researchers interested in the efficacy of the wireless intervention can track compliance. Pharmaceutical firms can monitor individual patient compliance, and they also may be involved in financing the Pill Box component of the service. The government and third-party payers also have access to various components of the data, as needed.

The wireless Web brings two things to the home monitoring space. The first is the *pervasive memory functionality* of the Web. Records that are stored on the Web in an appropriate format, such as XML or an SQL database, can be searched, manipulated, and analyzed by clinicians using expert systems and other analytical tools that have access to the Web. The second factor is *personalization*. A patient's particular condition often dictates specific medication frequency and dosage.

Bluetooth-enabled home or clinic monitoring is only one example of a potential use of wireless Web technology in medicine. It's one example of how wireless information and communications technologies can be used to save patients time and money, allow more independence and involved health care, and simplify a complex problem area.

CHANGE AGENTS

Every new beginning starts with the end of another beginning, and progress in the wireless Web arena is no different. Given the great potential of wireless Web communications as a component of a pervasive computing environment that will eventually touch every aspect of modern life, what are the change agents that will help the evolution come about? Although new technologies and applications, legislation favorable to wireless industries, and expectations fueled by the prospects of a second dotCom experience are core change agents, the most important change agent is vision.

With the maturation of the wired dotCom world that was highlighted by the market correction of 2000, it's clear that a prerequisite for success in the wireless space is a collective vision of the future. For example, one future is a world in which wireless computer technology is embedded in everything from appliances to toys and tools. Everyone is connected to the Web, especially children, whether for communications with their parents or to play video games, to download music from the Internet, or to watch Internet TV.

Another possible change agent is a corporate vision that empowers employees to contribute their expertise in problem solving regardless of time or location. In order for wireless to take off as a commercial success, what the wireless providers have to offer must fit what customers expect—which is in turn influenced by vendor-specific marketing and advertising.

The collective vision is ultimately reflected in legislation at some level. For example, consider the impact of the German Tax Reform of 2000, which reduced personal and business tax rates. This removed a large barrier to corporate mergers, and boosted momentum for the further economic restructuring of Europe. In short, it made the world's third largest economy friendlier to wireless activity.

The expectations of a second coming of the dotCom experience is also fueling more than casual interest in developing wireless touch points. Many individuals and corporations want to repeat the glory days when the wired Web was at its peak. For example, management at Marvel Comics, which licensed their superheroes to be deployed as comics on cell phones for a small monthly subscription fee, views the wireless Web as a potentially huge revenue stream. Other domestic and foreign companies want to replicate the success of NTT DoCoMo as soon as the technology becomes available.

Potential customers clamoring for the benefits of wireless Web connectivity include not only early adopters but also customers from all walks of life. Applications of wireless communications technologies, range from delivering Webucation through packet video; smart cars; networked appliances; fixed wireless services; commuting games, including collaborative games; universal remotes; and wireless eBooks that allow readers to download books from a virtually infinite library over the wireless Web.

Of course, the spark for the vision and the motivation behind the demand for these applications and services stems from the technologies that are on the horizon. The technologies discussed in Part 2, "Wireless Wonders," range from voice enabled interfaces, new tools for creating and manipulating content, and conversion utilities to convert current programs and content into wireless Web compatible form, to satellite systems, new protocols, wireless heads-up displays, and last-mile connectivity options.

Consider the potential change that the introduction of the Web and the Bluetooth standard, both major change agents, will bring about in how a typical business executive will keep track of her schedule, maintain her phone lists, and transact business over the phone. In the pre-Bluetooth scenario, the executive first looks up scheduling and to-call information on her PDA, and then manually enters the number into her cell phone to place a call. While this method of interaction has the advantage of privacy of data, the two-hand operation has an extended interaction time, even if she has both devices with her. Typically, however, the phone and PDA are stored separately, and the two devices are difficult to work with when there is no desk space.

Now consider a second scenario in which a Web-enabled cell phone provides access to the same scheduling and to-call information, but the data are now available on the Web. Not only can the executive review and manipulate her contact and to-do information from any Web site but she can also make calls and retrieve data with one hand free, and in much less time, since there is only one device to contend with. A benefit of the Web repository is the memory function described earlier.

A third scenario involves the use of a Bluetooth-enabled cell phone and PDA. Because local processing is involved, lookup is likely faster than through the Web. There is improved security, in that the data don't leave the executive's immediate area.

The natural extension of Bluetooth-enabled digital appliances is local storage of private data for rapid transactions and backup in the event that the Internet connection is temporarily lost. A Web connection allows the record of selected transactions to be stored on the Web for later analysis or manipulation. Alternatively, the Web provides a backup of all activities entered into the PDA. If the local storage device is configured such that it is unusable unless it is in range of the original owner's Bluetooth network, then the data on the device would be of no use to someone else if the device were misplaced or stolen. This provision for security is potentially a major change agent in the move to Bluetooth technology, given that an executive's stolen laptop computer makes front-page news.

For example, when the laptop of Qualcomm's chief executive containing several gigabytes of confidential corporate information was stolen in September 2000, the event made the front page of several national newspapers. The event highlighted the potential lapses in security that can be associated with the new high-capacity handheld and portable devices. Although Bluetooth and a variety of security-specific technologies may improve data protection, several companies have policies about what can be placed on a handheld or laptop device. Intel, for example, prohibits employees from working on confidential documents in public areas, such as airplanes, or from leaving laptops containing confidential materials unguarded.

THE CHANGE PROCESS

Returning to the high school students mentioned at the beginning of this chapter, another basic concept taught in physics class is the activation energy of a reaction. A chemical reaction involving several types of atoms that combine to form a new compound usually requires energy to move the process along to completion. That is, it isn't sufficient to simply put the ingredients in a container; they have to be stirred, heated, shaken, or pressurized, etc.

Without the extra energy required to promote the reaction—the activation energy—a chemical reaction may simply not occur under normal conditions. For example, the reaction might require an activation energy in the form of a very high temperature or pressure that's too difficult and expensive to maintain, given the value of the end product. The activation energy required to drive a reaction to completion depends on exactly how the reaction occurs. For example, adding a bit of platinum or a special surface on which the reaction can occur may drop the energy of an activation requirement enough so that a reaction can occur at a lower temperature than before. It's important to note that very small changes in the activation energy requirement can result in large changes in the rate at which the reaction occurs. In this relationship, the substance or environment, which isn't directly involved in the reaction but promotes it, is called a *catalyst*. The majority of chemical reactions and products would be economically unfeasible without catalysts.

The concept of activation energy and catalysts has parallels in the economics of technologic development. For example, the tax rate can be consider a catalyst, in that very small changes in the tax rate can profoundly increase or decrease the rate at which certain industries expand into a market. Providing a tax credit for certain business practices typically promotes that activity to a degree that is out of proportion to the direct investment required, often because there are competing demands for resources. A small advantage in one environment can shift capital and other resources from other activities, resulting in an abundance of activity in an area.

In many regards, the change agents discussed above—the vision, technologies, legislation, and economic projections—are catalysts for business to move into the pervasive computing space. The basic technologic ingredients and their catalysts appear to be in place; what remains to be found is a catalyst for the social process, which tends to progress much more slowly than the development of wireless hardware or software.

Often, the rate-limiting step in a business process is aversion to change, especially when there is a comfort level with the current process. For example, the field of medicine is notorious for its slowness to change, even when faced with new technologies that have proved their effectiveness in other areas. Many clinical activities are not yet computerized, for example, despite the virtually global acceptance of computer-based tools by knowledge workers in business, engineering, and other professions.

An Example in Medicine

Paradoxically, many of the early adopters of computer and communications technology were clinicians, in part because vendors see medicine as a lucrative market, and in part because clinicians, in general, have the capital to invest in technologies that may improve their practice. For example, the first commercially successful voice recognition systems in the United States were developed for medicine in the 1980s. However, except for pockets of activity in specialties such as emergency medicine, the technology has failed to spread to other medical areas. Similarly, even though electronic medical record systems were introduced in the 1950s in Russia and in the 1960s in the United States, most hospitals in the United States rely on a paper medical record.

The reason for the slow rate of acceptance of computers in medicine is a complex issue. It involves resistance to change, the initial impression that computers, like typewriters, are tools for secretaries and other support personnel, and a numbing to technologies with great promises. This latter factor is a result of clinicians' almost constant exposure to vendors promoting drugs and devices that are associated with fantastic claims, but which usually fail to deliver on the vendor's promises. Most clinicians will accept a procedure or technology only after a trusted colleague has proved the vendor's claims.

In medicine, the rate of computerization has increased at an exponential rate with new reimbursement guidelines that require complex coding and documentation procedures that are only practical with the aid of computer-based tools. Clinicians who don't embrace technologies such as wireless bedside computing simply don't have time to see patients and fill out the paperwork they need to be reimbursed by third-party payers and to cover themselves legally. The economics of health care in the United States are evolving almost as rapidly as wireless technologies, making home monitoring alternatives to hospital visits more economically viable. Because of the expectations of the government and third-party payers, it's becoming increasingly difficult for clinicians to maintain a pen and paper practice. There are similar situations in the financial and travel industries that seem ideally suited for wireless Web-enabled devices.

DISCUSSION

To many business executives, wireless is synonymous with a cell phone and, for the early adopters, a wireless PDA. However, wireless isn't a product, but part of a strategy for achieving a pervasive computing environment in which the ability to store and manage data is so ubiquitous that the technology becomes invisible. In this context, the value of the Web is much more than a mere collection of virtual storefronts that provide consumers with ready access to books, CDs, and inexpensive airplane tickets. In a ubiquitous, wired and wireless pervasive computing environment, the Web becomes a universal and timeless repository of personal and public data. The Web is transformed into a collective knowledge base that will eventually contain archives of every significant aspect of life, from medical records, educational and professional work, to purchasing and voting patterns.

Wireless technology is not the only enabler in creating a collective consciousness through pervasive computing. For example, consider the potential for the Zaplet technology, a class of lightweight applications built upon the convergence of email, the Web, and instant messaging. Zaplets, a kind of interactive, Web-based email, are automatically updated with either recipients' responses or external data. For example, a group of executives selecting the best time for their next board meeting might send out a calendar Zaplet to each board member. As each recipient indicates his or her preferred times for a meeting, their choices are automatically reflected in every other recipient's calendar. Similarly, a brokerage firm could email a single Zaplet showing a client's stock portfolio in the morning, and the graph would be automatically updated to reflect the current stock value when the customer opened the message in the evening. Zaplets and other crossover technologies can have a major synergistic effect on wireless, pervasive computing.

One day, subscribers will be able to ask, "Where is that old high school buddy of mine?", "What ever happened to my old girlfriend?", "What was that equation I derived in college physics?", "How much did I pay for that TV?", and "Is my TV still under warranty?" The ability to communicate directly with someone, search a high-school database of alumni, or check the status of a repair takes more than simply supplementing a communications cable with a digital walkie-talkie. It requires a technical and social infrastructure, and a collective vision that not only allows an incursion of technology into what people normally consider their private lives but actively encourages it.

To obtain this level of enthusiastic support for wireless technology, the personal benefits must be obvious, immediate, and affordable. Just as the vision promoted by the automobile industry (with added motivation supplied by the U.S. military) triggered the public outcry for the development of a national highway system, a collective vision of pervasive computing may help develop not only the information highway but also the educational systems and legal structures that will allow it to flourish.

Despite the technologic limitations of current devices, such as small screens and even smaller buttons that make casual Web browsing an exercise in frustration, wireless devices seem like a natural fit for transaction-based applications. Even with this humble beginning, it isn't difficult to imagine a future in which cell phones and other disparate wireless devices converge into a single communicator. This device, perhaps designed to be used with a docking station that provides a larger display and wired Web connectivity, will hold an archive of every event and action that the owner has been involved in since shortly after he or she was born.

For businesspeople in the United States who grew up with *Star Trek*, *Star Wars*, and the concept of time travel, the technologic leaps involved in creating a living, mobile Web consciousness seem almost trivial—from a technologic perspective. The issue, especially in the United States and Europe, is privacy. Despite the syntactical difference, pervasive is often synonymous with invasive, and what is deemed invasive computing is often viewed as con-trolled and elective computing.

There is also the issue of commercial privacy, privacy from the govern-ment, and the ability to turn off access to personal information. For example, that old girlfriend may not want to be bothered, but only notified that her for-mer boyfriend made an attempt to contact her. However, the government, whether in the name of national security or a suspected murder, may have access to detailed information to a degree never before possible. Consider that in Austria, where there is no division between church and state, citizens who denounce the Catholic faith aren't compelled by the government to pay the state-mandated church tax. However, if it's known by records of cell phone roaming charges that a woman visits a church every Sunday, should she be held liable for the tax?

On a more global level, since the Web isn't a company or government, and isn't responsible for any citizenry, where are the personal data stored? Who owns it? Who maintains it? Who can access it? Can it be erased? Is it per-missible as evidence in court? How is it paid for? For example, if a university allows students to record their academic lives on their servers, do they have a right to charge students to access that data years later?

Obviously, the wireless Web is ultimately not about simply reformatting what's on the Web to fit on a mobile device. It's also more than just about cre-ating a different platform that can support different needs. From business and sociopolitical perspectives, it's about redefining the way people communi-cate, conduct commerce, and transact business wherever they are in the world and, if possible, improving upon current processes.

From a personal perspective, the wireless Web represents a gateway into a new way of thinking about privacy, of contributing to society, and of leaving a legacy. Given the multitude of political, moral, and ethical views possible on these and other sociopolitical topics, it's clear that wireless technology is an enabler and not the rate-limiting step in the move toward pervasive comput-ing. The next chapter explores the technologic, business, political, and social issues that represent both challenges and opportunities for companies mov-ing into the wireless Web space.

EXECUTIVE SUMMARY

The potential of the wireless Web is much more than a new technology for creating another touch point for customers to interact with a business. Whereas the Internet provides the standard IP communications protocol, the Web provides a crucial memory component that has the potential to transform the Web-Internet combination into a pervasive communications and computing network. Pervasive computing involves both wired and wire-less Web connectivity. Predictions are for 1 billion wireless devices to be in use worldwide by 2003. Almost half of these devices will be connected to the

Internet, the same number of desktop devices projected to be connected to the Web.

The convergence of several enabling technologic, sociologic, business, and political factors strongly suggests that the time is now for wireless Web development. With the ability to provide anytime, anywhere, context specific, accurate, timely communications and computing, the challenge for creating the wireless component of pervasive computing is in deciding what needs to be wireless, and which markets have the greatest potential. There should be a focus on identifying the need for anytime, anywhere communications, tempered by a vision for where the technology and the industry as a whole is headed. In this regard, the key issue seems to be whether pervasive computing will be based on a post-PC, disseminated, virtual machine architecture or an extension of the existing PC operating system model.

Although there are multiple opportunities for wireless Web development in all industries, the most obvious areas appear to be medicine, travel, and financial services. For example, bedside computing for clinicians and Web-enabled home monitoring systems can simplify home monitoring to the point that elderly patients can operate the system without outside intervention. Often, the acceptance of these and other new Web-enabled technologies is impeded by a social momentum that resists change.

8

What's the Holdup?

A bend in the road isn't the end of the road —
as long as you remember to take the turn.

Joan Lunden

INTRODUCTION

In the face of profound marketing hype and what appears to be at least limited success for Europe and Asia in their wireless Web ventures, what's the
holdup? After all, isn't the wireless Web simply another touch point for an
organization? Why aren't more companies in the United States, Europe, and
Asia following the lead of the international telecom giants in their efforts to
provide subscribers with personalized, private, immediate access to information? Perhaps a better question is why the level of interest and activity isn't at
the level demonstrated during the action-packed nascent period of the wired
Web, the nearest technology to the wireless Web. Actually, thousands of
companies of various sizes around the world *are* jumping in, but many of
their activities aren't yet obvious because the CEOs of these companies are
wrestling with several challenges inherent in any new industry. The purpose
of this chapter is to highlight these challenges on the path to the wireless
Web, so knowledgeable executives can either address the challenges directly
or create a business around providing relief for other executives facing the
same issues.

The cautious approach that many CEOs are taking with the wireless
Web is related to factors common to the commercialization of a new technology. At the highest level, most of these factors are manifestations of a level
of fear and uncertainty. For example, there is a degree of uncertainty in the
investment community, in companies with a wired Web presence, and in the

general public regarding exactly what the wireless Web is and is not. Is it a completely new and separate touch point, like a fax machine or a telephone, or is it simply an extension of the wired Web experience onto new hardware? If a wireless Web initiative is undertaken at a company, who should own it— the IT division, the Web development group, telecommunications, or a new department? In addition to the uncertainty surrounding wireless technology, a lack of technical expertise, unproven business models, and the need to partner with or at least rely on start-up companies that have experience measured in months elicits fear in the minds of many executives.

In many instances, this fear and uncertainty are probably more appropriately labeled *issues of timing.* Many business executives are *certain* that they want to wait and see what happens in the wireless Web market. After all, there were major marketing efforts and a degree of initial success in the European and Asian markets for Laserdisc, HDTV, and the Interactive CD technologies—all stagnant or dead technologies today. Similarly, Clarion Corporation's AutoPC and the original Iridium Satellite systems were both launched with backing from major corporations, but neither of these technologies gained a critical mass of followers.

The issues outlined below are not offered as a body of information to be used by CEOs to rationalize waiting even longer before staking a claim on the wireless Web frontier. Instead, these challenges are offered to provide decision makers with a fuller understanding of ramifications of wireless Web technologies, so they can make better strategic decisions. With an understanding of the major issues related to the wireless Web, executives should be in a position to limit risk exposure while positioning their organization for maximum gain.

Many of the challenges listed below may be perceived as negatives by some executives, and as market opportunities by others, depending on the company's position in the wireless or supporting industry. For example, the prospect of having to support a new generation of wireless device hardware every 12 to 18 months may be perceived as a major challenge to the CEO of a company involved in developing and delivering content to wireless Web subscribers. However, for the CEO of a company that is involved in developing tools that can speed and simplify the process of supporting multiple hardware platforms, the stream of new hardware may represent her company's future revenue stream.

CHALLENGES AND OPPORTUNITIES IN THE EMERGING WIRELESS WEB SPACE

Continuing with the metaphor of the activation energy of a process that was introduced in Chapter 7, the primary challenges or issues that must be addressed in order for a company to move rapidly from a wired to a wireless Web presence. These issues, which are inherent to some degree in every emerging market, can be categorized as managerial, political, medical, legal, economic, technical, market-based, and social. For example, CEOs in virtually every industry have to deal with challenges surrounding the medical or environmental impact of their companies' goods or services, whether related to pollution resulting from the production and distribution of widgets, or from the potential hazard that the widgets pose to the health and well-being of end users.

These issues not only account for the bulk of the activation energy required to shift the progression from wired to wireless Web connectivity but they also represent opportunities for leaders of companies with solutions—catalysts—that can diminish the significance of these challenges for others. For example, many of the technical challenges associated with the current generation of wireless devices are being addressed in the R&D departments of companies throughout the world. In many cases, a solution to a challenge in any of the areas could catapult the wireless Web industry forward by years, for example, the introduction of a high-capacity, postage stamp-size energy source. The challenges and opportunities within each of the eight areas are described in more detail below.

MANAGEMENT ISSUES

The CEO's task of guiding his organization through the process of entering and exploiting the wireless Web space, regardless of the organization's position in the value chain, is characterized by uncertainty and volatility (see Figure 8-1). As such, a successful CEO in this arena requires a special mix of confidence, ambition, vision, genius, and fortitude. The key management issues are described in the following paragraphs.

MANAGEMENT ISSUES

Duality of Focus
Technologic Details
Volatility in the Space
Geographical Pockets of Expertise
The Wired Web
Diversion of Resources
Value Chain Positioning
Vendor Evaluation
Identifying Low-Hanging Fruit
The Huge Space
Management Strategies and Structures

Figure 8-1. Management issues in the emerging wireless Web industry.

Duality of Focus

The wireless Web can be divided into at least two major market segments, enterprise-centric and eCommerce-centric, each with its own goals, challenges, responsibilities, opportunities, and metrics for success. For instance, enterprise-centric initiatives, such as those providing a company's sales force with wireless EDA (Enterprise Digital Assistant) support are focused on providing employees with a competitive advantage over the competition through increased employee effectiveness and improved customer satisfaction. In contrast, eCommerce-centric initiatives (i.e., those providing an additional touch point to an online bookstore) are concerned with metrics such as an increased conversion rate (a measure of the number of visitors who initiate a business transaction within a particular period of time, relative to the total number of visitors), greater customer satisfaction, and, ultimately, greater customer loyalty.

From a management perspective, the eCommerce-centric segment is a much more volatile, unknown environment. Since the segment is characterized by unknown users employing a variety of hardware platform and operating system configurations, providing personalized, location-specific, timely content is much more of a challenge. Not only must a CEO whose company is focused on this space stay abreast of technologic developments so new devices and software systems can be supported as they hit the market, but she must contend with the competition as well. Many companies will eventually be involved in both market segments, requiring a support structure capable of addressing the challenges in each area.

Technologic Details

Because the wireless Web is a relatively new space, CEOs have to focus on technologic details that are normally the sole purview of Chief Information Officers (CIOs), Chief Technology Officers (CTOs), and technology specialists. Because wireless Web technology is evolving rapidly, standards are moving targets, and small changes in the technologic mix will provide some companies with an advantage in the marketplace, and cause others to fail. In other words, the successful management team in the nascent wireless Web space will have an understanding of the underlying technologies to a breadth and depth much greater than that of executives in, for example, the mature desktop PC industry. As the wireless Web matures and technology standards are established, executives will be able to focus more of their attention on the more compelling global strategic issues.

Volatility in the Space

The wireless Web space, like the early wired Web arena, is characterized by frequent acquisitions and mergers. Most of this volatility is found in the maturer, developed areas of the wireless value chain, such as the service providers.

Geographical Pockets of Expertise

As in most other industries, the political, business, and technical infrastructures favor one region and country over another in the availability of affordable skilled workers. For example, middleware developers seem to be crystallizing in Silicon Valley, hardware centers are in Japan and Sweden, and centers of expertise in infrastructure development are appearing throughout the EU. Companies that can't move to centers of expertise have a formidable challenge when attempting to recruit employees.

The Wired Web

The wired Web, the nearest technologic relative to the wireless Web, is also one of the greatest impediments to managing its development. Like a sapling growing in the shadow of a mature tree that prevents the sapling from absorbing enough sustenance from the soil to grow, the wired Web commands the limited resources that the wireless Web needs to grow and thrive. For example, the CEO of a company with a wired Web presence may have committed to wired Web maintenance and growth plans that have already strained hard to find and manage resources. For this CEO, the wireless Web is a diversion, or, at best, something to pursue *after* the next major overhaul of his company's wired Web system, which may be months or years away.

The wired Web is also a source of confusion for end-users. For example, because of their experience with the Web from the vantage provided by desktop PCs, many domestic subscribers have an unrealistic, preconceived notion of what the wireless Web should offer. Choosing which of these expectations to meet, and which to ignore, is a major management decision that has to take into account the resource requirements for implementing a specific feature versus the level of customer satisfaction.

Diversion of Resources

Information-based projects in other areas of a company may need to be put on hold or reduced in scope in order for the company to enter the wireless Web arena. Other touch points, including the wired Web, may have to be curtailed because they are less acute—with significant negative resource management repercussions. For example, if a CEO initiates a project to automate her company's internal sales force with wireless email and Web access, she may need to temporarily divert resources normally used to maintain core legacy systems. If these systems provide the backbone for communications for the sales force, and the wireless solution does not prove to be immediately effective, then the sales force may be at a competitive disadvantage for many months.

Value Chain Positioning

Because the wireless space is so volatile, many companies are constantly jostling for a place along the value chain. Uncertainties in the direction of the market reward executives of companies that can quickly adapt to change, and reposition their company's products and services along the value chain. For example, in the shift from B2C to B2B on the wired Web, in an effort to realize greater profits, many former suppliers became customers, and many former customers disappeared from the value chain.

Vendor Evaluation

Wireless vendor evaluation is a challenge for most executives. Wireless Web vendors with apparent technical competence, no track record, and headed by a CEO recently recruited from a dotCom are common. As such, because so many executives are new to the wireless arena, technically competent companies without knowledgeable leadership often fail to differentiate themselves in terms of providing credentials, identifying their unique features, emphasizing the value they provide relative to the competition, and communicating these differences in a professional manner. To complicate matters, many wireless technology vendors play on price-quality product confusion, setting an artificially high price to assert high quality to gain and retain market share.

Identifying Low-Hanging Fruit

CEOs of wireless Web companies are challenged to identify their most likely successes in order to demonstrate the viability of their business to early investors and to secure additional funding. For example, in the United States, financial, travel, and medical transactions are the three areas that seem to hold the greatest potential for early success in the wireless space.

The Huge Space

The wireless Web is a huge space that presents CEOs with seemingly infinite unknowns and options. As a reference point, consider the wired Web, which appears to many brick-and-mortar CEOs as a large, undifferentiated space filled with both opportunities and pitfalls, especially in the realm of eCommerce. However, to CEOs in the wireless Web space, the wired Web appears as a solid foundation where strategic decisions are most often based on an understanding of the wired Web trajectory, of the resources required, the relevant rules and regulations, the support requirements, and of where to find help. In contrast, for many executives new to the wireless Web space, there are dozens of technologies to contend with, even more standards, unknown and evolving federal, state, regional, and local telecommunications guidelines and laws, and an unclear endpoint.

Management Strategies and Structures

The above management issues highlight the need for a CEO to explore new management strategies and structures for her company to succeed in the wireless Web space. This shift in management strategy and structure occurred in the wired Web early on. As the wired Web evolved from its status as a marketing vehicle to a touch point of magnitude equivalent to that of the telephone, a new management structure evolved in most corporations, or, if an existing IT structure was in place, folded into existing structures.

Issues that may call for a CEO to explore new management strategies and structures include how to convert PDAs and other personal devices used by employees to EDAs. The challenge facing a CEO includes determining how best to provide benefits to her company without ostracizing or otherwise overcontrolling employees who are accustomed to owning and managing their own data. For example, as a company moves along the continuum from PDAs to EDAs for its employees, the CEO may be forced to establish a management structure for the enterprise devices. The higher level of technical support may require reeducation of employees as well as support utilities and other software to make device management as painless and as efficient as possible.

POLITICAL ISSUES

Wherever large sums of money and international corporations are involved, politics are soon to follow. The wireless Web space is no exception; it brings with it a veritable maze of international, national, state, and local political challenges for executives to solve. (See Figure 8-2.)

Standards Organizations

The main international standards organizations that every CEO in the wireless Web space needs to be familiar with are the International Telecommunications Union (ITU) and the Consultative Committee on International Telegraph and Telephone (CCITT). The ITU is a specialized agency of the United Nations and the CCITT is an operational entity of the ITU. Both of these organizations are intimately involved in issues such as spectrum assignments for cell phone users and other services.

POLITICAL
ISSUES

Standards Organizations
Contention for Limited Spectrum
Opposition to Foreign Investment
Local Governments as Stakeholders
International Politics

Figure 8-2. Political issues in the emerging wireless Web industry.

Contention for Limited Spectrum

One of the major political battles in the wireless Web space in the United States is over the fate of 3G services, since the FCC has yet to clearly designate where in the RF spectrum 3G services will be licensed. The Cellular Telecommunications Industry Association (CTIA), which represents the interests of the domestic telecommunications industry, suggests that the 1.7- to 1.8-GHz band is the most appropriate, in part because it would be consistent with plans for 3G services in Canada and Central America. However, a large segment of that band is occupied by the U.S. Department of Defense, which has invested more than $100 billion in its communications infrastructure to support almost 900,000 military systems, from weapons to military satellites.

The CTIA and Satellite Industry Association (SIA) propose the 2.5- to 2.7-GHz band as an alternative to the 1.7- to 1.8-GHz band for 3G services. However, their petition to the FCC is opposed by the Multi-channel Multipoint Distribution Service (MMDS) and Instructional Television Fixed Services (ITFS), which own licenses in that band. Educational institutions that own the ITFS licenses are reluctant to give up their spectrum licenses, but are negotiating leasing arrangements with domestic carriers. In other words, there aren't any uncontested spectrum slots remaining. In order for the FCC to award a new slot for 3G services, it would have to dislodge some other service.

Opposition to Foreign Investment

There is increasing political opposition to foreign-government—backed companies purchasing controlling shares in U.S. telecommunications companies. For example, a bill introduced by Senator Ernest Hollings in 2000 attempts to block any company from buying a U.S. phone company as long as a foreign government holds more than a quarter of the company. Politicians in Europe and Asia hold similar sentiments regarding investment from overly aggressive U.S. firms.

Local Governments as Stakeholders

Local governments are becoming aware of the leverage they hold in controlling access to the wireless Web. For example, Sweden's auction for G3 wireless licenses wasn't simply awarded to the highest bidder. As part of the bidding process, the telecom companies had to convince local regulators that they had the means to construct a G3 network and could guarantee excellent coverage and rapid development. In other words, Sweden didn't want to simply be a piece on a Monopoly board, with the licenses it granted to be used in some other business transaction, but required the recipients of their licenses to be committed to actually performing the development. The so-called beauty contest approach in which bidders compete to promise the best levels of service and most timely rollout, has also been embraced by Spain, Norway, France, and Portugal.

International Politics

The control of domestic telecom companies by foreign governments, especially as it relates to national security and market dominance, is a political issue in Asia, Europe, and the United States. For example, the FBI is concerned that a foreign-owned telecom company would be in a position to control or hide communications of a national security nature. As such, the FBI wants to maintain full access to all communications networks.

The value of wireless licenses as a card in international politics became obvious when China was desperate to join the World Trade Organization (WTO). At the time, there were indications that China's state-owned Unicom Telecommunications Company would use the CDMA standard popular in the United States instead of the European GSM standard. An agreement to use CDMA would have been a windfall for Qualcomm, Inc., the California company that holds the patents on CDMA technology. Similarly, Lucent Technologies stood to make millions installing the CDMA systems. In the end, the political carrot of WTO membership was insufficient, and China opted to use the GSM standard. However, there remains the potential for Qualcomm and other U.S. companies to work with China on CDMA-based systems in the future.

In potential agreements between U.S. corporations and foreign-owned companies, the FBI has concerns over giving a foreign government—controlled company access to U.S. government wiretapping activity, because it represents an espionage risk. The FBI's official stance is to bar disclosure of any classified or intercepted information to foreign governments. Increasingly, potential global wireless communications agreements face scrutiny from the

FBI, which often delays approval of agreements that have been approved by the FCC. The FBI apparently fears that it may lose the ability to wiretap communications outside of the United States, or that foreigners could eavesdrop on business conversations and steal trade secrets.

Another political issue is simply the time required to obtain approval from the FCC for mergers and acquisitions. A proposed merger or acquisition of two wireless carriers commonly takes one or two years to make it through the FCC gauntlet. Political snags also await U.S. and European companies involved in the wireless expansion in Europe, even though the EU is a strong proponent of wireless connectivity. Consider Britain's telecommunications industry. Even though Britain's was the first telecom deregulated in Europe, and has one of the most advanced telecommunications systems in Europe, old monopolies are creating political roadblocks that threaten to stall Britain's move to the wireless Web.

MEDICAL ISSUES

As mentioned earlier in this chapter, every business venture is associated with a medical or environmental impact of some type. For example, the manufacture of the electronic components found in every cell phone and PDA negatively impacts the environment because of the volatile solvents, heavy metals, and other pollutants released into the environment. More specifically, however, the medical issues related to cell phone use revolve around the *potential* radiation hazard that long-term use poses to subscribers, as well as the much clearer relationship between cell phone use and driving accidents. (See Figure 8-3.)

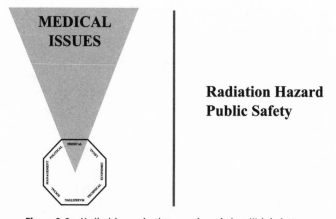

Figure 8-3. Medical issues in the emerging wireless Web industry.

Radiation Hazard

Speculation. The speculation surrounding the use of cell phones is that prolonged operation of a cell phone held against the head results in an increased incidence of certain brain cancers, and may adversely affect the functioning of the brain. It is theorized that localized heating of brain tissue may somehow hinder the DNA in brain tissues to repair itself, somehow resulting in brain cancer. It is also theorized that any health effect of cellular radiation will be more pronounced in children because cell phone radiation penetrates more deeply into a child's brain than an adult's brain. As a precaution, the British government officially discourages children from using cell phones for nonessential communications.

The speculation surrounding the possible ill effects of cell phone use was brought to the public's attention in 1993 with a lawsuit filed by a Florida man who claimed that his wife's brain tumor was caused by her mobile phone. In order to respond to the resulting public concern and to circumvent the potential of federal legislation on cell phone use, the CTIA, the U.S. lobby group for cell phone manufacturers and carriers, initiated a six-year study. The $25 million industry-sponsored study on the health risks of cell phone use, which ended in 1999, was inconclusive.

Objective Data. The biological effect of radio frequency radiation is quantified in terms of Specific Absorption Rate (SAR), a figure that reflects the absorption of RF energy by tissues. The SAR is a function of the cell phone's signal frequency, how the antenna is oriented relative to the tissue, whether the antenna is in, out, fixed, or internal, and whether the signal is continuous (analog) or pulsed (digital). It's clear, through objective measures, that cell phone radiation does affect brain tissue. Using a cell phone that generates the typical $1/4$-W output for a few minutes raises the temperature of nearby brain tissue by about 1/10th of a degree C. The implication is unclear, in part because normal brain temperature fluctuation in a 24-h period is about 1 °C.

An objective characteristic of low-power RF energy in the cell phone frequency range (about 800 MHz to 2 GHz) is that it's nonionizing. In other words, the photons or energy particles emitted by a cell phone aren't energetic enough to break down organic bonds in tissues or in a subscriber's DNA that could result in cancer-initiating mutations.

Several studies with mice suggest that cell phone radiation can affect mental performance. Although mice exposed to cell phone radiation displayed decreased reaction times, they took longer to find their way through a maze than nonradiated mice (the control group). However, results such as these are inconclusive, in part because of how the studies were carried out and interpreted. There are issues of disease incidence (number of new cases) and prevalence (number of cases that exist at a particular time), what constitutes a control group, correlation versus causation, and the relevance of animal studies in predicting human outcomes. In addition, studies vary in the statistical methods used, including selection of subjects, sample size, the nature of the subjects, experimenter bias, and the relative merit of epidemiology (studies of populations) versus limited lab studies. There is also a question of whether RF radiation has a cumulative effect and follows a dose-response curve, or is associated with threshold effect. The repeatability of studies is of particular concern, in that several key studies that have been repeated by other investigators reveal results very different from those documented by the initial experimenter.

The problem with epidemiological or population-based studies is that cell phones haven't been in use for the decades that it might take for significant health findings to become apparent. In addition, many cancers and tumors require multiple causation (for example, exposure to radiation *and* a toxic substance), and have incubation periods measured in years. In population studies, the distinction between causation and correlation is an important one. To illustrate, if 10,000 businesspeople hold bananas to their right ear for one hour a day, five days a week, for years, it's possible that, compared to businesspeople who never touch a banana (the control group) the banana holders will have a higher incidence of brain cancer—not to mention right elbow pain. Even though banana use and an increased incidence of brain cancer are corelated—that is, the use of bananas is related to an increased incidence of brain cancer—the cancer may have been *caused* by something else. A pesticide or other toxin on the banana peel, a virus carried by fruit flies that congregate near bananas, or some behavior of the businesspeople might have a causal link. For example, some of them might wash their hands with a special cleaner to get rid of the smell, and some substance in the cleaner actually causes brain cancer.

In appraising the relevance of cell phone radiation as a health risk, there is also the practical issue of quantifying cost and relevance. If the incidence of cancer in the control group is 1 in 1,000,000 businesspeople per year, a doubling of the incidence to 2 cases in 1,000,000 businesspeople per year may not be significant in the bigger picture of things. Every time a businessperson embarks on a business trip, her chances of succumbing to a violent death as a passenger in a taxi or airplane increases significantly, compared to the businessperson lounging at a poolside resort, conducting business over his cell phone.

Regulations. The FCC limits cellular and PCS base station output power to 500 W, depending on antenna height, and cell phones intended to be installed in cars with roof-mounted antennas are limited to 3-W output. Interestingly, in the United States, the FCC regulates personal exposure to RF radiation, not OSHA, which is normally charged with evaluating health risks, especially in the workplace.

The FCC's guidelines limit SAR to 1.6 W/Kg, measured over any 1 g of tissue. Typical values for cell phones range from as little as 0.22 W/Kg to almost 1.5 W/Kg, as measured using a lab test dummy filled with artificial brain matter. In addition to the SAR figure, the FCC limits radio frequency exposure at 869 MHz to 580 µW per square centimeter of tissue. At 1850 to 1999 MHz, the exposure limit is 1000 µW per square centimeter of tissue.

In a CTIA move to circumvent federal legislation against cell phone use, it requires cell phone manufacturers to disclose radiation levels produced by their devices. The initial phase of the policy requires makers to provide information on handset emissions, as well as details on the testing process *inside* each cell phone box. The industry-imposed regulation doesn't go as far as to require the emission figures to be listed on the outside of the box—a move that would make it easier for consumers to comparison shop.

Confounding Factors. One of the problems in looking for a causal link between cell phone use and certain cancers is that virtually everyone in a developed country is immersed in electromagnetic fields that may have detrimental effects. For example, the low-frequency fields produced by hair dryers and around high-voltage power lines have been implicated as initiators of cancer in a number of studies. Since the introduction of electricity in the home, most people in developed countries have been immersed in a 60-Hz electromagnetic field for their entire lives.

Secondary Gain. There are several groups with vested interests in both sides of the cell phone use and cancer issue. For example, while the major telecom companies are obvious stakeholders, there are activists that claim to be acting in the public's interest in order to gain personal attention and political clout. There are also multiple national and international political agendas and billions of dollars at stake. Wireless Technology Research (WTR), a private company with the responsibility of controlling and funding the CTIA's cell phone health research in the United States, and the Scientific Advisory Group of the CTIA have much at stake as well.

In the end, if a causal link between cell phone use and cancer or some other health condition is established, then the industry may experience a major setback. However, if managed properly, the findings could also represent an opportunity for companies that offer Bluetooth headsets and other low-power radio frequency communications technologies.

Public Safety

In contrast to the uncertainties surrounding the potential hazards of cell phone use on the physiologic health of subscribers, there is a direct, causal relationship between cell phone use and higher rates of traffic accidents when subscribers talk and drive. As such, the National Highway Traffic Safety Administration (NHTSA) advises drivers not to use cell phones and other electronic devices while driving. Restrictions have also been advanced at the state and city level. New York, for example, bans taxicab drivers from using cell phones while driving. Similarly, Merck Pharmaceuticals provides hands-free sets to its employees, and has an official policy that employees pull over before phoning. At least some of the motivation for cautioning employees on cell phone use is that employers may be held liable for employee accidents related to cell phone use while driving.

In the first U.S. criminal trial of a case involving a driver distracted by a cell phone, a Maryland man was convicted of negligence, but not manslaughter, in two deaths. The judge in the case was unable to convict the man on manslaughter charges because it was not illegal to talk on a cell phone while driving in Maryland or any other state.

Although additional restrictions have been proposed at the state and federal level, there is significant resistance from the domestic wireless industry against any form of legislation. Since the majority of wireless calls are made from vehicles, cell phone carriers depend on drivers for a vast amount of their revenues. Similarly, the auto industry is seeking to add navigation and other Web-based features to car-based cell phones in order to sell services to drivers. In an attempt to head off legislation that would negatively impact the sales of cell phones in the United States, the major handset manufacturers, including Nokia, are sponsoring public safety notices through radio and other media to urge drivers to use cell phones responsibly.

An additional public safety risk, although slight, is that the use of a cell phone near gas pumps may lead to explosions. In addition to potential danger from a cell phone's radio frequency signal igniting gas fumes, it's far more likely that dropping a cell phone in the proximity of gas fumes may lead to an explosion. The danger is that if a phone is dropped hard enough to dislodge its battery, then arcing at the point of contact between the phone and the battery pack may ignite gas fumes. Problems with arcing and batteries aren't new to the electronics industry; Apple Computer's initial Powerbook battery packs were known to burst into flames under certain conditions. In recognition of the potential risk of using a cell phone near open fumes—even if only risk from lawsuits—Exxon posts a "no cell phones" sign on their self-service gas pumps.

LEGAL ISSUES

With the technical convergence of voice and data, wireless Web executives face a clash of legal cultures. The Web industry, through major lobbying efforts, managed for years to keep the Web free of any tax, even while business conducted over the telephone or fax—wireless or wired—was subject to taxation. While the wired Web has maintained a relatively free-for-all attitude toward eCommerce, the telecoms face local, regional, and federally imposed taxes and regulations. To a CEO recruited from wired dotCom companies, the impact of dealing with the legal overhead associated with the wireless Web can result in culture shock.

Listed in Figure 8-4, and described below, are other issues that relate directly to the bottom line.

Figure 8-4. Legal issues in the emerging wireless Web industry.

FCC Licensing

To the CEO of a wireless Web company, the FCC can be a welcome friend or a formidable foe, depending on the size of the company and its place in the wireless Web value chain. For example, in order to give smaller carriers the ability to compete against larger, established companies for spectrum space, the FCC typically imposes limitations on bidders, such as total revenue and asset caps. As a result, smaller domestic companies can compete in markets they would otherwise be barred from.

The FCC also has a history of providing licenses in order to encourage experimentation on frequencies beyond what is considered commercially viable. These experimental licenses encourage development of future communications technologies. However, as higher and higher bands are conquered and commercialized, what constitutes as experimental continually changes. For example, the bands now occupied by cellular communications were once considered virtually unusable, and allocated to experimenters.

Intellectual Property

Like her dotCom counterparts, a CEO heading a company in the wireless Web space has to stay abreast of the evolving status of Web-based intellectual property issues, especially if her company is involved in content creation or repurposing. For example, MP3 was ordered to pay $250 million to the music industry for copyright violations. Similarly, the "conglomerates" face legal battles over repurposing Web content in browser environments that combine content from multiple sites into one page.

As wireless handheld devices increase in popularity, clipping services that selectively extract data from content originally developed for the wired Web will likely face legal challenges, as well. For example, if the clipped content doesn't provide the same subjective response from subscribers, does the company that developed the content have any recourse against the clipping service? Do advertisers and backers of content development have a right to have their ads and recognition of their contributions survive the clipping process?

For CEOs of companies developing wireless Web devices for internal employee support, there are an increasing number of intellectual property issues to contend with. For example, when a salesman leaves a company, from a practical perspective, how are lists of contacts and other corporate information on his personal wireless PDA and the synced information on his home PC reclaimed by the company? Can this dilemma be solved by issuing wireless EDAs in which the data are available to salespersons, but can't be synced or otherwise downloaded to other devices?

Revisiting the student introduced in Chapter 7 who had her classroom work during college stored on the Web, primarily with the assistance of wireless devices, what intellectual property rights can the college retain? Similarly, what rights do her college professors have over the use and repurpose of the content, since, in many respects, they are the originators of the intellectual property? Do universities have the right to sell a student's intellectual property to a third party without the student's permission? While there are obvious opportunities for legal firms in the area of intellectual property, there is also a place for companies that provide employees with information that cannot be easily extracted from handheld devices, and that allow only context-specific viewing of account information.

Fraud

When President Clinton signed the digital signature bill into law in June 2000, for many transactions, online signatures became as valid as pen-and-ink signatures. However, the bill doesn't specify what constitutes a legitimate, safe, secure digital signature. It's up to the online community to establish technology standards in secure digital signatures, which can range from smart cards to biometrics, including thumbprint, retinal, or voice-recognition.

Paradoxically, one area that isn't affected by the digital signature law is online sales, which continue to be a major risk for online merchants. If a hacker steals a credit card number and uses it to make a purchase online, the card holder isn't held liable. Instead, the credit card transaction disputed by the cardholder—the chargeback—is the merchant's responsibility. Although credit card companies usually absorb chargeback costs resulting from offline transactions, without a pen-and-paper signature, charge card companies won't honor a merchant's claim that a product was shipped. In short, the merchant pays even if a customer orders an item online and then claims that she never received it.

Chargeback is four times greater for online sales than for mail-order purchases, and almost 6 times greater than brick-and-mortar purchases. Of particular note for the CEO of a wireless Web company targeting the lucrative travel industry is that online credit card fraud is greatest with high-value items, such as airline tickets.

Although credit card fraud is an industrywide problem, it also represents an opportunity for companies offering solutions. Companies that create screening software that profiles and identifies suspicious charges, much like the closely guarded systems charge card companies use internally to detect fraud, would find themselves very much in demand. A fraud detection system that looks for high-priced airline tickets purchased at the last minute could potentially reduce fraud, assuming tickets are stolen for immediate resale to travelers.

Other solutions to credit card fraud involve more secure methods of payment. For example, American Express offers a disposable credit card, expressly for use with all Web-based transactions. Their Private Payments option allows cardholders to obtain a unique card number each time they purchase something through the Web, so they don't give out their actual credit card number. Once the card number is used, it becomes invalid. The service, which is free to cardholders and merchants, complements the AMEX Blue Card service that allows holders to transfer credit information directly to online retailers. The Blue Card system, which requires cardholders to use a card reader that is larger than most handheld units, isn't practical for wireless handheld devices.

An alternative card-based technology is available from ComSense Technologies (www.com-sense.com). The system uses a smart card that, when squeezed, sends an ultrasonic signal to a PC or wireless handheld's microphone. The signal routes an encrypted one-time code to an online retailer's server where it is decrypted and compared with a credit card database.

ECONOMIC ISSUES

Regardless of how sanguine the visions of the future wireless world are, and the impressiveness of the technology, at the end of the day the companies involved in creating a future wireless utopia must profit from their activities. As the wired Web has taught many dotCom CEOs, activity on the Web, even when offering obvious benefits, poses several questions regarding long-term viability. CEOs involved in applying wireless devices to external markets not only have to contend with the issues related to the wired Web, such as conversion rate, stickiness (how much time a user spends at a Web site), and developing customer loyalty but they also have to contend with a fee structure that raises expectations.

It's one thing for a dotCom to attract customers to a freely accessible Web site where they can be exposed to the products and services, and another for a company to offer a touch point in which customers have to pay for the privilege of receiving the same information. For example, other than a businesswoman who has connect charges paid for by her company, not many potential customers can afford to pay $90 per month for cell phone charges and another $50 per month for wireless PDA connect charges—on top of their wired service provider charges.

Multiple devices may be affordable, but the total cost of ownership may be prohibitive in the private sector where most of the potential wireless customers are. Domestic demographics continue to show an increase in consulting and other forms of self-employment. Few of these workers, who pay their own connect charges, can afford the expense of multiple service provider accounts.

Listed in Figure 8-5 and described below are other issues that relate directly to the bottom line.

Speculation

Much of the Web—wireless or otherwise—is speculative. A CEO must deal with the uncertainty of which technologies and companies will survive after each business cycle. Some companies go after market share, speculating that sacrificing short-term profit for visibility will pay off in long-term viability. Other companies invest in securing a high-profile customer, often at a loss, expecting to improve their credentials through the association.

Many questions regarding the ultimate ROI of the wireless Web activities are unanswerable because of lack of experience with the medium. For example, will captive portals, such as the MODO wireless pager, which can be personalized to reflect preferences for social events, be a hit outside of New

ECONOMIC ISSUES

Speculation
Competition
Infrastructure Investment
Moving Targets
Support Structures
Scarcity of Expertise
Time Pressure
Strategic Partnerships
Critical Mass
Popularity vs. Profitability
Existing Processes
Lost Opportunity Costs
Billing Structure
Sensitivity to Pricing
Wanted: Killer App

Figure 8-5. Economic issues in the emerging wireless Web industry.

York, Los Angeles, and San Francisco? Will an investment in a wireless infrastructure serve as a hedge against being one-upped by the competition? Will increasing the stickiness of existing customers through increased personalization and adapting applications for customers and their businesses pay off?

The stickiness issue is especially relevant on the wireless Web because of the freedom the technology affords customers. For example, of the major players in the wireless Web space, the hardware vendors, software vendors, portals, ISPs, carriers, banks, and the stream of new entrants, it seems that banks are in the best position. After all, people don't often change banks, but everything else seems negotiable. That said, consider the effect on the retail industry of a bank and a hardware vendor getting together to provide a hip-mounted ATM with a bar-code scanner front-end.

Competition

Not only are there multiple entrants in the wireless Web space that are attempting to dislodge legacy technologies in favor of their own, but there are companies in other, nonwireless areas positioned to claim the same space. For example, CEOs and other executives of cell phone and smart card technology companies are stalking the lucrative charge card business. Smart cards have an advantage of increased security over conventional cards, without requiring the customer to learn or do anything new. Web-enabled cell phones that can initiate secure business transactions, in contrast, offer little to the customer, other than the advantage of receiving one less statement at the end of each month. For the telecoms, however, the capability of becoming a financial institution represents a huge potential market.

Infrastructure Investment

As wireless companies in the EU and Japan have shown, supporting a successful wireless Web initiative requires a significant investment in the underlying communications infrastructure in order to provide the security and bandwidth necessary for the development of wireless Web applications. This investment may be direct in an enterprise-centric model, such as allocating funds for servers, routers, and database management systems. It may also be indirect, especially in an eCommerce model, in the form of licensing arrangements with service providers.

Moving Targets

One of the most frustrating aspects of leading an organization through the wireless Web space is that what constitutes a deliverable product or service is a constantly moving target. In any emerging wireless Web market, what the customers want will certainly change by the delivery date, requiring more time and money to deliver what they actually want and need. For example, a wireless PDA without an always-on feature may be sufficient initially for the exchange of corporate communications, until some employees realize that they need the feature to receive immediate communications.

Support Structures

One of the side effects of activity on the wireless Web is the emergence of support structures and services that feed on and feed the early movers. Many of these support services, such as advertising, banking, and headhunters, benefit from the increased business activity. For example, radio broadcast stations benefit from ads for cellular services, battery manufacturers are pressed to supply new battery configurations for new wireless devices, and, accessory manufacturers attempt to profit from add-on cases, chargers, and long-life batteries. The issue for the CEO of a wireless Web company is whether these structures are serving only to divert capital away from their activities, or if they add to the validity of a product line by extending it.

Scarcity of Expertise

The new experts in the field of wireless Web communications and computation are in short supply, and these experts are demanding increasingly higher salaries. As a result, much of the workforce of wireless Web start-ups tend to be expensive consultants with no long-term commitment to a company, and who may take the knowledge gained through working on a problem with one company with them when they go to work for the competition.

Time Pressure

Executives in wireless Web companies are actively pursuing the highly coveted first-mover advantage in a variety of niche areas. Activity on the wired Web demonstrated that the first movers generally realize a competitive advantage by claiming a niche first; later movers are forced to do so simply to keep up with the competition. Many of the niches in the domestic wireless Web space have yet to be claimed—or defined.

Strategic Partnerships

The wireless Web space is too big to go it alone, even for the CEOs of the largest dotCom and telecommunications companies. Some strategic partnerships are more obvious than others, especially when they are between market leaders. For example, Motorola, the number two cellular handset supplier, and Palm formed a strategic partnership to codevelop a Web-enabled cell phone. Similarly, Phone.com, which produces WAP and microbrowsers for cell phones, partnered with application developer Software.com to provide a more rounded portfolio of products. However, few strategic partnerships are this clear or synergistic.

The issue of choosing a strategic partner is much more complicated when relatively new, minor players are involved. Typically, the strategic partnerships that form in a nascent industry such as the wireless Web are between established, high-profile companies and customers and new entrants in the field. Because the high-profile companies understand their positioning in the industry, they are able to demand very favorable partnership arrangements with smaller companies.

Critical Mass

The critical mass—or chicken-and-egg—problem that most wireless Web CEOs face is that there aren't enough customers to buy their products or services, in part because there isn't a large enough delivery platform. For example, even though the Palm VII is one of the most popular wireless PDAs in the United States, the installed base is insignificant compared to the number of PCs on the wired Web. Because of variation in the devices developed for the wireless Web, no one device has the critical mass necessary to attract customers or developers to a particular platform to the exclusion of all others.

The lack of a critical mass of wireless subscribers causes many application developers to take a wait-and-see approach. Early adopters are an important component of the user population, but they are usually insufficient in numbers to move a new wireless product or service into profitability. For example, although Bluetooth products were released in 2000, devices supporting the standard aren't expected to reach critical mass before 2004.

Popularity versus Profitability

As the wired Web has demonstrated, the popularity of a Web site doesn't necessarily translate into profitability. There are tens of thousands of popular Web sites that have yet to turn a profit, either because of flawed business plans or because it's easy for a company to create a popular Web site when the site is provided free of charge. Although there are notable exceptions, for example, the cartoon subscription service offered by NTT DoCoMo, profitability on the Web continues to be elusive, regardless of whether a cable or a wireless link provides the connectivity.

Existing Processes

A wireless solution has value if it saves a subscriber time, money, or both, relative to other competing solutions. For example, in the United States, where virtually every office worker has email, and most have wired Web access, simply offering these desk-based workers a wireless email solution isn't likely to sell millions of wireless Web appliances.

In countries like Czechoslovakia, where few adults carry or use credit cards, and most transactions are made with cash, Web-enabled cell phones may preempt the credit card. Because there is no legacy of plastic money, Czech businesspeople are more likely to accept the use of their cell phone as a method of payment. In contrast, in the United States, where the typical businessperson carries at least one charge card, there is little need for a new payment system, especially if it's slower or more complex than simply handing a salesperson a charge card. The challenge for CEOs of businesses that depend on wireless eCommerce for survival is to provide a compelling reason why cellular subscribers should use their cell phone instead of cash or a charge card.

Lost Opportunity Costs

Cellular voice services are now commodity items with decreasing profit margins. With the possible exception of pager services, voice makes up the bulk of billing time for wireless operators, even in Japan and Europe. One challenge that the CEOs of these wireless operators face in developing and supporting bandwidth-hungry 3G wireless services is evaluating lost opportunity costs. Since hundreds of voice calls can fit into the bandwidth proposed for 3G services, and as long as there are potential customers for wireless voice communications, providing affordable 3G-level multimedia services will cost the wireless operators potential revenue.

The potential for lost voice business isn't a major concern in Japan and Europe, partially because operators that run out of bandwidth can license new spectrum for 3G services. In contrast, lost opportunity costs are significant for operators in the United States because of the lack of spectrum for expansion. For example, PCS operators in the United States already occupy the 2-GHz spectrum that other countries are licensing for 3G services.

Billing Structure

A key business issue in the United States is the billing structure for wireless services. In most cases, the cell phone subscriber pays for calls initiated and received at a cell phone. This is a major deterrent for ubiquitous cell phone use—simply because most businesspeople don't give out their cell phone numbers to casual acquaintances as they might with a wired phone number. Most of the wireless carriers are actively experimenting with a variety of billing schemes in order to attract and keep customers. For example, AT&T was the first major domestic cell phone service provider to offer voice subscribers wireless Web browsing without extra fees.

Sensitivity to Pricing

The sensitivity to pricing demonstrated by wired telephone subscribers in response to special calling plans pales in comparison to price sensitivity along the wireless Web value chain. Because the basic assumptions of CEOs of companies along the value chain are so volatile and based predominantly on predictions, small changes in the pricing structure can decimate entire categories of product and service providers.

Several wireless middleware vendors offer systems that assume that subscribers pay for connect time, regardless of the amount of data transferred to their wireless PDAs. In this scenario, the middleware products, which download all potentially interesting information at once and then quickly disconnect from the network, provide value to subscribers in part because they can work with the data offline. Not only are connect charges lower, but systems that take advantage of local processing power for tasks such as compressing and uncompressing text, can provide subscribers with greater interactivity.

If, however, the wireless carriers change their pricing structure to reflect the amount of information transferred, regardless of the connect time, then these same middleware applications become much less attractive to subscribers. Although the advantages of local processing potentially provide a more enjoyable subscriber experience, the economic and time penalty subscribers pay for downloading several KB of content they won't view may outweigh any advantages of the middleware.

Wanted: Killer App

The dream of every dotCom CEO, wired or wireless, is to offer that one "killer app" that everyone simply has to have. In Japan and the European countries with a low penetration of desktop computing, the killer app, not surprisingly, appears to be email. However, aside from infrastructure developers, there isn't a very large market for email suppliers; the challenge for CEOs in the United States is to find a wireless must-have application other than email, which virtually every businessperson has at home or in the office.

In Europe, a must-have application that's also economically viable has yet to surface. While Web-enabled vending machines frequently make the news, simply because of the novelty factor, the soft drink industry isn't large enough to support all of the activity planned for the wireless Web. A killer app hasn't yet appeared that will make accessing the wireless Web an indispensable part of everyone's daily routine.

TECHNICAL ISSUES

The primary focus of all the wireless Web activity at this stage in its life cycle is technology. CEOs in the industry contend with issues such as how to best support wireless eCommerce, synchronization of data and applications, partnering with a wireless ISP, and how to develop a wireless Web portal. But for their technology to succeed in the wireless marketplace, five core criteria must be satisfied: performance, reliability, availability, ease of use, and security.

Although these criteria may seem self-evident, they are difficult to realize in practice. For example, product availability is susceptible to disruptions in the supply chain. In late 2000 and early 2001, there was a worldwide shortage of LCD panels, due in part to the increased worldwide demand for laptop and handheld computers. As a result, prices for LCD panels skyrocketed. In order to avoid forfeiting market share, many companies priced their wireless hand-held devices below cost. The situation parallels the events in the late 1990s, when the desktop PC market suffered from the scarcity and expense of RAM chips following the destruction of a RAM factory in Taiwan caused by an earthquake.

Because new technologies create shortages by their very nature, the supply of electronic components will likely periodically adversely affect wireless hardware production and distribution. Since only a few manufacturers in the world produce the leading-edge technologies used in wireless handheld devices, political or natural disruptions can easily upset the supply chain, and derail the projected progress of the wireless Web technologies.

Additional technology-related challenges associated with the wireless Web are described in Figure 8-6.

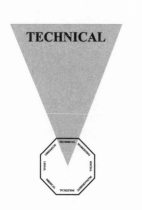

Complexity
Device Diversity
Scalability
Testing standards
User Interfaces
Security
Network Capacity
Development Tools
Infrastructure
Interference
Competing Standards
Bandwidth Projections
Content, Personalization
Localization
Timeliness
Hardware Limitations
Platform Standards
Communications Quality

Figure 8-6. Technical issues in the emerging wireless Web industry.

Complexity

The overriding technical concern of CEOs and CTOs in the wireless space is increasing complexity. With billions of two-way communications, glitches and down time will be unavoidable. The eventual move to a single wireless standard will mean that a computer virus may be able to cover the globe within minutes.

In addition to challenging executives, complexity also negatively affects the subscriber's experience. For example, although NTT DoCoMo I-Mode customers can subscribe to and unsubscribe from wireless Web access service with a few key clicks, the process is much more complicated for most U.S. and European subscribers. In order to subscribe to wireless Web services, wireless subscribers in the United States typically need to wade through several postage stamp-size pages of menus, and may even have to use the wired Web to finalize the transaction. For example, if a businessman in the United States wants to personalize the home page for his Web-enabled cell phone, he typically has to log on to the Web from his home or work computer. Interestingly, unsubscribing tends to be a much more arduous process than subscribing.

Device Diversity

The early, evolutionary phase of wireless Web development is characterized by incredible device diversity. There are PDAs designed for children, systems designed for automobiles, cell phones designed to be attached to clothing, and dozens of Web-enabled cell phone formats, and each device has its own development environment and standards, such as WAP, XML, or Palm.

Not only are the choices confusing for potential consumers, but software developers, system integrators, and executives with companies that want to add wireless touch points to their business are pressed to select the most viable options from a constant stream of hardware options. For example, the CEO of a company that needs to support customers or employees in the field must choose between dozens of two-way pagers, Web-enabled phones, and wireless PDAs. What's worse, the expected lifetime of these devices is typically less than 12 months, in part because better models are constantly being introduced.

Scalability

Virtually all wireless connectivity technology solutions have inherent scalability limits. For example, the Bluetooth standard is a viable technology for use with a handful of wireless devices. However, the system doesn't scale past nine Bluetooth units. Similarly, database connectivity and other infrastructure characteristics typically have a scalability limit, based on assumptions made by the original equipment designers. The challenge for the CEO of a company developing or delivering end-user wireless solutions is to correctly assess the scalability of the components and subsystems used in her company's products and services.

Testing Standards

Because wireless Web devices and software applications have not yet stabilized, there are no universally agreed-upon testing standards, especially in the areas of usability and ergonomics. In contrast to the desktop computing world, testing methodologies for user interface designs have not been fully developed, and those that have been advanced have not been fully adopted by the development community. Ease of use criteria, user testing, and other subjective tests are in their infancy in most wireless Web application development initiatives. Part of the challenge is that the criteria for optimum handheld device configuration take time to establish and disseminate. In addition, wireless handheld devices vary considerably in their physical user interface design from model to model, even with devices produced by the same manufacturer.

User Interfaces

The common denominator of wireless handheld device user interfaces is that they're new. It remains a challenge for even the most experienced desktop PC interface designer to develop and test a cell phone user interface that is limited to 16 characters per line or a wireless PDA with 200 characters per screen. The art and science of developing and testing wireless handheld device interfaces will likely remain a major challenge until a universal wireless communicator is designed.

Security

Security is perhaps the greatest challenge—and opportunity—for CEOs in the wireless Web space. Not only are wireless handheld devices subject to most of the same security limitations that plague wired desktop and unwired handheld units, including theft and attacks by viruses, but wireless communications can be intercepted more easily than signals traveling through a copper or fiber optic cable. The opportunity for CEOs of companies with security solutions for wireless handheld units rests in the fact that most potential customers understand that security has a cost, and many are willing to pay for peace of mind.

Network Capacity

Adding new wireless users to an already stressed network requires technical expertise, investment in infrastructure, and, if the legacy network system doesn't scale very well, a new network design. Larger, public networks tend to be configured for scalable growth. However, small and medium-size companies that add a few thousand new wireless network accounts to their existing network may have to invest considerable resources in network infrastructure and support staff.

Development Tools

The wireless Web value chain is inhabited by software tool builders and tool users. To some extent, the initial stages of wireless Web development parallel those of the wired Web, in that even software tool users end up performing some low-level development. For a company to create application- and hardware-specific features requires highly trained developers who can either work without advanced software tools or modify tools developed by others. The unknown and shifting standards in the wireless Web space make toolset development problematic.

For companies involved in tool development, the lack of mature development tools is a good thing. However, for companies interested in delivering their content to customers, the lack of tools presents a time and resource challenge. Software toolsets tend to be expensive when they are initially introduced, in part because the developers need to recoup their investment as soon as possible. Although most wireless development projects demand a suite of tools, costs can be prohibitive, especially if licensing significantly increases the price of the end user product.

Fortunately, the lack of development tools for wireless Web applications isn't a universal problem. Palm Computing and RIM, for example, offer a complete suite of development and testing tools for building wireless applications that run on their respective platforms. One of the Palm's strengths in the market is the thousands of applications that run under Palm OS. The large number of applications available for the Palm is in part due to the availability of tools from Palm, as well as a variety of high-level third-party tools that can minimize time to market.

Infrastructure

Nokia, Motorola, and Ericksson can continue to create miniature, lightweight, multifunction Web-enabled phones, but without a supporting infrastructure, they are valueless as communications devices. While there are standards evolving to provide support for wireless devices in the home and office environments, the infrastructure is by no means in place.

A wireless Web presence assumes that there is an infrastructure that can deal with issues from file distribution and email to security and systems management. Moving up the structure, from a PC with wired Web connectivity to a wireless handheld device should be accompanied by increased ease of use. For example, there are no disks to deal with, no waiting for a system to boot, no archiving to a server, or other routine maintenance tasks associated with a desktop PC. Conversely, moving up the pyramid represents increasing system complexity. Hiding all of the details of the underlying system takes more effort from programmers and device designers. This situation is similar to when Apple's Macintosh GUI was introduced at a time when MS-DOS was the predominant operating system on desktop microcomputers. DOS programs were much easier to write because, except for games, there was little attention paid to the user experience. The added overhead imposed by the Macintosh, and later Windows GUIs, complicates the programming and systems design tasks considerably because they shield the user from unnecessary details of computer operation.

Although, with outside help, some third-world countries can jump directly to wireless without ever developing a wired infrastructure, most companies in developed countries require experience and expertise with the wireless Web in order to realize the full potential of the medium. If the CEO of a company doesn't have a managerial, economic, and technical handle on his company's wired infrastructure, then moving to a handheld or wireless handheld system has a high degree of risk. Similarly, for a company to move to wireless handheld devices, it should first deal with the added challenge of handhelds, from the perspective of security, theft, and display limitations.

Interference

Dealing with radio frequency noise pollution is a major technological hurdle for the wireless Web industry, even without the addition of a billion cell phones. There is an increasing amount of radio frequency noise from commercial, military, police, airplane, and entertainment services, as well as devices such as microwave ovens and desktop PCs and peripherals. Some sources of RF noise are more problematic for the wireless Web than others. For example, desktop computers emit signals at and above the frequencies used for cellular communications.

Most countries set limits on the maximum incidental radio frequency that a device can emit at different frequencies, measured a set distance from the device. In the United States, desktop computers and other potential sources of interference designed for home use are limited in the maximum permissible radiation in the range of frequencies that includes the cellular band. Computers and other devices intended for business use have much less stringent requirements. For example, computers intended for business use are allowed to emit potentially interfering radiation at nearly 40 times the level permitted for consumer devices.

Competing Standards

Multiple operating systems, nonstandard display formats, new user interface designs, and, most importantly, evolving communications protocols will continue to challenge wireless application developers and service providers, especially in the United States. In Europe, where GSM is the standard for 3G wireless communications, there are still multitudes of unresolved communications issues, such as the fate of WAP versus SMS for email.

Bandwidth Projections

Worldwide, wireless carriers are predicting that they will need to double their current bandwidth in order to adequately support the demand for wireless communications by 2010. Part of this needed bandwidth will undoubtedly come from technologic advances in data compression and encoding. However, there will also be a real need for spectrum real estate, especially in the United States. Given the history of wireless communications in the United States, this real estate will most likely come from increasingly higher frequency bands, including light-wave communications.

Content

The lack of compelling content on the wireless Web, especially in the United States, is part of the challenge facing most CEOs whose companies do not have wireless connections. The wireless community recognizes that at least part of the success of ITT DoCoMo's I-Mode can be attributed to content. I-Mode customers are willing to pay for the premium wireless service over the other three wireless data services available in Japan because I-Mode is faster, has better service, and, most importantly, provides more and better content. In the United States, it's almost impossible to attract and maintain Web designers for Web projects because demand far outstrips supply. Given this reality, it isn't clear where the talent for creating wireless content will come from—much less the applications for hotels, restaurants, and other markets. If a pervasive computing environment based on wireless virtual machines becomes a reality, then the search for content will include libraries of applications as well.

Personalization, Localization, Timeliness

The three big draws of wireless Web access—personalization, localization, and timeliness—are still promises, since the technology simply cannot yet deliver. The companies most likely to succeed first in delivering on some of the promises have experience in developing infrastructures capable of providing transaction-based customer profiling on the wired Web.

Hardware Limitations

First-generation wireless handheld devices, like the first desktop microcomputers, are hardware limited. Web-enabled cell phones have very little local RAM and insignificant local processing power, and all wireless Web devices are bandwidth limited. For example, it might take a half hour for a business-woman to download her incoming email onto her wireless PDA, compared to a few minutes for the same operation on a desktop PC with a high-speed wired connection to the Internet. There is also the ergonomic issue in evalu-ating the adequacy of a particular device when used to support given tasks. For example, the clamshell design used in some Motorola two-way pagers, is more likely to survive clipped to the belt of a telephone lineman, compared to a standard, not very rugged Palm or RIM wireless PDA with a larger exposed LCD panel. Every device has idiosyncrasies that must be addressed in a man-ner that makes sense to the intended user and the application.

Platform Standards

Whereas the desktop PC operating system has stabilized, Java OS, Palm OS, Symbian, Windows CE, Linux, and a variety of other platform standards, includ-ing DOS, compete for market segments on the wireless Web. For example, for-mer Borland CEO Philippe Kahn's company, LightSurf, developed a wireless digital imaging infrastructure based on Linux. Although the future of the oper-ating systems under development for wireless devices is uncertain, Palm has apparent support in the low-end market, Symbian dominates the cell phone market, while CE devices are positioned for the higher end and specialized ver-tical market applications. Linux has potential in the embedded device market, whereas Java OS, DOS, and other platforms have only pockets of support in niche areas. As noted earlier, it's premature to assume an OS environment, given the great interest (reflected in investment dollars) surrounding the use of vir-tual machine environment architectures based on some flavor of Java.

Quality of Communications

The ultimate technical challenge for a CEO, regardless of the other issues involved, is for his company to provide reliable, clear, timely communications. A great user interface isn't very helpful to a trader on the stock exchange floor if she has to wait more than a few seconds for a stock quote. Similarly, extended battery life for a wireless PDA is inconsequential if a complex or awkward user interface makes sending an email an exercise in futility.

MARKETING ISSUES

The process of promoting the wireless Web includes the four classic compo-nents common to marketing most products and services: defining the product or service, establishing a price, selecting and designing distribution channels, and promotion. In addition, as described below, marketing in the wireless Web space shares many of the characteristics associated with new technologies. (See Figure 8-7.)

Unknowns
Business Myopia
Product Confusion
Heightened Expectations
Wait and See Attitude
Product Divergence
Evangelists

Figure 8-7. Marketing issues in the emerging wireless Web industry.

Unknowns

The wireless Web market is like a multivariate equation with multiple unknowns in that the customers, competition, and market potential have yet to be fully defined. Although much more is known about the wireless markets in Japan and parts of Europe than in the United States, no one CEO, company, or country has all of the answers on how to best capture the global, evolving wireless Web market.

In the United States, where most households don't yet use charge cards, how likely are Americans to embrace the concept of a cell phone as an eWallet? How is the marketing department of a service provider going to convince a subscriber that it's in his best interest to use his cellular phone as a charge card? After all, a charge card has a small form factor, there's a chance to visually inspect the bill before it's signed, and there's a hard copy of the transaction for reimbursement and budgeting purposes. Using cell phones for credit purchases has worked in several European countries, but the success has been the most pronounced in countries without charge cards. That is, given a choice between a charge card that never needs batteries and is virtually indestructible, and a fragile electronic phone, why would someone choose the phone? Perhaps the "coolness" factor will help, or creating the impression that only a select few million people can use the services. After all, exclusivity works for the millions of consumers who have bought into the proposition that membership with a credit card company has its privileges.

Business Myopia

One of the challenges facing CEOs in assessing the market potential of wireless Web technology is how to critically evaluate the wireless Web market potential beyond their work environment. Executives in the fast-paced dot-Com industries that spend much of their time in airports, toting cell phones, laptop computers, and PDAs can easily get a distorted image of the "real" world. While the industry debates over what constitutes the best handheld device, less than 5 percent of U.S. households own a PDA. Similarly, while frequent business travelers long for ubiquitous, worldwide cell phone coverage, the majority of domestic subscribers live and work in the same community. For most potential subscribers, whether or not their cell phone works seamlessly in Sweden or even in the next state isn't a concern—as long as it works from the grocery store.

Product Confusion

With so many wireless Web options on the market, it's difficult for most potential consumers to critically evaluate products and services with same degree of certainty that they are accustomed to with comparable desktop PC technologies. With the elevated level of hype, relatively high prices, and lack of a critical mass of wireless Web devices, evaluating the options is a challenge for most customers. As a result, customers are more likely to rely on review articles and other sources of secondary information, including early adopters, instead of promotional materials from manufacturers.

The challenge for the marketing executive is to reach the early adopters, arrange for product reviews, and target users more likely to purchase their technologies. The goal is to create localized concentrations of satisfied users that can serve as references for other potential customers.

As an example of potential product confusion, consider the current generation of two-way pagers and wireless PDAs. As pagers become more powerful, the distinction between pagers and wireless PDAs is diminishing. Even the name of Motorola's two-way pager, the Talkabout T900 Personal Interactive Communicator, is a potential source of confusion. The communicator allows subscribers to send and receive text messages, receive email, and review market updates, news, and sports. Similarly, the RIM two-way pager, with its miniature keypad and email functionality, has more in common with a full-function PDA than a traditional pager.

Heightened Expectations

Because of the hype surrounding wireless computing, including selective reporting of the apparent success of companies in Japan and Europe, as well as the general trends in the electronics industry of decreasing price and increasing functionality, customer expectations are constantly increasing. Whereas a CEO may think that her company's thinner, lighter, more capable device is the next "new thing," potential customers may take little notice because miniaturization and other advances are expected. Customers who are aware of the computer and consumer electronics industries know that if they wait long enough, the current model of whatever they're interested in will be available in a form that is cheaper, smaller, and with more features.

Against this backdrop, marketing a new product or service is a challenge, simply because wowing a potential customer is virtually impossible. As it is, wireless customers in the United States are more likely to be disappointed with the slow speeds and limited displays of wireless PDAs and Web-enabled cell phones.

Wait-and-See Attitude

In part because of increased customer expectations and the inability of the current wireless technologies to replicate the wired Web experience, many prospective customers are taking a wait-and-see attitude toward wireless Web technology. A CEO willing to take on the challenge of dislodging these potential customers has to properly highlight the features and benefits of her company's *current* products.

Product Divergence

Web-enabled device manufacturers are creating mutations and seemingly random combinations of features and forms to explore the potentials of the marketplace. For example, there is a proliferation of specialized handheld devices that combine wireless connectivity with music, alarm systems, pagers, and wearable computers in a variety of form factors. Similarly, service providers are experimenting with pricing schemes that are attractive to both business and nonbusiness customers.

In the short term, the challenge facing a CEO at one of these companies is to focus the company's marketing activities in areas that are most likely to be receptive to the particular mix of features and benefits offered by the device or service. For example, wireless PDAs with enough memory to hold and play MP3 music titles that have been downloaded from the Internet may have greatest potential in the college student market. In the long term, as products converge on one or two standards, the marketing challenge will shift to highlighting small distinctions in features and capabilities between the standards.

Evangelists Wanted

When the benefits of a new technology aren't readily apparent, someone needs to create a level of excitement that translates into product awareness. To this end, a successful marketing program often includes enlisting a personality that can articulate a vision that is understandable to a wide customer base. For example, Guy Kawasaki helped create the Apple Macintosh through his evangelism. Products for the wireless Web need similar evangelism in order to break into and succeed in the general marketplace.

SOCIAL ISSUES

Business executives, homemakers, and professionals are all social creatures, and the introduction of a technology, no matter how advanced, doesn't change their basic human needs or traits. In many respects, the hardware and technical infrastructure in the wireless world today has far outpaced the social systems.

With the exception of restaurants that distribute pagers to patrons waiting to be seated so they are free to walk around without blocking the restaurant entrance, most retail outlets don't use cell phone or pager technology. A doctor's office could easily page or phone a patient when the doctor is ready, instead of making her sit for an hour in a crowded waiting room. Similarly, a dry cleaning service could page a businessman to let him know that his shirts are ready. Although the technology for these types of services has been available for years, societal expectations haven't created a demand for it. There are additional social aspects of wireless Web technology, from both the producer and consumer sides of the equation, as described in Figure 8-8.

A New Technologic Elite

Because of intense interest and development in wireless Web technologies, communications and network engineers are displacing traditional programmers as the technologic elite. Executives and managers who have experience in the communications field are achieving a new level of prominence, both financially and professionally. This emergence of a new technologic elite in the United States, Asia, and Europe is having a ripple effect throughout the educational system as well as the economy. In the United States, where the majority of programmers do not hold computer science degrees and come from other disciplines, there is an increasing demand for corporate or self-funded education on the technical aspects of wireless communications.

SOCIAL ISSUES

A New Technologic Elite
Local Culture
Global Worker Shortage
Reality Distortion
Privacy
Tech Burnout

Figure 8-8. Social issues in the emerging wireless Web industry.

Local Culture

In Japan, mobile messaging fits the compact, always on the move, public transit, small living and working space culture. Unlike businessmen in the United States, Japanese businessmen don't sit down to surf the Web to search for the best airline ticket prices. As such, it will take time to work wireless Web technology into the social fabric of the United States.

One advantage of the U.S. wireless market is that the typical businessperson is familiar with cell phones and PDAs, and relies on them regularly in the course of the business day. These businesspeople are likely to have a level of trust in the technology that may help them make a painless transition from the wired to the wireless Web.

Global Worker Shortage

The severe global shortage of skilled technology workers acts as a brake for many wireless technology companies. For example, Nokia can no longer fill positions with Finns, but relies on a global recruiting effort to bring in programmers from India and China on a regular basis. Consider that, in 1998, Nokia's workforce of 44,500 was 50 percent non-Finns. By 2000, the total workforce jumped to 56,500, with 60 percent non-Finn workers.

Similarly, in the United States, CEOs with dotCom and wireless companies are looking to Korea and India for skilled technology workers. Telecom companies in the United States are cannibalizing each other's workforces, enticing employees to stay or move to their company through cash and incentives such as on-site daycare, generous vacation time, and more. For example, one in every three Cisco employees is a millionaire, and employees with Nortel and Lucent are compensated handsomely, as well. Because employees with engineering and telecommunications experience are so difficult to find, companies are increasingly training employees in-house. Paradoxically, although the United States attracts foreign technology students to attend school, U.S. laws don't allow them to work in the United States once they've graduated.

Bounty fees for turning in candidates and other incentives that hark back to the early days of the wired Web are common. Unfortunately, the churn rate is also similarly high. High growth areas, such as optical networking, are attracting the brightest talent, in part because they're cash-rich from venture capital. Because demand outstrips supply, there is a major disequilibrium in the wireless and wired job market. Workers skilled in both communications and programming are encouraged by economic realities to change jobs often, creating a disincentive for employers to invest in employees. The move by the U.S. Senate to provide 600,000 new visas from 2001 through 2003 may help the domestic high-tech worker shortage.

Reality Distortion

As noted in the marketing section above, life in Silicon Valley is rarely representative of how "real" people spend their time. Despite the hype regarding how wireless computing is changing the world, most doctors in the United States use paper and pen to create patient records. Most families can't afford the monthly service charge for cellular service, much less a wireless PDA or pager. Many schools are without Internet access. Some segments of the U.S. population, for example, many Native American reservations, don't even have basic phone service.

Vendors are quick to point out how their wireless communications products can be used to provide telemedicine in remote areas of the United States, but fail to point out that federal laws prohibit physicians from practicing remotely without a license to practice in the patient's state. Most families in the United States plan a dinner out at an expensive restaurant weeks in advance, simply because of the cost, and don't need a wireless device to help them find an appropriate restaurant within seconds of realizing that they're hungry. In other words, the world that the current incarnation of the wireless Web caters to is a select, somewhat rarified subset of the general population.

Privacy

One of the most highly touted advantages of the wireless Web is the proposition that customers appreciate the convenience of 24x7, location-based, personalized attention from businesses. However, with the possible exception of a businessman who is interested in receiving the best rates for a rental car and a hotel room soon after his plane lands, most people regard their private time as just that. After a long day at the office, most executives don't appreciate an intrusive phone call at dinnertime, nor do they appreciate a fax advertisement printed with their ink and paper. In this context, 24x7 customer access, especially when the customer pays for the access, has to provide more value to the customer than the cost of the call and the intrusion into the customer's private life. Voice or email ads that are unsolicited, out of context, disregard subscriber preferences, and interfere with other services, such as the receipt of important voice and email messages, won't be tolerated. Similarly, merchants that violate privacy relationships, offering subscriber profiles to other merchants without subscriber approval, for example, won't be tolerated.

In general, Europeans perceive cell phones as trusted, personal devices. As such, for a European subscriber to pay for something with a cell phone doesn't require a huge leap of faith. However, typical cellular subscribers in the United States tend to perceive the use of cell phones in place of their credit cards as a threat to their privacy. Because of the way the U.S. cell phone system is designed, there may be some reason for concern. For example, if a business-

E-911 Federal Regulation
GPS Independent **Location by Latitude and Longitude** **Location within 125 meters** **Available at least 2/3 of the time** **Effective Oct 1, 2001**

Figure 8-9. Summary of the E-911 Federal Regulation.

woman uses her cell phone to make an appointment, according to FCC regulations (see Figure 8-9), the cellular provider has to have the ability to track the location of her phone to within 135 meters (443 ft). The businesswoman's location, specified in terms of latitude and longitude, is based on the triangulation of her cell phone signal from several adjacent cells. That is, the relative signal strength of her cellular signal from adjacent cells is used to estimate the position of the phone. In order to give carriers time to work out the bugs in the system, the location-tracking capability, which must be independent of GPS technology, initially has to be available only two-thirds of the time.

Privacy advocates and many of the CEOs of ISP providers in the United States are concerned about the implications of the FBI's Carnivore system. Carnivore is a hardware device and software that can track a subscriber's email, instant messages, the log of Web sites visited, and Internet relay chat sessions over an ISP. One source of concern is that there is no way for an ISP operator to know what the software and hardware are doing, or whether monitoring is being performed on a person named in a court order or someone else. ISPs take the stance that they don't want the privacy of all users on a system compromised on the basis of one user's presumed activities.

There are several potential solutions to these and other privacy issues, however. For example, context-specific, personalized, time and place—appropriate advertisements over a cell phone can be made a tolerable and even a positive event. Compensating subscribers for the right to offer them advertising, which has to include more than simply paying for the airtime, is one approach. Timely offers that parallel subscriber-defined filters can be welcome and convenient. For example, a woman who is an avid cyclist and in the market for a new helmet could be given the ability to set her wireless microbrowser to filter for advertisements from local bike shops for a sale on bike helmets. If this filtering is presented as an RFP (request for proposal), where merchants are given the opportunity to bid on the subscriber's business through a personal invitation, then notices become personal services. Consider the utility of a wireless handheld device placed in a cab that presents the same woman with information on retail shops in a two-block radius of the cab's destination—especially if she is given a reduced cab fare for using the system. Yahoo.com has tried captive wireless portals on a limited basis in New York City.

Even though everyone enjoys their privacy, there are times when some people simply can't be out of touch, and are willing to pay for the service. For example, a businessman who is a subscriber to British Telecom who is flying Virgin Atlantic can receive calls while in flight. He inserts a card containing his mobile phone information through a seat-back phone, which registers his cellular phone account information and seat information with the plane's onboard network. When someone calls the businessman's usual cellular phone number, the call is routed through British Telecom's satellite system, and to the businessman's seat-back phone.

Tech Burnout

For an increasing number of executives and the cities in which they live, the days of dotCom euphoria are over. Productivity tools such as email, once promoted as time savers, are now seen as time stealers that can consume precious hours every day. Many CEOs are restricting the use of email at their companies, simply because their employees are spending too much time initiating and responding to electronic messages. CEOs and other executives have to deal with the prospect of data overload on a daily basis. Even for the techno-savvy early adopters, having to remember yet another username and password for every wireless device is becoming an arduous task.

Social disapproval of cell phone use in restaurants, museums, and other public places is on the rise. Some restaurants restrict phone use or have a designated phone area. Many public areas, such as the San Francisco Museum of Modern Art and the Philadelphia Museum of Art, ask patrons to refrain from using their cell phones. It's becoming common etiquette to turn all phones and pagers off during meetings, even in technology companies. At least one company, BlueLinx, is developing a Bluetooth-based system that automatically lowers the ring volume of a cell phone within designated areas, such as theaters.

There is also a public outcry against the speeding motorist who has one hand on the wheel and one on a cell phone. Some wireless carriers, such as Bell South, are proactively addressing the public backlash against drivers who dial with a series of radio commercials that suggests safer driving habits.

DISCUSSION

The challenges and opportunities that lie ahead for CEOs in the world of the wireless Web are almost limitless. With the proper focus, visionary leaders can map out a path through the diverse space, navigating their companies to a rewarding future in spite of shifting standards and evolving technologies. The high degree of global interdependence in wireless Web hardware and software suppliers, and the pockets of expertise appearing in certain countries, demand communications that far exceed the norms established for the wired dotCom world. For example, decisions made by engineers in Japan on cell phone screen size and button layout dramatically affect the task of software developers in Europe and the United States.

Even the underlying rules for company involvement in domestic wireless commerce are changing. For example, in late 2000, the FCC changed the rules for PCS auctions, allowing large companies to bid on the broadband licenses that had been reserved for smaller companies. Under the new rules, companies with more than $500 million in assets and $125 million in revenue can acquire up to two-thirds of the spectrum in large markets, and up to one-third of the spectrum in smaller markets. This change should at least partially address the problem of multiple, noncompatible standards in most wireless markets.

A hot issue in companies that are adding a wireless component to their wired Web presence is ownership of wireless Web projects. When the Web first became popular, it was seen as a media for advertising, and so became the preview of marketing. However, as the full potential of the Web emerged, and executives began to take note of the new potential touch point, the Web took on a life of its own. Today, in many organizations, there is a head of Web development, usually at the VP level or equivalent, who is in charge of Web initiatives. However, because the eCommerce landscape is changing so rapidly, most companies have yet to fully develop their wired Web touch point. In addition, less than 1 percent of the eCommerce sites have shown a direct profit of any type.

Given the lack of resources in the dotCom space, should wireless Web development be considered separate from wired Web activity? The answer to this and similar questions must be answered on a case-by-case basis, because every wireless Web activity, like every dotCom project, is different. The theme of differences and the opportunities available to executives who are committed to exploring the potential of the wireless Web space continues in the next and final chapter.

EXECUTIVE SUMMARY

The challenges and opportunities in the emerging wireless Web space can be categorized as managerial, political, medical, legal, economic, technical, market-based, and social. Management issues include an enterprise-centric versus eCommerce-centric duality of focus, the need for CEOs and other executives to focus on technologic details early on, volatility in the wireless Web space, the crystallization of geographical pockets of expertise, competition with wired Web projects for resources, the diversion of resources from other information—based projects, volatility in value chain positioning, difficulty evaluating vendors, the need to identify and act on low-hanging fruit, the challenge of working in the vast space of the wireless Web, and the management strategies and structures that need to be developed in order to address these and other challenges.

The political issues for CEOs in the wireless Web space include dealing with standards organizations; contending with political organizations for limited RF spectrum; understanding the general opposition to foreign investment in the United States, Europe, and Asia; realizing that local governments are major stakeholders in the wireless Web; and working through international politics.

The top medical concerns revolve around the potential radiation hazard that long-term cell phone use poses to subscribers, and the threat that driving while dialing presents to other motorists. Legal issues include the status of FCC licensing, how intellectual property is evaluated, especially for firms that use clipping and other technologies to dynamically repurpose content, and how to deal with fraud.

The economic issues surrounding use of the wireless Web include the speculative market, competition from wireless and wired systems, the need for infrastructure investment, the challenge of moving targets, working with support structures that either are fed by or feed on the success of other companies, the scarcity of expertise, time pressure to acquire the first-mover advantage, the challenge of acquiring a critical mass of users and devices or services, the difference between popularity and profitability, the competition from existing processes, lost opportunity costs associated with moving to 3G wireless services, changes in cellular billing structures, sensitivity to pricing, and the need for a Killer App to move things along.

Technical issues include dealing with complexity, device diversity, scalability, a lack of testing standards, new user interface issues, the challenge of providing adequate security, providing added network capacity, the lack of development tools, creating a supporting infrastructure, dealing with interference, competing standards, increasing bandwidth requirements, the lack of compelling content, providing personalization, localization, and timeliness, hardware limitations, evolving platform standards, and providing an overall high quality of communications.

Marketing challenges revolve around the unknown customers, competition, and market potential, the potential of business myopia, product confusion, heightened customer expectations, a wait-and-see attitude from customers, product divergence, and the need for evangelists to promote a vision.

The social issues facing CEOs of wireless Web companies include the creation of a new technologic elite, the significance of local culture, the global high-tech worker shortage, the reality distortion created by executives living in the center of technical innovation, the threat that the wireless Web poses to privacy, and the technology burnout that many knowledge workers experience from being continuously plugged in.

9

Timing Is Everything

Long-term planning does not deal with future decisions,
but with the future consequences of current decisions.

Gary Blair

INTRODUCTION

Following the line of reasoning that every new beginning starts with some other beginning's end, the wireless Web begins with the resolution of dot-Com fever. As the wired Web stabilizes and consolidates, the CEO who was once in charge of an adrenaline-packed roller-coaster ride through the dot-Com space is now managing a fleet of tour buses. This CEO, who proved himself in the wired Web and is now looking for adventure in the wireless space, isn't the only one affected by the lure of the wireless Web. Rising customer expectations of the Web now include the notion that anything can and should be available to them at any time—for a price. This and similar expectations are fueling the consumer market for time-saving conveniences such as wireless home shopping, cellular voice communications, two-way pagers, and wireless, Web-enabled digital cameras.

Assuming that the industry projection that 1 billion wireless hand-held devices will be in use worldwide by 2003 is correct, most subscribers will experience the Web for the first time through wireless portals. However, not only does the wireless Web offer a very different user experience compared to the wired Web but it also requires that the CEO from the wired Web world stand back and appraise the differences between the two touch points.

The differences between the wireless and wired Web are significant, even though the wireless applications of the Web are a natural outgrowth of wired

Web technology. These differences include technology focus, staffing requirements, complexity of the space, and the rate-limiting resources.

For example, the technology focus of the wired Web is primarily software development. Furthermore, software innovations developed for the wired Web tend to be related to applications that assume a stable hardware and network infrastructure. Innovations such as P2P (person-to-person) eCommerce, popularized by the server-based Napster and server-less Gnutella models, assume a standard user hardware configuration and connectivity infrastructure. In contrast, the technology focus of the wireless Web tends to be intimately related to specific hardware features of handheld devices, such as the number and placement of keys, battery life, communications range, and the variety of input and output of modes supported. Because the universal communicator has not yet been invented, wireless software development typically focuses on applications for a specific hardware platform, such as a Palm wireless PDA or RIM pager. Furthermore, wireless device developers are concerned with issues such as battery life, the ergonomics of user interaction, and how to make the best use of limited screen real estate.

User interactions with wireless, minimum bandwidth, small-screen handheld devices tend to be surgically precise, transaction-directed activities. Except for pockets of early adopters in Asia and Europe, most handheld subscribers don't use wireless devices for browsing the Internet. U.S. subscribers are especially averse to handheld browsing, given that they are accustomed to surfing the Web on high-speed desktop PCs. In addition, as noted in the previous chapter, whereas the user interface design for the wired Web is grounded in established principles, expertise on user interface design for wireless devices is scarce.

To the CEO most familiar with the wired Web, the wireless Web space represents a vast, expanding, and virtually unknown business opportunity. In contrast, the wired Web is relatively contained and expanding at a steady but moderate rate. Even with the millions of pages of content that are posted to the wired Web daily, the major wired Web players have staked their claims in the space. For most companies, whether or not to have a wired Web presence is no longer a topic of discussion—it's assumed.

Staffing tends to be more of a challenge with wireless Web development, in part because Human Resources (HR) executives and middle management are more familiar with what is required to create and maintain a wired Web presence. For the wired Web development shop, Web designers, C++, Java, and HTML programmers, and graphic artists are all known quantities, in terms of cost and what can be expected from each employee. However, on the wireless Web, communications engineers, network specialists, and XML and WAP programmers are not only in short supply but their skills, roles, and expected contributions are less well defined. Furthermore, since workers skilled in communications and networking are in demand in other areas, such as the burgeoning field of high-speed optical networking, they are more challenging to recruit and retain.

The projection is for parity in numbers of wired and wireless Web devices in the near future, with an explosion in the number of wireless subscribers shortly thereafter. In contrast, only moderate increases are projected for the wired Web. This explosive growth in the number of wireless Web subscribers represents a significant potential customer base for wireless Web companies throughout the entire wireless Web value chain.

Because of the inherent uncertainties in the wireless Web space, the lack of readily available expertise, and an overall increased complexity, creating a wireless Web presence is more challenging than simply erecting a home page on the wired Web. In addition, there are significant risks associated with the wireless space, including short-lived, rapidly changing hardware platforms, unstable standards, and unknown and potentially unreliable business partners. As such, the cost of entering the wireless space tends to be prohibitive for many companies. Although skilled workers and the intellectual property they generate are scarce commodities in all areas of Web development, the rate-limiting resources in the wireless Web space additionally include scarce hardware and software tools.

At a minimum, the CEO who is developing a wireless strategy for her company should have an appreciation for the differences between the wired and wireless Web, an understanding of the historical context of the wireless Web, an overview of the technologies involved, and at least an awareness of some of the challenges involved in achieving a wireless Web presence. However, for an intrepid CEO to develop and execute a *winning* wireless strategy, she must also have a blueprint for the process of moving her company from where it is to where it needs to be, as well as a knack for timing. The purpose of this chapter is to provide the CEO with that blueprint; she must be able to accurately anticipate her customers' needs before they do.

DEFINING A WINNING WIRELESS STRATEGY

Before a CEO can embark on the path to defining a wireless strategy for his company, he has to build a foundation of knowledge. At the most basic level, he must thoroughly understand his organization, in terms of its strengths, weaknesses, and goals, and the environment in which it operates. To this end, the CEO must acquire knowledge of the issues and the technologies relevant to establishing a wireless Web presence. In order to quantify the value of a wireless touch point to his organization, he may have to survey his organization to identify the relevant issues. This, in turn, will help him determine, for example, whether the market focus for wireless technology should be primarily enterprise-centric or eCommerce-centric. Once the technology, business, and political issues have been identified, the CEO can decide where to invest his company's resources, for example, in enterprisewide wireless network infrastructure development or in a pilot study using a few dozen handheld wireless devices. Finally, the CEO should develop the metrics for quantifying his company's success in creating a valuable wireless Web presence.

A practical implementation of this general process description is to follow the five-phase strategy illustrated in Figure 9-1. Phase I of this process or strategy, deciding whether to develop a wireless Web presence now or to wait until some point or event in the future, is probably the most critical. The issues at Phase I include the overall focus of the plan, gathering knowledge of the issues and technologies involved, and determining the type of wireless Web presence that should be developed. The tasks in Phase II of the process are to define the development approach, in terms of the tools and resources required, and to determine whether these will come from inside the organization or outsourced to those with external expertise.

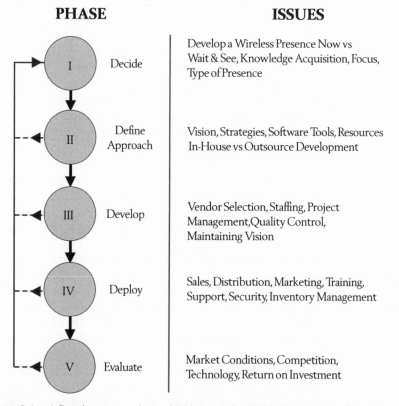

PHASE

I — Decide

II — Define Approach

III — Develop

IV — Deploy

V — Evaluate

ISSUES

Develop a Wireless Presence Now vs Wait & See, Knowledge Acquisition, Focus, Type of Presence

Vision, Strategies, Software Tools, Resources In-House vs Outsource Development

Vendor Selection, Staffing, Project Management, Quality Control, Maintaining Vision

Sales, Distribution, Marketing, Training, Support, Security, Inventory Management

Market Conditions, Competition, Technology, Return on Investment

Figure 9-1. A five-phase process for establishing a wireless Web presence. Because of the rapid rate of change in the wireless Web environment, the assumptions made in Phase I of the process should be revalidated at each subsequent phase.

The goal of Phase III involves actually developing the wireless presence, whether it involves hardware development, software development, or both. At this phase, issues include vendor selection, project management, and quality control. Phase IV, the deployment phase, entails the use of a distribution system, training, security, and, if the distribution of handheld devices is involved, inventory management. Phase V, evaluation, is when the CEO should critically evaluate the market conditions, competition, technology, and return on investment for his company's activities.

As suggested by the dotted lines leading back to Phase I at each subsequent phase in Figure 9-1, the tasks of knowledge acquisition, defining a focus, and the type of wireless presence that should be developed are revisited at each phase in the process. The wireless Web is a dynamic, rapidly changing environment, and the introduction of a new technology or standard and internal changes in the company may alter the basic assumptions made in Phase I, necessitating a major shift in other phases of the process. Depending on the change, it may be better for the CEO to adjust the approach instead of investing time and other resources in a product or service that may have less than optimum results. The impact of some changes in basic assumptions is more obvious than others. For example, if a hardware manufacturer discontinues the production of a PDA that the CEO targeted as the sole deployment platform for her company's wireless product, then it probably makes sense for the CEO to at least revisit Phase I, regardless of which phase of the process her company is in.

The issues and milestones related to each phase of the five-phase model are described in more detail below.

PHASE I: THE DECISION

In Phase I of the process of developing a wireless Web presence, the CEO must decide whether or not the timing is right for his company to move into the wireless space. The CEO should make his decision after gathering as much information as is practical. The CEO should evaluate the risks of starting a wireless Web project based on his estimate of the investment required relative to its likely return, the project's duration, the technical challenges to be addressed, the internal infrastructure changes required, the availability of skilled workers with the competencies needed to complete the project, and the overall likelihood of success.

In order to make the decision of whether to move immediately to the wireless Web or wait, the CEO should determine the type of wireless Web presence that will provide the greatest value to his company and its customers. The value of the wireless Web depends on whether customers are internal, such as an internal sales force, or external and focused on eCommerce. For a retail company that sells services to primarily mobile customers, providing a wireless touch point may provide a means of cementing customer relationships with the company. That is, by making the company's services available to existing customers at an additional touch point, the value of the wireless Web has the potential to increase customer loyalty—as long as they're recognized as existing customers.

The value of a wireless Web presence also depends on the company's experience with the wired Web. For example, a typical brick-and-mortar company without a Web presence of any type should consider developing a standard wired Web site first, for the reasons outlined in Chapter 8. The prudent CEO will guide her brick-and-mortar company to use tools and techniques—either directly or through an outside vendor—in developing a wired Web presence that facilitates a future move to the wireless Web. A parallel wired and wireless Web development project, while possible, will require significant resources, and is probably unrealistic for most companies. For example, creating a seamless click-and-mortar entity from a brick-and-mortar company by simultaneously adding wireless and wired Web touch points requires the best of the physical world and the best of online technology. The disruption in normal business processes resulting from the addition of wired and wireless touch points is compounded by the time and energy required to establish an infrastructure of customer call centers, data mining applications, and online features such as personal shopping assistants, gift registries, and other parallels of retail operation.

For a click-and-mortar company with a wired Web presence or at least a mature intranet, supplementing a wired Web site with "thin" pages designed expressly for wireless PDA or cell phone access may be a viable initial step. For example, Nissan and Infinity dealers access customer relationship management information from the showroom floor via two-way pagers. In this way, dealers are freed from breaking the focus of the sales process to go to their desks and access information with their desktop PCs. After a company gains experience with supporting wireless devices, it can add transaction capabilities, perhaps transaction-processing hardware and software for faster responses.

The primary business challenge for the CEO involved in Phase I of the process is to estimate how a wireless presence will affect his company's bottom line. Working with early adopters may not be profitable in the short term, but may create a test bed of customers who will help companies work out the kinks in their wireless strategies, in preparation for a larger market. Potential cost savings over alternative approaches to supporting a mobile workforce should also be considered in Phase I. For example, deploying a handheld wireless device in the field has a Total Cost of Ownership (TCO) of about $2700, compared to over four times that for a laptop computer.

Some paths to profitability are less obvious than others. For example, NTT DoCoMo is a deep-pocketed company with millions of subscribers who pay for content and this positions the company as a credit house with

$200 million per month of content-related business. Consider that NTT DoCoMo's I-Mode phones are thriving with its microbilling system. In addition to an added monthly service charge, which is typically paid by automatic bank withdrawal, accessing certified I-Mode sites incurs an additional monthly fee. Although any site can be accessed on the Web by tapping out an address, certified I-Mode sites can be accessed with a thumb-controlled joystick from a list on a cell phone screen.

The small monthly fee (about $3 U.S.) charged for accessing certified sites appears on the subscriber's monthly statement. Since the fee is split between DoCoMo and the content provider, the relationship is a win-win, with huge profits for NTT DoCoMo and successful sites. For example, a service run by Bandai Company that ships different animated characters to cell phones every day has over 2 million customers—representing a $6 million revenue stream. Even the local Tokyo weather site hosts over a quarter of a million subscribers. In addition to positioning itself as a bank, NTT is using its customer contact and financial strength to offer insurance to subscribers over the wireless Web.

Another business model involves positioning a wireless touch point as a captive portal. Several financial institutions are giving away wireless handheld devices as part of pilot programs for their best clients. The instant-on handheld devices, which are locked to the financial institutions' Web sites, allow clients to trade stocks and direct other financial transactions through secure, real-time communications.

The issue in taking a wait-and-see approach toward a move to the wireless Web is defining the criteria for reexploring the wireless space in terms of either time or events. For example, revisiting the Phase I decisions in six months, or when a clear hardware device standard has emerged in a particular industry, are both reasonable criteria.

PHASE II: DEFINE AN APPROACH

Once a decision has been made to establish a wired Web presence, the CEO's next step should be to define an approach. The milestones for the CEO involved in Phase II of the process include creating a vision for her company and defining what the customers experience from their interactions with the wireless Web. The CEO should also define an overall strategy for her company, in terms of technology, management, and the business model, including an inventory of resources required to realize success.

For a CEO to help her company achieve these milestones, she must consider issues ranging from choosing potential technology and business partners, performing a risk analysis, considering integration of existing touch points, selecting hardware, locating software tools, defining a network infrastructure, developing contingency plans, defining timelines and budgets, and identifying a reasonable home for the project within her organization.

Technology Strategy

The most appropriate strategies for achieving a wireless Web presence necessarily follow from the CEO's vision of his company, which should also reflect the corporate mission. Similarly, defining a technology strategy, including a plan for securing the most appropriate devices, the type of connection or infrastructure provider, and application areas, must also reflect customer requirements. For example something as simple as the characteristics of a handheld device, such as its need for frequent recharging, may cut too deeply into the customer interaction time for a mobile sales force for the device to be practical.

The CEO evaluating the *connection* associated with a particular wireless technology approach should consider three primary parameters: speed, coverage, and mobility. Consideration for speed or bandwidth should encompass not only top speed, but also the typical speed, which takes the contention of limited channels and interference from other services and the environment into account. Coverage, the geographic percentage of urban and rural areas covered by a wireless service, should be evaluated in terms of inside and outside building penetration. For example, if the intended wireless customers are a mobile sales force who will connect to the Web while they are in their cars, then inside building coverage isn't relevant. However, for a copier repair business that needs to contact its repair people at any time, then the in-building coverage is critical. Mobility factors, such as the ability to roam, and the associated charges, are important if the CEO's company routinely does business outside of a single metropolitan area.

In evaluating the appropriateness of wireless *applications* for her company, the CEO and her technical staff typically have industry standards to use as a guide. For example, medical applications, which usually trail applications in the financial area in terms of technical sophistication, should be evaluated relative to competing solutions, wired or wireless, in the medical space.

The technologic strategy should also focus on the range of handheld *devices* and other hardware supported, from wireless PDAs to wireless modem cards for laptops. Because the wireless device is the primary interface between customers and the Web or some custom application, the appropriateness of the device to the task is central to its evaluation. There are many parameters that go into the wireless hardware evaluation mix. There are obvious factors, such as connectivity options, in terms of the protocols supported, and the total cost of ownership for the devices, including initial and recurring costs, such as monthly connect charges, insurance, and keeping an inventory of spares in stock. Additional factors include the mean time before replacement (MTBR), the modalities supported (text versus voice, for example), power requirements, theft potential, portability, and fragility. Some features are orthogonal to others, and their relevance depends on the application and the customer environment. For example, increased portability tends to increase theft potential. Special security features, such as password protection, tend to diminish ease of use. Similarly, a small form factor may require a hard-to-find, expensive battery pack.

In evaluating the appropriateness of the range of wireless devices available, the CEO should consider the information needs and processes required by potential customers. The most appropriate wireless device depends on the degree of portability required by customers and the tasks that must be supported. As the task moves from simple data viewing to data acquisition to data creation, the optimum hardware power increases, moving from cell phones and two-way pagers to PDAs and wireless laptop computers. For example, Web-enabled cell phones support data viewing in a highly portable form factor. PDAs with bar-code scanners and other data acquisition features are more portable but less powerful than wireless laptops.

Although laptop computers are capable of supporting bar-code scanning with the appropriate attachments, they tend to be overpowered for the task. Conversely, for creating a large number of email messages and graphic data, the processing power and screen size provided by wireless laptops are usually necessary. Because portability is also a consideration, the optimum device category depends on where the company's customers lie on the Power-Portability curve. The exact position of a device on the Power-Portability Curve depends on the particular device characteristics. The miniature, full-featured keypads supplied on two-way pagers from Motorola and RIM, for example, tend to be easier to use to write email messages than the limited keypad of a cell phone.

There are additional, subjective metrics that a CEO and his technical staff can use to evaluate the applicability of wireless Web technologies to their mission. For example, the maximum tolerance a businessperson typically has for device availability is related to her intended interaction time or the perceived value of the interaction, as well as to her expectations. For example, if the businesswoman is working in her hotel room, she may be willing to wait two or three minutes to boot up and connect through her wireless laptop computer. Conversely, she won't wait for more than a few seconds for her wireless PDA to be available—unless her PDA holds vital information that she simply must have. Instant-on devices, such as most PDAs, have interaction times measured in minutes and seconds; high-latency devices, such as wireless laptops, have extended boot times and interaction times measured in hours and minutes.

Rising expectations, either because of the technologies that the competition offers or because of alternative channels available to customers, shift the delay tolerance—interaction value curve downward. That is, customers are less willing to tolerate a delay when they know that the technology exists for better responsiveness. For example, even though most patients will wait two hours in a stuffy waiting room in order to spend five minutes with a doctor, most PDA users won't tolerate a PDA that doesn't provide instant-on capabilities, in part because all PDAs on the market provide that capability. Similarly, the 5- to 15-s latency associated with data accessed through the first-generation wireless Palm PDA is becoming less tolerated as more wireless customers become familiar with other PDA designs, such as the RIM Blackberry, that support always-on, instant wireless Web connectivity.

Clearly, the intended application of wireless Web communications must define the hardware device and connectivity characteristics. In the end, a mobile salesperson doesn't care about the make and model of his PDA or cell phone; what he cares about is providing service to his clients. To this end, the wireless device should be transparent to the customer and the task.

The final milestone in defining a technology strategy is for the CEO to identify an infrastructure capable of supporting the company's wireless Web initiative. A short-term approach is to outsource, picking the best of breed. Alternatively, there is the long-term approach of slowly acquiring a suite of infrastructure tools. However, there are no universal infrastructure development tools that work across a wide range of devices. Given the uncertainties in the wireless space, an agnostic infrastructure should be created, as long as the lack of support for specific device features doesn't detract from the customer's experience.

An increasingly popular, low-risk infrastructure approach on the wireless Web is to use Wireless Application Service Provider (WASP) technology, either supported in-house or outsourced to a wireless enabler, such as OracleMobile (www.OracleMobile.com). As listed in Figure 9-2, there are several advantages to using WASP architecture. For one, the WASP design supports the integration of third-party content, as well as data from intranets and the Internet in one seamless presentation. That is, content from a variety of sources, including different pages from the same Web site, whether on the Internet or from a corporate intranet that is located behind a firewall, can be formatted and displayed on a single page or series of pages.

Secondly, because of the degree of integration possible, the WASP design is compatible with smart linking. With this technology, wireless subscribers can be presented with the links they are most likely to use from any data display. For example, when a customer lists restaurants in an area on a Web-enabled cell phone, links to the restaurants' Web sites and to a separate online reservation service can be provided next to the listing of the restaurant names.

A third advantage of the WASP design is that it is inherently scalable, in that the architecture can be developed for internal use on an intranet and then opened for general access by simply adding processing power. Multiple levels of security can be provided as well. For example, sensitive, password-protected information can be kept behind a secure firewall, allowing customers to access general information on a server outside the firewall, and a mobile sales force with the appropriate access privileges, for example, can use the same Web site to access sensitive corporate data.

In addition to simplifying the distribution task to a variety of hardware devices through the use of a central database and XML or other language that supports models of handheld device characteristics, the WASP model sup-

WASP Advantages
Allows Integration of Third-Party Content
Can Combine Intranets with the Internet
Compatible with Smart Linking
Scalability
Security Through Firewalls
Simplification of Distribution
Supports: Alerts
Alternative Interfaces
Content Filtering
Data Mining
Location-Based Services

Figure 9-2. The advantages of Wireless Application Service Provider (WASP) technology in achieving a wireless Web presence.

ports the generation of alerts on always-on hardware. Because a minimum of local processing power is used on the subscriber's hardware, a variety of high-computational load processes can be supported, such as data mining, content filtering, and location-based services. Finally, the server-based processing of the WASP model is also compatible with alternative user interfaces, such as voice recognition.

Management Strategy

Defining an approach to the wireless Web is not only a question of having the right tools but using them correctly—which is where management strategy comes in. A primary issue in this area is developing contingency plans in the event that the wireless system fails or even fails to be realized. For example, the implementation plan may take longer than estimated, requiring alternative forms of communications and support for a field sales force for several months.

Ownership of the wireless space, at a corporate level, is also at issue. As introduced in the previous chapter, the nature of the business should dictate where the wireless Web development team lives. Although a wireless communication system may be connected to the Web, the main components may fall under what would normally be considered the purview of telecommunications or the IT department. For example, email, one of the major applications used on Web-enabled handhelds, is normally administered through a company's IT department. Similarly, pagers are typically administered by telecommunications, which assigns user IDs and access numbers. These and other administrative tasks don't normally fall under the heading of Web development. However, if the purpose of a wireless Web presence is to supplement the Wired component by mirroring functions, which may include transaction processing, then it may make sense to keep the administration of wired and wireless Web development projects under the same management.

Business Models

In order for a wireless Web development project to succeed, the business model must incorporate an integration effort, define the legacy processes that will have to be updated to support the wireless effort, identify the most likely business and technology partners, and target the resources needed to complete the project on time and on budget. Business partnerships are especially crucial for success, given that no one company is large enough to go it alone in the wireless space.

Maintenance costs, life cycle, time to market, and likely return on investment figures should be part of the business model. The model should also define a limited time and budget for the project in order to avoid escalating cost due to added features not considered—and perhaps not available—at the time the project was started. From a strategic business perspective, the CEO should evaluate business decisions in light of her company's overall eCommerce technology strategy. For example, the technologies employed in development of a wireless Web presence for an international company should scale globally. For this reason, voice recognition and synthesis systems that are limited to English, databases that support only ASCII, search engines that only work with English, and computer languages that can't support the character sets of a variety of international languages are strategically poor business choices that should be avoided, even though they may satisfy the immediate technologic requirements.

PHASE III: DEVELOP

Given a decision to go ahead and a definite approach, the next step for the CEO to take toward providing her company with a wireless Web presence is to simply plan the work and then see to it that the appropriate resources are focused on working the plan. Planning involves the steps typical of any major software or hardware project, including creating written requirement and functional specifications, establishing a budget, developing timelines, defining deliverables, and creating milestones. If the decision is to work with outside vendors because of the expense or disruption of using internal staff, the CEO needs to identify vendors, establish quality control standards, and set definite timelines. Similarly, if the work is to be done using internal staff, then the CEO will need to work with project management issues, including staffing, productivity, and quality control.

The selection of a wireless technology vendor is one of the most important decisions in the process of developing a wireless Web presence. There are various levels of vendor involvement, from supplying a piece of middleware, such as an application server, to a virtually complete solution that includes hardware, application software, and the underlying infrastructure. The basic components involved in wireless vendor selection are the connection or infrastructure, the application, and wireless device characteristics.

Vendor evaluation criteria should include examining the vendor as a stable, financially sound business, including bank references, number of years in business, credentials of the CEO and management team, references from clients, the proximity of their physical plant, the breadth and depth of their technical knowledge, and customer support capabilities. If the vendor is supplying a mission-critical software application, then it must be amenable to establishing a software escrow account that provides the CEO's company with access to application source code and documentation in the event that the vendor goes out of business.

Aside from vendor selection, the CEO's most important role in Phase III is to develop, maintain, and articulate a clear vision of what the project will provide the customer and the company. A clear vision of the final product is especially crucial with wireless Web development, given that the rapidly changing environment can distract an unfocused development group away from the task at hand. Without a clear vision, it's easy for development staff to divert too much energy and time into second-guessing the development plan and exploring possible alternatives to the selected approach.

PHASE IV: DEPLOY

After the months of work developing the software and infrastructure necessary for a wireless Web approach, the CEO's next step is to deploy the product or service. The milestones in Phase IV include establishing a sales and marketing center, creating distribution channels to customers, providing support and training, developing security procedures, and, if wireless devices are distributed to employees, inventory control.

Subtle but significant differences in this phase of the process exist between internal and external deployment. For example, if a wireless application is developed for an internal sales force, then relevant issues include the impact on the bottom line, infrastructure demand, training, monitoring results, security, and employee feedback. If the product or services are aimed at external eCommerce, however, there will likely be more of a focus on the sales and marketing process, a potentially more complex and difficult distribution mechanism, cost containment, and customer support.

All of these factors come into play to some degree in both internally and externally focused wireless products and services. For example, inventory control may be a major factor in enterprise-focused deployment, especially if several hundred handheld devices are in service simultaneously. There must be a mechanism to rapidly replace defective or stolen devices, adequate inventory for providing loaner devices while an employee's unit is being repaired, and enough stock to adequately equip a wave of new employees.

PHASE V: EVALUATE

German science, technology, and business are known for their reliance on outcome measurements, in which evaluations are based on hard, objective data. Although soft, subjective measures certainly have a place in evaluating the impact of a wireless Web presence, there is something to be said for critically quantifying the impact of a new technology on an existing business process.

Milestones at Phase V include evaluating the new technologies, assessing the competition, identifying new business opportunities, continually monitoring the status of the implementation, and modifying the overall approach as necessary. At this phase, the CEO should be prepared to modify the system based on customer feedback, regardless of how well the system fits the original functional specifications document. For example, given the rapid rate of technologic change, there is a good chance that, as technologies evolve, reliance on multiple operating systems and protocols will shift to one or two standards. WAP may prove too limited and fail to scale when higher bandwidths and larger displays become available. Heads-up displays, biometric security, and other technologies may fundamentally change how users interact with their devices.

EXPECTATION MANAGEMENT

A key issue in developing a wireless Web presence is to appropriately manage customer expectations. Since the wireless Web won't be able to meet most of the market hype for several years—if ever—there is the potential for customer frustration and wholesale rejection of the wireless Web. As such, expectation management requires a careful marketing strategy. The wireless Web won't succeed as a touch point unless the companies involved manage to capture the hearts and imaginations of the subscribers. In other words, the CEO should provide customers with a clear vision of where the technology is heading and a clear list of benefits customers can expect from the technology today, all the while generating an air of excitement about his company's wireless products and services.

Consider how NTT DoCoMo manages customer expectations in Japan. DoCoMo doesn't even mention the terms *Web* or *the Internet* in its marketing materials, thereby avoiding any expectations, especially that the Web is a free library of information.

In the United States, however, wired Web users have a preconceived notion of what the Web is or should be, based on their experience with the multimedia Web. However, if U.S. subscribers approach the wireless Web as a portable version of the wired Web, they'll be extremely disappointed. For example, the wireless Web is not based on the model that everything is free.

THE WIRELESS FUTURE

Even the most driven, time-limited CEO has a profound need to communicate her thoughts, experiences, desires, dreams, and ambitions to others. Although nothing can come close to the quality of a face-to-face exchange of ideas, over time, technologies have been developed to support communications over increasingly greater distances. Today, distance is no longer an obstacle; given access to the appropriate technology and the knowledge of how to use it, virtually anyone on the planet can communicate with any one of the other billions of inhabitants. The keys to ubiquitous communications, including access to technology and a supportive social infrastructure, remain as unanswered challenges—and business opportunities.

As the number of wireless users worldwide exceeds a critical mass of a billion businesspeople, homemakers, professionals, and students, the limitations of technology access may no longer be an issue—for those who can afford it. Even so, there will continue to be haves and have-nots owing to technologic, economic, social, and political factors. For example, in the United States, the sign that wireless communications technology has reached a level of general usability will be when a working knowledge of the wireless Web migrates from the well-heeled early adopters in business and technology to the mothers and fathers of the current generation of decision makers.

Although the wireless Web market only started at the turn of this century and is in an early-adoption phase, the market is large enough to provide many companies with sufficient incentives to court the high-value early adopters. Part of this incentive is short-term monetary reward, and part is gathering knowledge that may be useful in future business. For example, information from the businesses serving the early adopters thus far strongly suggests that the wireless communications solutions developed in each market must stand on their own. That is, they must reflect the social needs of local markets and corporate cultures. For example, when the business practice of quality circles—a wildly successful practice in Japan based on a small group that performs voluntary quality control activities within the same workgroup—was instituted in the United States, it failed. The U.S. business culture simply didn't support the practice. Similarly, the particular successes with the wireless Web demonstrated by ITT DoCoMo in Japan won't necessarily translate to subscribers in Europe and the United States.

Technology transfer doesn't always occur smoothly or predictably, even when the benefits have been demonstrated for decades in other cultures. For example, through the use of smart card technology, Poland is moving from a cash economy directly to a credit economy, bypassing checks and credit cards altogether. Although the smart card technology is stable and mature, the social and economic issues of dealing with buying on credit are being resolved very slowly. Even though credit is a normal part of contemporary life in the United States, it may take a generation or more for customers and businesses in Poland to fully understand the inherent benefits and limitations of living on credit.

It's clear that the goal of pervasive computing will be achieved, at least on a technologic basis, within the first decade of this century. What is unclear, and much more significant, are the social, political, and cultural consequences of billions of subscribers connected to each other and to the knowledge repository of the future Web. At least one possible future is both very similar and very different from a typical scene in downtown New York or Tokyo today. Businesspeople, customers, and couriers will be walking around with wireless wallets in their pockets, talking into their wireless communicators. However, instead of talking and listening to others in real time, they'll be conversing with the wireless Web through multimedia communicators equipped with speech synthesis and voice recognition interfaces. Web-centric communications will allow businesses and customers to transact business on a global scale and on a 24x7 basis, without having to wait for a human operator. In order to provide a semblance of a human touch and thereby develop some degree of customer loyalty, businesses will use synthetic, personable, animated sales personalities that are age, race, and affect-appropriate to fill the video screens of Web-enabled cell phones and PDAs.

Another possible future is one in which every man, woman, and child is encouraged or required to accept ingestible and injectable Web-enabled biochips. These chips will be used to communicate with Internet appliances, automating the tasks of daily living, such as opening refrigerator doors and turning on room lights as a person stumbles into the kitchen in the middle of the night. The devices will also allow self-communications—a form of biofeedback—that will allow athletes to train better and diabetics to more easily monitor and control their blood glucose levels. This level of intimacy and immediacy with the wireless Web will also bring the focus to the political arena of social compliance, in which rules communicated by the government or an employer must be obeyed. For example, if a diabetic patient fails or refuses to take her medications, she may lose her medical insurance coverage. For some subcultures, this type of Web presence has the potential to take on the characteristics of the compliance collars that prisoners were forced to wear in *The Running Man*. In addition to monitoring each prisoner's location, the collars allowed the government to administer painful shocks to prisoners who did not comply with established behavioral norms.

While it's important for every CEO to be responsible and look ahead to the possible social consequences of introducing a new technology into a culture, the short-term issues are much more pressing. They are the prerequisites for either of the above scenarios to become reality, and ones that will most assuredly be met by innovative, entrepreneurial executives. These include the carriers that will serve as pipelines to consumers, applications and protocols for wireless devices, and content to attract customers. In addition, there are the PDAs, pagers, and other wireless devices needed to serve as platforms for communications and content display, and the infrastructure to provide transmission technology to network carriers. Finally, there are the software tools needed to provide meaning to the huge quantities of data that will result from the billions of wireless devices that will soon populate the planet.

The wireless Web is just beginning, and yet, as every CEO knows, by beginning to live, it's also beginning to die, with another new beginning just over the horizon. The current incarnation of the wireless Web, like every technology, has a finite, fairly predictable life span. As such, the prudent CEO is positioning her company to exploit the wireless Web, either directly or indirectly, while looking for an opportunity to develop and introduce the next evolutionary or revolutionary application of wireless Web technology. After all, the best way to predict the future is to create it.

EXECUTIVE SUMMARY

A practical approach for a CEO contemplating a move to the wireless Web is to follow a five-phase strategy that considers the company's resources, including available capital, other ongoing projects that require IT resources and their relative priority, the type of business the company is involved in, and what the competition is doing.

Phase I. Decide whether to develop a wireless Web presence now or to wait until some time or event in the future, based on technologies involved and the type of wireless Web presence to be developed, from a limited pilot program to a full-scale eCommerce service.

Phase II. Define the development approach, in terms of the tools and resources required.

Phase III. Develop a wireless presence with vendors and/or in-house expertise.

Phase IV. Deploy the product or service, which may entail establishing a distribution system, training, security, and inventory management.

Phase V. Evaluate market conditions, the competition, the latest technologies, and the projects likely to produce return on investment.

Because of the hype surrounding wireless Web technology, it's imperative that the rollout of wireless technology be accompanied by a carefully orchestrated plan of customer expectation management.

As the upheavals in the valuation of dotComs so adeptly demonstrated, it's imperative to separate form from the substance of communications; a clear communications channel will only have value if someone has something of relevance to say. Simply existing on the Web as an electronic billboard, wireless or otherwise, doesn't add value to the customer relationship. Although the early movers in the wireless Web space will bring public attention to—and eventual acceptance of—the wireless Web as a valid form of communications, when the dust settles, it will be business as usual, albeit at a faster pace. A wireless touch point will be as expected and as commonplace as a wired Web, telephone, or fax touch point.

Given these realities, a prerequisite for any CEO contemplating a move to the wireless Web space is to have her brick-and-mortar house in order. This means understanding her company's current and potential customers as well as the perceived or real advantage of its products and services in the market-place. This also means having the infrastructure in place to support the seam-less integration of all touch points, thereby avoiding the frustrating "you can't get there from here" encounters many customers initially associated with the wired Web. Customer relations management should be empowered—not supplanted—by wireless Web communications technologies.

With a solid business infrastructure in place, a wireless Web touch point has the potential to become a value-added multiplier of sorts, much as the telephone has been to business. In this respect, the wireless Web is to the wired Web as the cell phone is to the wired phone. For many potential cus-tomers, communications now extends beyond the confines of a pay phone or desk and into the very fabric of daily living. However, a ubiquitous, universally available communications channel to and from customers is only useful if cus-tomers want the company's products or services, especially when the cus-tomer pays for the communications.

It's the CEO's charge to lead her company through the inevitable grow-ing pains of adding and supporting a wireless Web touch point. However, in order to decide when and where to invest in wireless Web technology, she needs to understand the current status of wireless Web technologies, the probable trajectory of these technologies, and the likelihood that they will survive into the next decade. She must also have a firm grasp of the repercus-sions associated with selecting one technologic approach over another, in terms of resource requirements, return on investment, and interoperability with other technologies on the horizon.

With time, selecting a wireless Web strategy will be akin to picking an office telephone system today. The decisions involved will be as commonplace and as obvious as selecting the number of phone lines, special features, such as caller ID and conference calling, and perhaps the color of the handset. Until then, how-ever, there will be years of technologic evolution, battles over standards, the need to develop new communications infrastructures, and marketing to cus-tomers, whether they're employees, other companies, or end consumers.

Grounded with the knowledge of the technologies and business issues involved in the wireless Web, the decisions that a company will have to make to gain a stable foothold in the wireless Web space can be based on sound business principles, as opposed to dotCom hype. For the technologically savvy CEO, the journey into the technologically and economically complex space of the wireless Web will be a marvelous adventure.

Glossary

1G: First generation wireless communications infrastructure. Synonymous with first generation analog cellular services.

2.5G: A wireless communications infrastructure somewhere between second and third generation in terms of bandwidth. ITT DoCoMo's I-Mode is generally considered to be a 2.5-G network infrastructure.

2G: Second generation wireless communications infrastructure, which includes digital cellular and PCS.

3G: Third generation communications infrastructure, designed to deliver information to handheld wireless devices at speeds of up to 2 MBps.

A/D Conversion: Analog-to-digital conversion. The process of converting voice and other continuous signals to discrete digital signals.

Advanced Wireless Access (AWA): A high-speed wireless system based on ATM technology.

Alpha Testing: The first stage of testing a new product, carried out by the manufacturer's own staff.

AM: Amplitude Modulation. Varying the amplitude or strength of a signal in relationship to another signal, such as voice.

Amplifier: An electronic circuit that increases the strength or amplitude of a signal.

Amplitude: The extent to which the voltage or current of a signal varies in time. Higher swings in voltage or current correspond to greater amplitude.

AMPS: Advanced Mobile Phone System. The analog cellular system in the United States.

Analog Network: A network in which voice and data are sent "as is," without going through a digitization process.

Analog Signal: An electronic signal that is represented by varying levels over continuous range rather than in discrete steps (digital).

American National Standards Institute (ANSI): A voluntary standards organization that develops and publishes standards for transmission codes, protocols, and languages in the United States.

Application Service Provider (ASP): A technology that provides access to software through a Web browser, negating the need for the customer to purchase and run the software locally.

Architecture: The general technical layout of a computer system.

Asynchronous: A property of an event that occurs at an arbitrary time, without synchronization to a reference clock.

Asynchronous Transfer Mode (ATM): A telecommunications method for relaying images, sound, and text simultaneously at very high speeds.

Auction: A form of bidding for G3 licenses in which the highest bidder wins.

Bandwidth: A measure of the information-carrying capacity of a medium. On the Internet, bandwidth is commonly measured in bits per second (Bps).

Beauty Contest: A form of bidding for G3 licenses in which wireless providers vie to promise the best levels of service and most timely rollout. This approach to granting wireless licenses has been embraced by Sweden, Spain, Norway, France, and Portugal.

Beta Testing: The second stage of product testing, carried out by typical users in a variety of settings that mimic those in which the final product will be used.

Binary: A system of expressing numerical values as 0's and 1's.

Bit: The smallest unit of data in a computer system. Any specific data bit can either be high (1) or low (0).

Bitmapped Screen: A display screen where every pixel is represented by a memory location.

Bits Per Second (Bps): A measure of the speed at which data is transmitted or received. Maximum Bps is limited by the bandwidth of the connection. KBps, MBps, and GBps refer to thousand, millions, and billions of bits per second, respectively.

Bluetooth: A very short-range wireless connection standard. Its aim is to link a wide range of computers, electronics, and telecom devices.

Brick and Mortar: A traditional business with a physical presence.

Broadcast: One-way communications from a single transmitter to many receivers. As in broadcast TV and radio.

Browser: A software program that interprets documents on the Web. Netscape Navigator and Microsoft Explorer are the two most popular browsers in use today.

Code Division Multiple Access (CDMA): A wireless communications protocol that is based on digital spread-spectrum technology. Each transmission is identified by a unique code, allowing multiple calls to use the same frequency spread.

CDMA2000: A third generation wireless technology derived from CDMA.

Cellular Digital Packet Data (CDPD): A wireless transmission protocol in which each wireless device has a unique network IP (Internet Protocol) address and remains connected as long as the modem is on. Broken connections are automatically and transparently resumed.

Cell: The area covered by a single cellular base station transmitter and receiver pair. A typical cell is a few hundred meters or more in diameter.

Click and Mortar: A traditional business with a significant Web presence. A hybrid between the pure dotCom and brick-and-mortar companies.

Client: A PC or wireless device that communicates over a network both with its peers, other clients, and with a larger computer, called a server, which typically stores data that many workers need to use. The client has just one user, the server many.

Client-Server: A computer architecture in which the workload is split between desktop PCs or handheld wireless devices (clients) and more powerful or higher-capacity computers (servers) that are connected via a network such as the Internet.

Common Carrier: Licensed utilities that provide communications services for a fee, under nondiscriminatory terms. Companies usually rely on common carriers to send data between offices in different cities.

Compression: Manipulating a signal to minimize bandwidth requirements.

Convergence: The merging of all data and all media into a single digital form.

Cross Talk: An unwanted signal on one channel due to an input on a different channel.

CTIA: Cellular Telecommunications Industry Association. The U.S. trade association representing the interests of the domestic telecommunications industry.

Customer Relations Management (CRM): The process of managing the relationship between a business and its customers.

D/A Conversion: Digital-to-analog conversion. The conversion of a discrete digital signal into a continuous, time-varying analog signal.

Digital Advanced Mobile Phone System (D-AMPS): Digital cellular.

Data Mining: The process of extracting meaningful relationships from usually very large quantities of seemingly unrelated data.

Data Warehouse: A central database, frequently very large, that can provide authorized users with access to all of a company's information.

DCS1000: Digital collection system, version 1. A program, formerly known as carnivore, developed by the FBI to locate and read the email of people targeted by court-ordered investigations.

Digital Encryption Standard (DES): A communications encryption standard defined by the National Bureau of Standards.

Dial-Up: Connection to the Internet through an Internet Service Provider's (ISP's) host computer over standard telephone lines. The most common type of Internet account for home users.

Digital Network: A communications network in which speech and data are first converted to digital form (A/D Conversion) before being transmitted on the network.

Digital Signature: An encrypted digital tag added to an electronic communication to verify the identity of a customer. Also called an electronic signature.

Digital Subscriber Line (DSL): A digital phone connection that skips the analog-digital-analog conversions and sends data directly in digital format. DSL supports simultaneous voice and data communication on the same line.

Digital Switching: A means of supporting multiway conferencing in a fully digital network.

Direct Sequence Spread Spectrum (DSSS): A wireless spread spectrum method that breaks each transmission into pieces, scatters them across the designated spectrum, and reconstructs the pieces at the receiving end.

DSP: Digital Signal Processing. The manipulation of digital information, often with the aid of specialized hardware.

DSP Filtering: The use of computer-simulated filters for processing digital information. The original information is usually an analog audio or video signal that has been digitized for DSP operations.

Early Adopter: In marketing circles, a customer who must have the latest and greatest gadget, regardless of cost or inconvenience.

Ease of Learning: Regarding a user interface, the ease with which a particular interface can be learned. Contrast with Ease of Use.

Ease of Use: Regarding a user interface, the ease or efficiency with which the interface can be used. An easy to use interface may be difficult to learn and vice versa.

Elliptic Curve Cryptography (ECC): A method of encryption and digital signatures that is optimized for computationally limited devices, such as wireless PDAs and cell phones. ECC is more efficient than RSA, the standard encryption used on the wired Web.

Enhanced Data Rates for Global Evolution (EDGE): A technology that can be used to boost data speeds on both GSM and TDMA networks.

Electronic Data Interchange (EDI): A standard transmission format for business information sent from one computer to another using strings of data.

Encryption: The alteration of transmitted information to keep it secret.

EPOC: An operating system for wireless devices, developed by Psion.

Ethernet: The most common form of network used in corporations, with a top speed of 10 MBps. Because it works like a party line, if too many users try to send messages at once, the network slows dramatically.

European Union (EU): The EU member nations are Austria, Belgium, Denmark, Finland, France, Germany, Greece, Ireland, Italy, Luxembourg, Netherlands, Portugal, Spain, Sweden, and the United Kingdom.

Federal Communications Commission (FCC): The U.S. governmental office responsible for radio emissions, including wireless signals, and for assigning different parts of the radio spectrum for a variety of reasons. The FCC does not license the optical spectrum for communications.

Fire Wall: A network security device that can limit unauthorized access to parts of a network.

Frequency-Hopping Spread Spectrum (FHSS): A wireless spread-spectrum method that "hops" its transmission across multiple channels instead of remaining on one signal.

Fuel Cell: A battery that creates electricity by separating protons from electrons in hydrogen atoms. Fuel cells often use methanol and water for a source of hydrogen atoms.

General Packet Radio Service (GPRS): A method of sending Internet information to "always-on" wireless devices.

Global Positioning System (GPS): A usually handheld navigation device that receives transmissions from several satellites, enabling users to plot their positions in latitude, longitude, and altitude.

Graphical User Interface (GUI): The point-and-click interfaces first popularized by the Apple Macintosh and now used by Microsoft Windows.

Global System for Mobile Communications (GSM): A digital cellular standard that uses time-division (TDMA) to carry multiple, simultaneous calls on the same frequency. The vast majority of European mobile phone networks are built in accordance with the GSM Communications standard.

Home Audio Video Interoperability Organization (HAVi): A consortium of consumer electronics companies that is developing a wired and wireless standard for home entertainment systems. HAVi is compatible with JINI and UPNP, the competing smart home communications standards.

Handheld Device Markup Language (HDML): A proprietary language for coding Web sites so that the content can be downloaded quickly onto handheld wireless systems.

High Data Rate CDMA (HDR): A proposed third generation network standard.

HomeRF: An inexpensive wireless network designed for home applications.

HyperText Markup Language (HTML): The most popular programming language used to create documents on the Web.

Human-Computer Interface: The combination of hardware and software elements that provides the communications channel between a computer and the computer operator. Also called the user interface.

I-Mode: I(nternet)-Mode. NTT DoCoMo's proprietary wireless Internet service that is popular throughout Japan.

International Mobile Telecommunications for 2000 (IMT-2000): The third generation global wireless initiative by the ITU-T.

Infrared (IR): Light just below the frequency of the visible light spectrum. IR wireless communications are used in devices from TV remote controls to PDAs.

Infrastructure: In the context of the Internet, the system of servers, cables, and other hardware, together with the software that ties it together, for the purpose of supporting the operation of the network.

Instant Messaging: A type of communications service that allows someone to establish a private conversation with another individual.

Internalization: The process of matching the content in a Web site to suit the language and culture of specific customers.

Internet: An internet is a collection of local area networks (LANs) connected by a wide area network (WAN). The Internet is the World Wide Web, one of many internets.

Internet Phone: A wireless phone that can access the Internet. Smart Phones are also Internet Phones.

Internet Protocol (IP): The most important protocol on which the Internet is based.

Integrated Services Digital Network (ISDN): A digital circuit-switched telephone system that integrates voice and data services.

ISM: The Industrial, Scientific, and Medical frequency band that is shared with the Bluetooth wireless standard.

Internet Service Provider (ISP): A commercial organization that provides clients with access to the Internet.

International Telecommunications Union (ITU): The international standards organization, based in Geneva, Switzerland, that standardizes telephone service throughout the world.

ITU-T: The Telecommunications Sector of the International Telecommunications Union.

Java 2 Micro Edition (J2ME): Sun Microsystems's development platform for Internet phones. J2ME is a potential competitor to the Wireless Application Protocol (WAP).

JINI: The standard proposed by Sun Microsystems, Inc., for the wired and wireless connection of appliances to the Internet.

Local Area Network (LAN): A group of computers, interconnected through wired and/or wireless communications, so that they can share data, software, and storage devices. LANs are part of a client-server computing architecture.

Latency: The delay inherent in wireless systems, such as the time it takes for a file or a program to arrive once a request has been sent.

Legacy System: An existing information system in which a company has already invested considerable time and money. Legacy systems usually present major integration problems when new, potentially incompatible systems are introduced.

Liquid Crystal Display (LCD): The flat display technology used on laptops, cell phones, and wireless PDAs.

Lithium Polymer: A form of lithium battery that can be molded into virtually any shape. Polymer batteries, while expensive, offer a high energy density in a package that can complement the form factor of a wireless device.

Local Exchange Carrier: The telecommunications company that provides public switched network access services.

Localization: The process of adapting a Web site to a particular country or region.

Loyalty: A positive inner feeling or emotional bond between a customer and a business or a brand. Loyalty can't be assessed directly, but can be inferred from a customer's actions.

Loyalty Effect: The quantifiable behavior normally associated with loyalty, such as repeatedly transacting business with a particular retailer or Web site.

MCommerce: Mobile Ecommerce or eCommerce on wheels. Web-based transactions made with the help of wireless PDAs, Internet Phones, and other nonfixed Web-enabled devices.

Metropolitan Area Network (MAN): A high-speed network that links multiple locations within a city.

Minibrowser: An application, similar in concept to Netscape Navigator or Microsoft Internet Explorer, that enables handheld wireless devices to access to the Web.

Mobile Telephone Switching Office (MTSO): The connection between cellular services and the wired telephone network, as well as connectivity to the wired Web.

Noise: An undesirable electrical signal.

Packet Switching: A data transmission technology that breaks down a stream of data into smaller units, called packets, and routes them separately over a network.

Personal Communications Network (PCN): Originally conceived as a very low-power, city-based communications system, but implemented in the form of PCS.

Personal Communications Service (PCS): A digital service similar to cellular phone service.

Personal Digital Assistant (PDA): A handheld electronic organizer that may have Internet access and email functions.

Personal Digital Cellular (PDC): One of several alternatives to the GSM standard.

Pocket Video: A proprietary technique for delivering pictures to wireless handheld devices.

Portal: A Web site that offers a broad array of resources and services, from e-mail to online shopping.

Process Management: An evaluation and restructuring of system functions to make certain processes are carried out in the most efficient and economical way.

Protocol: A set of standards that defines communications between devices.

PSTN: Public Switched Telephone Network.

Push Technology: The automatic delivery of information without continuous prompting from the user.

Radio Frequency (RF): Any frequency that corresponds to signals that can propagate through the ether, including those used by cellular telephones and wireless networks.

Radio Frequency Identification (RFID): The use of electronic tags that emit or reflect signals for nearby readers that are part of a wireless network. RFID tags can be used to wirelessly track stationary and moving objects, from pallets in a warehouse to missiles in transit to a battlefield.

RSA: An encryption algorithm that forms the basis for security on the Internet.

Server: The computer that serves data or applications to one or more client computers.

Shared Wireless Access Protocol (SWAP): The standard behind the HomeRF wireless network.

Short Message Service (SMS): A technology used to send limited (a few hundred characters) text messages to Internet phones. SMS is an inexpensive alternative to the Wireless Application Protocol (WAP).

Smart Phone: A cell phone with Internet access as well as onboard PDA capabilities. That is, an Internet Phone with PDA capabilities. Every Smart Phone is an Internet Phone, but not every Internet Phone is a Smart Phone.

Spread Spectrum: A wireless communication method that spreads transmissions across a spectrum instead of transmitting over a fixed radio frequency. The two types of spread-spectrum transmission, direct sequencing (DSSS) and frequency hopping (FHSS), deter eavesdroppers because the signals are either encoded or are difficult to intercept.

Time Division Multiple Access (TDMA): A wireless communication method that divides the designated frequency into time slots. Each frequency can carry multiple transmissions, with each call taking a turn in a time slot.

Telecommunications Infrastructure: The telecommunications spaces, cable pathways, grounding, wiring, and termination hardware that together provides the basic support for the distribution of all telecommunications information.

Text-to-Speech (TTS): Voice synthesis, using email or other text source to drive the voice synthesis process.

Thin Client: A "stripped down" application designed specifically to run over a low-bandwidth communications channel.

Touch Point: The point of contact between a customer and a company. Touch points include the wired Web, the wireless Web, telephone, fax, email, and person-to-person conversations.

Universal Mobile Telecommunications Systems (UMTS): In Europe, third generation networks built with Wideband-CDMA (WCDMA) technology.

Universal Plug and Play (UPNP): The standard advanced by Microsoft for connecting appliances to the Internet via wired and wireless communications.

Voice Portal: A connection to the Internet based on voice recognition and speech synthesis instead of graphical or textual input and output.

Voice Recognition: The automatic conversion of the spoken word into machine-readable text or computer commands. Voice Recognition is especially attractive as an alternative to keyboard and stylus input on handheld wireless devices.

Wide Area Network (WAN): Multiple local networks tied together, typically using telephone company services. WANs may connect users in different buildings or countries.

Wide-Band CDMA (WCDMA): A third generation wireless technology derived from code-division multiple access (CDMA) that is officially known as IMT-2000 direct spread. Referred to in Europe as UMTS, WCDMA is a rival to CDMA2000.

Wireless Application Protocol (WAP): A standard for delivering information to Internet and Smart Phones.

Wireless Application Service Provider (WASP): The wireless equivalent of an ASP. Also known as a wireless enabler.

Wireless Markup Language (WML): A derivative of XML optimized to create Web pages that are compatible with the Wireless Application Protocol (WAP).

World Wide Web Consortium (W3C): An international organization that develops programming and interoperability standards of the Web.

Extensible Hypertext Markup Language (XHTML): A hybrid between HTML and XML, designed specifically for creating documents on the Web.

Extensible Markup Language (XML): A markup language used to create Web pages that can be automatically reformatted to suit the needs of a variety of devices, from Internet phones with postage-stamp—size displays to large desktop monitors. Unlike HTML, XML specifies not only the appearance of data but also defines what the data represent.

Index

265

About the Author

Bryan Bergeron has over 30 years' experience designing and working with wireless systems and has been writing about leading-edge technology and envisioning the future for most of that time. He teaches at Harvard Medical School and MIT, is editor-in-chief of e.MD, technical editor of Postgraduate Medicine, among others, the author of over 275 articles and chapters on business and technology, *The Eternal E-Customer: How Emotionally Intelligent Interfaces Can Create Long-Lasting Customer Relationships, The Hitchhiker's Guide to the Wireless Web,* and several commercial software packages, including many "firsts" in the industry. He is president of Archetype Technologies, Inc., a technology consulting firm, and speaks internationally on a variety of technology and business issues.